THE INTUITIVE SOURCES

OF PROBABILISTIC THINKING IN CHILDREN

SYNTHESE LIBRARY

MONOGRAPHS ON EPISTEMOLOGY,

LOGIC, METHODOLOGY, PHILOSOPHY OF SCIENCE,

SOCIOLOGY OF SCIENCE AND OF KNOWLEDGE,

AND ON THE MATHEMATICAL METHODS OF

SOCIAL AND BEHAVIORAL SCIENCES

Managing Editor:

JAAKKO HINTIKKA, *Academy of Finland and Stanford University*

Editors:

ROBERT S. COHEN, *Boston University*

DONALD DAVIDSON, *Rockefeller University and Princeton University*

GABRIËL NUCHELMANS, *University of Leyden*

WESLEY C. SALMON, *University of Arizona*

VOLUME 85

E. FISCHBEIN

THE INTUITIVE SOURCES
OF PROBABILISTIC THINKING
IN CHILDREN

D. REIDEL PUBLISHING COMPANY

DORDRECHT-HOLLAND / BOSTON-U.S.A.

Library of Congress Cataloging in Publication Data

Fischbein, E.
    The intuitive sources of probabilistic thinking in children.

    (Synthese library ; v. 85)
    Translation of Le concept de probabilité chez l'enfant.
    Bibliography: p.
    1. Cognition (Child psychology) 2. Probability learning.
    3. Intuition (Psychology) I. Title.
BF723.C5F5713   155.4'13   75–22376
ISBN 90–277–0626–3

Published by D. Reidel Publishing Company,
P.O. Box 17, Dordrecht, Holland

Sold and distributed in the U.S.A., Canada, and Mexico
by D. Reidel Publishing Company, Inc.
306 Dartmouth Street, Boston,
Mass. 02116, U.S.A.

Printed in The Netherlands by D. Reidel, Dordrecht

To my wife and my daughter

TABLE OF CONTENTS

PREFACE

About a year ago I promised my friend Fischbein a preface to his book of which I knew the French manuscript. Now with the printer's proofs under my eyes I like the book even better than I did then, because of, and influenced by, new experiences in the meantime, and fresh thoughts that crossed my mind. Have I been influenced by what I remembered from the manuscript? If so, it must have happened unconsciously. But of course, what struck me in this work a year ago, struck a responsive chord in my own mind. In the past, mathematics teaching theory has strongly been influenced by a view on mathematics as a heap of concepts, and on learning mathematics as concepts attainment. Mathematics teaching practice has been jeopardised by this theoretical approach, which in its most dangerous form expresses itself as a radical atomism.

To concepts attainment Fischbein opposes acquisition of intuitions. In my own publications I avoided the word "intuition" because of the variety of its meanings across languages. For some time I have used the term "constitution of mathematical objects", which I think means the same as Fischbein's "acquisition of intuitions" – indeed as I view it, constituting a mental object precedes its conceptualising, and under this viewpoint I tried to observe mathematical activities of young children. Constituting the number 3, or the whole number as such, precedes conceptualising it, constituting linear order or geometrical space may take place without ever being followed by conceptualising. The mental constitution of sets is indispensable in mathematical development but it can only be hampered by teaching set concepts even if concretised by physically constituted sets, as is now fashionable. So for various reasons I consider Fischbein's shifting the stress from concepts to intuitions as a cognitive advance which may benefit teaching mathematics.

In a more general sense I think mathematics teaching will profit by Fischbein's studies. For a long time developmental psychologists focused on spontaneity. Learning by more or less formal teaching has gradually become accepted as a feature worth studying, though in experiments the laboratory setting still continued to prevail both as to environment and problems. I feel in both respects Fischbein's approach is closer to real teaching and classroom practice than even much frankly didactical research. Interested as I am in teaching theory and practice, I interpret and welcome Fischbein's work as a major breakthrough in mentality of research in the field of developmental psychology.

HANS FREUDENTHAL

TRANSLATOR'S ACKNOWLEDGEMENT

I would like to thank Arthur Still, who helped me at many points in this translation.

CAROL A. SHERRARD

Note. This translation was made from the author's original manuscript in French, except for Appendices III and IV which have been previously published in English.

ACKNOWLEDGEMENTS

The Author is grateful to Mrs Melania Turcu for her excellent secretarial assistance and to Miss Carol A. Sherrard for her kind and competent cooperation in the achievement of the English version of this book. The author is also grateful to Mrs Doina Doneaud for preparing the first English version.

The Author is very much indebted to Mrs C. E. Brand-Maher from the D. Reidel Publishing Company for her constant and friendly help with the editorial work on this book.

Thanks are due to my colleague and friend R. Codirlă whose critical reading of the book in the first version was so useful.

I express my thanks to Mr Reidel and his staff for their helpful and efficient cooperation.

Above all I am particularly grateful to Professor H. Freudenthal who from the very beginning was so encouraging about writing this book and who has always been a mentor and a great friend to me.

I am indebted to the University of Chicago Press, to the Authors and to the Publishers for their permission to reproduce in this book some tables taken from different issues of *Child Development*. The table reproduced on page 44 is from: B. M. Ross, 'Probability Concepts in Deaf and Hearing Children', *Child Development* **37** (1966), p. 924. The table reproduced on page 78 is from P. Yost, A. E. Siegel and J. N. Andrews, 'Non Verbal Probability Judgement by Young Children', *Child Development* **33** (1962), p. 778. The tables reproduced on pages 80–81 are from E. Goldberg, 'Probability Judgement by Preschool Children; Task Condition and Performance', *Child Development* **36** (1966), pp. 159, 163.

In the Appendixes of the book there are reproduced some of our own papers concerning the probabilistic thinking in children, which have been previously published in different journals of child and educational psychology. I am very thankful to the Publishers of *Enfance*, *The British Journal of Educational Psychology*, *Educational Studies in Mathematics* and *Child Development* for their permission to reproduce these papers in my book.

E. F.

CHAPTER I

INTRODUCTION

Psychological Research and the Concept of Probability

Probability is a concept of increasing importance in scientific thought. Over the 300 years since the famous correspondence between Pascal and Fermat about games of chance, the theory of probability has become an important branch of mathematics with wide repercussions in science, philosophy, and practical human activity.

In psychology, it is only during the past 30 years that the concept of probability has played an important part. What are the reasons for this comparatively recent interest?

First of all, there is the fact that behavioural phenomena themselves are probabilistic in character. An explanatory model in psychology, whether mathematical or causal, must involve probabilistic considerations in its axioms and structure. Scientific psychology has only recently arrived at the idea of the need for probabilistic models in the interpretation of behaviour. Of the great doctrines, such as behaviourism, Pavlov's conditioning theory, and Gestalt psychology, to mention just three, none has provided explicit probabilistic considerations within its conceptual system.

There are many possible reasons for this delay. The fact cannot be overlooked that, historically, psychology has emulated the so-called *exact* sciences. It has always been concerned with finding, within the complexity and variability of the behavioural event, possibilities of prediction comparable in exactitude to those of, for example, physics or chemistry.

Secondly, the belated interest of psychology in probabilistic models may be ascribed, more pragmatically, to the difficulties experienced by psychologists in using this mathematical tool. It is only during the last decade that the theory of probability has been sufficiently adapted to practical use in the interpretation of behavioural phenomena.

It is a remarkable fact that the first important attempt – that of Hull – to achieve a quantitative, deductive system of psychology, was not a probabilistic, but a determin-istic theory. It was not until 1950, with the first theoretical paper on stimulus-sampling theory by Estes, that the new direction of research was embarked upon in a systematic way.

The real beginnings, however, are somewhat earlier than this. Already in 1935, Tolman and Brunswik had made a point of the fact that stimuli in the natural environment are stochastic in character, which meant that predicting them entailed probability considerations. In 1939, Brunswik, working on rats, introduced a stochastic sequence of reinforcements. Food was available sometimes on the right, and sometimes on the left, and the matching of behaviour with the stochastically successive stimuli was observed. Brunswik's research initiated an important line of study in what has been termed 'probability learning'.

It is not the intention here to trace the detailed development of various stochastic models in mathematical psychology, but to point out that one source of the interest which psychology has taken in probability has been the probabilistic nature of behaviour itself – a fact which has only recently been systematically acknowledged in psychological theory.

Another source of this interest has been the development of new fields in other sciences which are based on probability theory and which, because of their relevance to behavioural phenomena, have caught psychologists' attention and have influenced research, hypothesis and interpretation in psychology. We are referring particularly to decision-making theory, information theory, and cybernetics.

Furthermore, the work on the axiomatic basis of probability theory has re-opened discussion on the meaning of the concept of probability itself. It has been recognised that, regardless of the theoretical solution adopted, the subjective aspects of estimation cannot be ignored. Some of the solutions have directly expressed the subjective approach in interpreting the concept of probability. According to this point of view, probability is the degree of belief a given person has with regard to a given statement on the basis of given evidence (see, for instance Kyburg and Smokler, 1964). This characterisation gives rise to a set of problems with direct psychological implications, such as the consistency or coherence of belief, the relationship between hypothesis and data (in connection with Bayes' formula), intuitive estimations of probabilities and of the form of distributions, and so on.

Finally, the interest of psychology in the area of probability is part of a general trend toward the probabilistic approach and statistical methods in contemporary scientific thought. Psychology is extremely sensitive to scientific 'fashion', not in the pejorative sense, but in the sense that it is quick to exploit new methods which are readily adaptable.

The Concept of Probability in Child Psychology

Genetic psychology has, also comparatively recently, concerned itself with the area of probability – in particular, with chance, the estimation of probabilities, and combinatory capacity.

The source of this interest should certainly be sought, in the first place, in the orientation of contemporary scientific thought in general, and in that of contemporary psychology in particular.

This cause has also acted indirectly on child psychology via educational preoccupations, at least in recent years. The attempts of schools to bring their curricula in line with scientific advances have had to take account of the increasing interest in probabilistic and statistical ideas and methods. In the area of mathematics itself, the area of probability has been given much greater weight in the past few decades. Consequently, we have witnessed in the past few years, and in many countries, the attempt not only to introduce the theory of probability in schools, but also to start teaching it to very young children.

In addition, mathematical education today aims as far as possible to develop independent and creative thought in children, and probability can be an excellent medium for achieving this. "In no mathematical domain" writes Freudenthal "is blind faith in techniques more often denounced than in probability; in no domain is critical thought more often required" (Freudenthal, 1970, p. 167).

The teaching of a new branch of science raises, however, many problems concerning curricula, methods, and materials; and these in turn raise further questions concerning the psychological and psycho-genetic implications of such a step. What, for example, is the best age to start teaching it? In what order should the concepts be taught, in order that the acquired body of knowledge should be as reliable and viable as possible? What should be the proportion of concrete to abstract elements, intuitive to axiomatic presentation, *ex cathedra* exposition to the encouragement of independent discovery?

There can be no answer to such questions until systematic research in genetic psychology has produced some findings, based on an analysis of the conceptual system in question from the point of view of mathematical psychology.

These problems arise also, of course, in the teaching of mathematics itself, including the theory of probability. The systematic construction of a new conceptual system within the process of education cannot afford to ignore the intuitive endowment of the child. A conceptual system cannot be built in a vacuum, but only by making use of the (sometimes contradictory) pre-existing intuitive biases.

Productive reasoning of any kind is achieved through heuristics, and motivated by an anticipatory approach structured as intuition. This recognition has had important consequences in thinking about probability, since the intuitive substrate available in this domain is relatively inconsistent and ambiguous. A proper curriculum of probability learning should, then, take into account this primary intuitive substrate, and concern itself with improving it and with finding methods of building new intuitions which are readily compatible with it.

Two main directions of research have been taken in relation to the formation of the concept of probability.

The first, originated by Tolman and Brunswick, concerns what has been termed *probability learning*. The subject predicts, on successive trials, which of two or more possible events is going to occur. The events occur randomly, but with a specific frequency. When, without special instructions, the probabilities of the responses approximate the probabilities of the events, it is possible to assume that the subject possesses a particular intuition of chance and probability. This line of research has not been limited to children. The majority of studies in probability learning have, in fact, been carried out with adult subjects.

The second main line of research concerns the organisation of conceptual schemas in the domain of probability: the development of concepts such as chance, proportion, and the estimation of odds, and the development in children of the concepts and procedures of combinatorial analysis.

These two directions of research are focussed on rather different problems, and the techniques they use are, consequently, different. Yet, as will be seen in the following chapters, their findings can be successfully combined in an effort to reach a unified view of this area.

CHAPTER II

INTUITION AND INTELLIGENCE

The intellectual development of the individual involves more than the assimilation and organisation of conceptual systems. In addition to such structures, whose dynamics are explicitly determined by definitions and combination rules, intellectual activity involves cognitive and problem-solving modalities which are less explicit, though not necessarily more primitive. These are intuitions, that is, forms of immediate cognition in which the justifying elements, if any, are implicit.

In this book, we will study the relationship between intuition and intelligence in the ontogenesis of probabilistic thinking. The role of intuition in mathematical creativity and in mathematical learning has been frequently discussed. We shall not dwell on this general aspect of the problem, which is far beyond the scope of this work. There is, however, a quotation from Felix Klein which is particularly relevant to this general question, and to the orientation of this book: "...on this point Pasch does not agree with me, the point in question being the rigorous value of axioms. He believes – and this is the traditional approach – that it is possible, eventually, to give up completely intuition and base all the science on axioms only. As far as I am concerned, I am convinced that, in research, one should always combine intuition with axioms" (Klein, 1898).

What Felix Klein has stated for research is even more true for the teaching of mathematics: the pupil must, on the one hand, reinvent learnt truths, and on the other hand *learn to invent*, to be creative.

As we have said, we do not wish to dwell on this general aspect. But it is important to stress that the relationship between intuition and logical structures plays an essential part in the domain of probability, perhaps more conspicuously and strikingly than it does in other domains of mathematics.

In the present work, the results obtained from this area of research will be analysed from the point of view of relationships between intuition and reasoning in the ontogenesis of probabilistic thinking, in particular the development of probabilistic intuitions in relation to the development of operational schemas of the intellect.

The work by Piaget and Inhelder *La genèse de l'idée de hasard chez l'enfant* (1951) is the classic in this field. But they deal almost exclusively with the stages of logical organisation of the concepts of chance and probability. The interpretive, explanatory, and problem-solving predispositions generated by the intuitive base appear only sporadically in their account.

In the following pages, we shall deal first of all with the concept of intuition.

Our main hypothesis is that *human cognition is fundamentally unitary*. It is unitary by virtue of its original adaptive character, and by virtue of the fact that, on any level, it envisages a single reality, and provides essentially concordant sets of information, even though they may be expressed in different codes.

Consequently, our starting-point is that intuition and intelligence (or intuition and reasoning) tell us about the same reality, even though, superficially, the mechanisms or the codes may be different. *The 'immediacy' of intuition is explained by its close link with action.*

According to Janet, Piaget, Galperin, and others, mental operations are internalised actions, carried out via imaging or symbolisation. But if mental operations are internalised actions, *the action itself must possess cognitive features even before it is translated into figural or symbolic terms.* The proposition would otherwise make no sense. The fact is that adaptive responses, from simple to complex ones, imply assimilative and accommodatory schemas which are characteristic of any living organism, and which prefigure cognitive activities. Conversely, a sensation, perception, or idea not only precedes action, but is itself an incipient action. No doubt there are times when splits occur, and mental operations become organised in comparatively autonomous structures (like the group-structures of operations in Piaget's theory).

Yet this splitting does not occur spontaneously, and is never definitive. The immediacy of intuition results from the intimacy that cognition, in any given situation, shares with action. Intuition has the same adaptive fluency which is characteristic of the total organism in action.

The immediacy of intuition is initially attained through the anticipatory simultaneity of the action programme, which consists of spatial images.

Intuition provides something analogous to Tolman's cognitive map. It may be accompanied by a spatial representation, or it may consist of a global synthesis in which visualisation is secondary.

The affinity between image and intuition is not based on a superficial analogy. Their immediacy is a common feature which reveals their relationship with action as tools of adaptive, anticipatory behaviour.

Consequently, visualisation alone is not the same as intuition. It *becomes* intuition to the extent that it constitutes an action programme, whether motor or cognitive.

The feeling of conviction, of certitude, which accompanies intuition expresses a stabilised, and therefore long-verified mental organisation. This certitude or immediacy which characterises intuition does not result, as Kant held, from its *a priori* nature, but from the stability of patterns broadly verified through active contact with reality.

According to our hypothesis, then, the essential quality of intuition consists in the fact that, through its functional characteristics, it maintains intimate contact with action, and serves action by direct articulation with it, more effectively meeting its requirements of continuity, fluency, and readiness than explicit reasoning could do.

The immediacy of intuition does not entail absolute spontaneity. It denotes, on the contrary, the existence of long-verified mechanisms, stabilised by experience. It is possible that certain hereditary patterns facilitate the generation of some intuitions. It is certain that social learning and experience contribute to the organisation of intuitions through logico-verbal schemas, and spatio-temporal systems of reference. Yet, *in addition to all this, individual experience is an essential component of the consistent articulation which characterises intuition.* The explanation of this lies in the very nature of intuitions, in the fact that in their origin and properties they are intimately tied to action.

Intuition seems, then, to represent an intermediate stage between outward action and internalised action (or operation, in Piaget's sense). This is only partly true, however, and holds only for certain intuitions. *In general, intuitions do not represent mere transitional events; they constitute autonomous cognitive processes with unique and important functions.*

An analogy can be drawn between intuitions and representations. Representations are, primarily, mental patterns which schematise a given perceptual experience, and they are therefore precursors of concepts.

But the representation is not *only* an intermediate stage between percept and concept. Representations, i.e. mental images, are components of the process of reasoning; they are part of the idealised experiences which characterise productive thinking. Representations are, then, not merely precursors of concepts, but also *figural tokens of constituted abstractions.*

Intuitions have analogous functions in the relation between action and intellectual operations. They may be antecedent to the operations, or they may occur during the operations, facilitating their continuity and fluency. They may also occur *after* the analytical operations, synthesising the results of analysis in a global view of unitary significance, and thus assisting in the transfer of decision to the level of action.

In our view, then, intuitions are not confined – as they are in Kantian terminology, for example – to the constitutive elements of sensibility. They are intrinsic to reasoning.

Internalised and autonomous actions in the form of intellectual operations acquire the character of intuitions as they become automatised and stabilised. These operations lose their discursiveness, but acquire, instead, the speed and fluency required for efficient action.

Broadly speaking, intuitions may be divided into three categories: pre-operational, operational, and post-operational.

In the first category are those intuitions which, by synthesising experience in a given domain, confer speed, adaptibility, and efficiency on the appropriate action. Such intuitions are not merely cognitive echoes of the actions concerned, but are real cognitive syntheses of previous experience relevant to the present action. The most suggestive example is probably to be found in the elementary spatial intuitions which enable us to judge distances and locate objects on tacit criteria, thus adapting our reactions to the objective data.

In our view, then, pre-operational intuitions are not only to be found in the developmental period termed as pre-operational by Piaget. They may survive throughout the life-time of an individual.

Operational intuitions are those intrinsically involved in reasoning. They are the intuitions which make us hold a conclusion to be true on the basis of given premises, and, in general, the intuitions that are expressed in the formal rules of logic. These might be considered as *basic operational intuitions.*

Ewing (1941), among others, has accepted the idea of a close relationship between intuition and reasoning. There seem to be primary intuitions of causality, deduction, and so on. Ewing, however, views intuition and inference as irreducible: truths exist that are not empirical generalisations, and that are not demonstrable. In deductive reasoning, the conclusion follows from the premises, but the deduction itself remains undemonstrable. It is the expression of an intuition. Ewing does not accept that intuitions are implicit inferences. Implicit inferences do, of course, exist in the form of very rapid reasoning; but Ewing would not call these intuitions. True intuitions are 'justifiable beliefs' which are irreducible, and which are intercalated in this form in our reasoning.

On the other hand, one could speak of *derived specific operational intuitions*, like those which anticipate solutions in problem-solving, and which correspond to what Selz has called 'anticipative schemas'.

Finally, *post-operational intuitions* are intuitions which, by synthesising previous experience into automatised operational structures, permit prompt solutions to current practical problems. This is illustrated by the doctor's intuition in making an initial diagnosis before all the test results are known, or the mechanic's intuition in detecting a fault in an engine by its sound, and so on.

Such post-operational intuitions have been described by Berne (1949). Working as a psychiatrist at a military selection centre, he had to examine a great number of cases. He became skilled in making very rapid appraisals, and even in predicting responses from the patient's general appearance; for example he was able to predict profession from appearance.

Intuitions could also be classified into *primary* and *secondary* intuitions.

Primary intuitions are formed before, and independently of, systematic instruction. Spatial intuitions, as described previously, belong to this category, as do the fundamental operational intuitions which regulate logical thinking.

Secondary intuitions are those which are formed after a systematic process of instruction, and they enable the individual to transcend primary cognitive acquisitions. They convey the products of social experience in the form, mostly, of scientific truths. The mathematician's intuitions, or those of the scientist, fall into this category. Felix Klein (1898) used the term 'refined intuition', and Severi (1951) the term 'second-degree intuition' for related meanings.

If our view of the close relationship between action and intuition is correct, it follows that secondary intuitions also, even though attained through social experience, would be reconstituted through individual experience, from which they are distilled.

What distinguishes intuitions from information or intellectual habits (which also imply a process of assimilation through rehearsal)?

The French Revolution took place in 1789; the dilation coefficient of gases is 1/273; the ratio of circumference to diameter is 3.14; the formula for the solution of a 2nd-degree equation is:

$$x_{1,2} = \frac{-b \pm \sqrt{b^2 - 4ac}}{2a}$$

and so on, are all examples of acquired information and mental skills, *but not of intuitions*.

Repetition is required for the acquisition of these mental skills, just as it is for the acquisition of intuitions; but in these cases it is 'local', small-scale repetition of comparatively short duration. When recalling such facts or formulae, we do not feel motivationally committed; we do not perceive them as necessarily deriving from our basic intellectual mechanisms.

Secondary intuitions, like all intuitions, involve large areas of intellectual activity (however specialised they may appear), and represent vertical syntheses of motor, imaginative, and conceptual elements.

Secondary intuitions therefore presuppose extensive practice and familiarisation.

Because of this, it is clear that a new, secondary intuition is formed neither through listening to explanation, nor through rote learning. *An intuition is never simply the cognitive echo of an isolated habit.* The feeling of conviction is not, as Bunge (1962) states, the result of confusing psychological certainty with rigorous proof, but the result of the coherence, stability, and efficiency of the cognitive organisation.

"If a coin is tossed three times and the result is heads every time, what will be the result of the fourth toss?' An educated man, perhaps even a professional mathematician, unfamiliar with the theory of probability, may answer "tails are more likely on the fourth toss". This is an erroneous intuition, but an *intuition* nevertheless (the so-called negative recency effect, which we shall discuss later).

As an intuition, it represents an amount of stored and consequently verified experience. We seem to be dealing with a paradox here. It is a fact that the reasoning in this case is wrong; it confuses two approaches.

Take, for example, sets of six coin-tosses; the probability of obtaining heads 5 times and tails once within a set is less than the probability of obtaining heads 4 times and tails twice, which, in turn, is less than the probability of obtaining heads and tails 3 times each. This hierarchisation is intuitively assimilated from experience (without any explicit reasoning, of course), and leads to the belief that, in the case of equally probable events, long runs of events are less probable than short ones, or than alternations. This belief is an unwarranted extrapolation from the correctly hierarchised sets of events.

If a coin is tossed 6 times, each of the following sequences of events is equally probable, viz. $(\frac{1}{2})^6$:

```
H  H  H  H  H  H
T  T  T  T  T  T
T  H  T  H  T  H
T  T  T  H  H  H
T  T  H  H  T  T   ...and so on.
```

The probability of getting heads 5 times and tails once is less than the probability of getting heads 4 times and tails twice, *provided there are no restrictions on order*.

A sequence of 6 events of which 5 are H and one is T may occur in 6 different ways (according to the position of T). A sequence of 6 events, 4 of which are H and 2 are T, may occur in 15 different ways

$$\binom{6}{4} = \binom{6}{2} = 15.$$

Correct understanding of this reasoning involves a body of knowledge and calculation skills with quite wide repercussions on the thinking processes of the individual. The consolidation of these acquisitions, their integration within the current way of thinking in the form of synthetic views, takes even more time, all the more so as they have to substitute themselves for a long established mode of interpretation (as expressed in the negative recency effect). It is in this connection that we speak of *secondary intuitions*. Simple theoretical explanation is not sufficient to convert the information into stabilised acquisitions, involving the basic features of intuition. The use of the information in action and prediction is necessary during periods of intellectual development, in order for this to occur.

Once the basic cognitive schemas of intelligence have stabilised (after 16–17 years of age) modifications to the intuitive substrate seem to be difficult, if not impossible.

It also follows that the creation of secondary intuitions would require a learning programme which would include motor, representational, and conceptual elements, and further representational and motor components at a higher structural level.

In Galperin's theory of mental actions (Galperin, 1963) we find roughly the same elements. He sees them, however, as the stages of concept-formation, while *in our view they result in the constitution of intuitions.* Both views are sometimes correct, as when a concept is accompanied by intuitive certitude. Yet, in many cases, concepts do not require intuitive conviction; they are not accompanied by a feeling of inward necessity.

In our view, then, the concept-building stages described by Galperin are all valid, *but for intuitions, not concepts. Automatisation of the internalised action is not the final stage in the formation of a concept, but the final stage in the formation of an intuition.* Those concepts which do not have a specific intuitive substrate do not go through these stages of formation, and they are acquired through ordinary learning. These considerations imply that Galperin's theory is subject to certain restrictions as far as its application in educational practice is concerned.

Affirmatory intuitions and anticipatory intuitions. A third dichotomy that may be proposed is that between affirmatory intuitions and anticipatory intuitions. In fact, any intuition involves a feeling of affirmation, of conviction and certitude. But in certain cases, the intuition itself is nothing more than this self-evident affirmation. It is intuitively true that the shortest distance between two points is a straight line; that if $A = B$ and $B = C$, then $A = C$; that if one box contains 5 black and 4 white beads, and another box contains 5 black and 2 white beads, the probability of drawing a white bead from the first box is higher. (It is clear that each of these intuitions presupposes some personal experience, plus a certain background of elementary knowledge.)

Anticipatory intuitions are the global views of the solution to a problem, which precede the detailed explicit steps of the problem-solving process. Bruner in his book *The Process of Education* (1960) refers to these intuitions as being complementary to analytical thinking.

Westcott (1968) has defined intuition as "the event which occurs when an individual reaches a conclusion on the basis of less explicit information than is ordinarily required to reach that conclusion" (p. 100). To some extent, Westcott's definition accords with our notion of *anticipatory intuition*. However, an anticipatory intuition can manifest itself not only in cases where information is lacking, but also in cases where all the information is available, but needs to be organised before a solution can be embarked upon.

The distinction between affirmatory and anticipatory intuitions is far from being sharply delineated, and this is for two reasons.

Firstly, anticipatory intuitions derive at least part of their plausibility from affirmatory intuitions. When the mathematician contemplates the possibility of a new theorem, he 'feels' that this is likely to be correct *before* he has discovered all the steps of the proof. Yet, this preliminary impression which anticipates the full demonstration of solution is generally based on affirmatory intuitions (frequently fixed in axioms, rules of inference, and so on).

Secondly, affirmatory intuitions may derive from anticipatory intuitions which have passed the test of demonstration (and are eligible, on that account, to acquire the status of secondary intuitions). I expect that, if I draw a line inside a triangle parallel to one of the sides, this line will divide the other two sides into proportional segments. Once this truth is demonstrated and has become routine thinking, it becomes, in time, self-evident and acquires the status of an intuition. Any affirmatory intuition is also anticipatory in that it prefigures the result of a possible action. The intuition that the relation of order implies transitivity expresses, not only the feeling of obviousness about a result obtained, but also, and especially, the firm belief that this result will always be obtained. The intuition expressed by the so-called 'law of large numbers' anticipates the fact that relative frequencies approach their theoretical probability as the number of trials increases.

Furthermore, the anticipation by intuition of an original solution is 'committing', expressing a belief in the self-evidentness of the path chosen before the detailed steps of demonstration are taken.

It should be stressed that it is their close relation to effective action that causes intuitions to be so specific, as compared to the other cognitive modalities. It is not their global nature, as such, that is the distinctive feature of intuitions, but the fact that they synthesise experience in the service of action. Intuition is the means whereby cognition meets the requirements of speed, fluency, and coherence of effective action.

Intuitions, then, according to this point of view, are nothing but intelligence. They are components of intelligence in action. They develop along with the individual; they are changed and modified through contact with the reality which otherwise could not be effectively coped with.

This refers not only to practical action, but also, and this is important, to mental action, which may precede or temporarily replace practical action.

The terms 'intuition' and 'intuitive thinking' appear in Piaget's work, but with the restricted meaning of 'representational' thinking, dependent on perceptual experience. "It is these prelogical schemata, still very closely representing perceptual data while at the same time truly recentring them, which can be called intuitive thought" (Piaget, 1964, p. 156).

In a different context, Piaget mentions the connection between intuition and action, but he restricts it to the pre-operational level. "In general, if intuitions are considered as the representations of internalised actions, then an operation arises out of an intuition as soon as that intuition is reversible" (Piaget and Inhelder, 1951, p. 236).

In Piaget's theory, the psychology of intelligence is, after all, a psychology of logic; "...the psychologist" writes Piaget "studies the way in which the factual equilibrium of actions and operations establishes itself, while the logician analyses the same balance in its ideal form, i.e. the way it would be if it was integrally achieved and the way it enforces itself as a rule to the mind" (Piaget, 1964, p. 71).

Yet, the fact is that constructive, productive thinking is more than a process of linking operations, analysable in terms of logical mechanisms. Global anticipation, and guessing, are also part of reasoning.

Intuitions are *structural acquisitions*; this implies their active integration into the overall structure of intelligence at a given period during its development. Yet, the structural character of intuitions does not explain their immediacy, their anticipative and creative capacity, or their role in ongoing activity. According to Piaget, structures are stabilised systematisations of operations which become autonomous with respect to practical action, and whose autonomy is secured by their internal coherence.

In reality, however, human practical or intellectual activity does not confine itself to closed circuits governed by internal consistency rules. The consistency is always being disrupted, and the restoration of consistency always presupposes *invention*. Invention means at the same time belief in success (stemming from long-validated experience) and the possibility of transcending experience; in other words, involvement in new action. *Intuition is the mechanism whereby a structural acquisition can be involved in a novel action.*

The great stability of intuitions follows from their structurality. But the degree of confidence that is attached to them, the leap through extrapolation, and their efficiency, all result from the vertical synthesis which they entail and which enables cognition, without losing any of its cognitive qualities, to convert itself into action.

We may recall that, for Bergson (1930, p. 191–192) intuition and intelligence are radically distinct functions. For him, intelligence is basically a tool of action. Intuition, as the extension of instinct, is able to directly apprehend the core of phenomena, the continuous flux of life, by a sort of innate sympathy. This divorce between intelligence and intuition is the result of Bergson's opposition between cognition and action.

Intelligence is, without doubt, a tool of action. But it is precisely *because* it is a tool of action that intelligence is at the same time, and to the same extent, *cognition*. In its elementary forms, intelligence is adapted only to take account of the knowledge of solid physical properties. But there is also a more complex and sophisticated modality – dialectic thought – in which the intelligence is able to grasp motion, development, and the contradictory nature of the processes of reality.

Intuitions, within the structure of intelligence, perform the function of gearing knowledge into action. The suddenness of the 'Einsicht' (insight) phenomenon first described by the Gestaltists is what might be called a 'quantum leap' in the flow of thought. But, as we have been at pains to point out, the suddenness of a solution in the form of an intuition does not imply the absence of antecedents in the subject's experience. The moment of 'insight' is merely the moment at which the cognitive steps are converted into incipient action. In the first (cognitive) stage, *I know what I am looking for*: this is the 'searching' of intelligent behaviour. In the second stage *I know what to do*. Intuition (in our case, anticipatory intuition) is the moment of transition from the first to the second stage.

Probability is a particularly appropriate area in which to test these hypotheses and their possible practical applications.

The theory of probability, first of all, requires cognitive attitudes which are, to a great extent (and probably more than in other branches of mathematics) 'unnatural'. The primary intuitions which are so important in geometry are of little use in probability. "Why has the theory of probability failed to influence mathematics to the same extent that geometry has?" asks A. Engel. "Because we possess a natural geometric intuition but no probability intuition." (A. Engel, 1970, p. 8).

We do not entirely agree with this statement of Engel's, as will become clear later, but it is certain that we possess only a very meagre intuitive substrate regarding probability. This fact will enable us to observe the creation and development of probabilistic intuitions while analysing the behaviour of subjects of various ages in situations where they have to predict probabilities.

Secondly, the area of probability is particularly appropriate for the study of intuition because probabilities are closely tied to action. Stochastic experience is to probability what spatial experience is to geometry. In both cases, even though one eventually arrives at a strictly axiomatic form of the exposition, the fundamentals, the problems, the nature of the solutions, and the style of thinking are closely coupled to the specific character of the domain. The construction of the concept of probability starts from specific experiences which are stochastic in character, and whose results are inventoried according to a logical classification.

We are undoubtedly dealing here with ideal, conceptualised experiences which can be integrated into a logical structure. When we need to solve a problem, however, the intuitive substrate becomes actively involved, conferring meaning on concepts and reasoning, suggesting solutions, and generally providing the scaffolding (according to Poincaré's expression) on which the formalised reasoning is erected.

Actions are involved also in the intuitive substrate of geometric measuring, sectioning, superimposing, etc.), but the final result is *images* – totally conceptualised images, *figural concepts*. The spatial image is the 'soul' of geometry, even though we may sometimes pretend to ignore it.

Probabilistic intuitions also involve images – images of dice, coins, boxes, and so on, but these images have a merely auxiliary function. They are not intrinsic to the reasoning, in the way that spatial images are in geometry.

The germ of intuitive reasoning about probability lies in natural 'experiments' with stochastic results, which involve predictions and random draws or other equivalent actions.

The distinction between geometry as based intuitively on images, and probability as based intuitively on 'experiments' is of course artificial to some degree. In both cases, as for any intuition, we are dealing with hierarchical structures in which conceptual schemas, crude or refined figural elements, and programmed actions are involved.

Nevertheless, there are grounds for supposing that the intuitive substrate of probabilistic thinking bears a more manifest relationship to action, and should therefore be easier to observe.

A third fact which makes probability a suitable area in which to study the relationship between intuition and action is that human behaviour is itself probabilistic. It matches, more or less correctly, the probabilistic character of events in the environment.

The responses of an individual cannot be reduced to either built-in stereotypes, such as instincts, or acquired stereotypes, such as classical conditioned reflexes. The complexity of circumstances frequently compels the individual to respond on the basis of a global intuitive estimate of odds. Such statistical intuitions are an intrinsic feature of behaviour. How do they take shape and develop within the structure of the adaptive behaviour of the individual? To what extent can we speak of a true stochastic conditioning, causing responses to match the probabilities of stimuli? How can the relationships among the three modalities of representation described by Bruner – iconic, enactive, and symbolic – be translated into probabilistic terms, which would help explain the development of probabilistic intuitions?

These problems are not only important from the theoretical point of view. We would like to know whether conceptual understanding of probability could benefit from practical training. Conversely, we would like to know whether everyday practical behaviour, to which the estimation of odds is intrinsic, could benefit from instruction in the theory of probability.

These introductory considerations lead us to the following five hypotheses about the ontogenesis of probabilistic behaviour.

(1) We can hypothesise the existence of a natural intuitive substrate for the notions of chance and probability, because the day-to-day experience

of the child comprises stochastic processes. If intuitions provide the mechanism whereby intelligence can rapidly insert itself into the flux of practical or mental action, then we can assume that day-to-day experience would create this adaptive tool in the pre-operational child. Among the child's adaptive mechanisms should be included the ability to intuitively estimate proportions and make predictions. (The age at which probabilistic intuitions are acquired is one of the problems we shall consider.)

(2) If intuitions are syntheses of individual experience, probabilistic behaviour should develop in step with general intellectual development.

(3) The formation of a natural intuitive substrate must be distinguished from the development of secondary intuitions which are the result of systematic instruction. Since the intuitive substrate of probabilistic thinking is relatively poor (and, as we shall see, contradictory) the problem of the formation of secondary probabilistic intuitions is particularly important from the point of view of mathematics curricula. "Indubitably intuition can be trained and developed" Feller writes in a well-known text-book on probability theory; and further: "...mathematical intuition increases with experience and it is possible that a natural feeling develops for concepts such as that of quadri-dimensional space" (Feller, 1968, p. 2).

(4) If the theory of probability is supported by a specific intuitive substrate, and if this substrate is largely to be acquired through the process of education, then the teaching of probability theory should start at the concrete operational level, or at the latest during the period of organisation of formal operations (12–14 years).

(5) It is clear, however, that before the novel intuitions and conceptual system of any branch of science can be imparted through educational procedures, it is necessary to know the primary intuitive substrate underlying the science.

We therefore believe that the introduction of new curricula in schools should be preceded by research into the primary intuitive substrate of the relevant subject. The primary intuitions may facilitate the assimilation of new knowledge if they correspond to scientific truth; on the other hand, if they do not correspond to scientific truth, they may impede the assimilation of new knowledge.

The concept of probability, which is a synthesis of chance and necessity,

of the random and the deterministic, involves sometimes dramatic con-
frontations in the developing intellect. As we shall see, there is a variety of
possibilities, facilitating and impeding intuitions on different levels of
complexity of understanding and having many different relations with
adaptive behaviour, perceptual information, and conceptual schemas.

CHAPTER III

PROBABILITY LEARNING

Intuition and Probability Learning

As we have already indicated, intuition is, according to our hypothesis, the means by which intelligence secures for cognition an immediate control over action. An intuition is a stabilised action programme * which is derived from experience, and which is effective because of its global, immediate, and flexible qualities.

Deriving from action, it summarises, concentrates, and determines the anticipatory cognitive qualities of adaptive action in general, and of certain classes of adaptive actions, in particular.

The implications of this point of view will be sought in subjects' predictions of relative frequencies in experiments of the 'probability learning' type.

We have already pointed out that the natural conditions of individual existence are stochastic in character. The so-called deterministic laws, i.e. those revealing fixed dependencies, do not govern all phenomena. The possible, as opposed to the determined, should be allowed for in any account of adaptive responses. The individual, before being able to carry out any explicit computation of probabilities, must adapt to an environment in which the accidental, the uncertain, and the possible are all part of ongoing existence. Under such circumstances, adaptation cannot be achieved through a classical form of conditioning in which the repeated and constant conjunction of a stimulus and a response gradually establish a stable connection. In reality reinforcements are intermittent, and both predictions and responses are inconsistently reinforced; given that this is the case, behaviour must adapt in such a way that the minimum of failures occurs. In such conditions, predictions, and, correspondingly, adaptive responses, are only possible to the extent that relatively stable dependencies can be found beyond the uncertain and the accidental. It is the stability of relative frequencies which is the basis of successful prediction in these circumstances.

But before the individual is able to compute relative frequencies (and draw conclusions relevant to behaviour) there must be available some method of storing frequencies and proportions that experience has revealed to be important for adaptive behaviour; and this method must be intrinsic to the action programme.

An action programme of this kind has all the characteristics and functions of intuition which have been discussed in the preceding pages.

The adjustment of behaviour to the frequencies of events obviously implies a certain amount of *individual experience*. This adjustment of behaviour is not reducible to mere habit, because it is not an aggregate of stereotyped, automatised connections. It is a *cognitive phenomenon uniquely serving action*, since the anticipative element is not co-extensive with individual responses. It is part of a schema which is relatively autonomous and detached from the repertoire of responses. In other words, what we are dealing with is not just a series of responses which are automatically and uniquely determined by stimuli, but with responses which follow from an action programme *which includes storage of antecedent events*. We are therefore dealing with probability matching by a representative schema, an anticipatory function whose existence is relatively independent of the string of responses, as is any cognitive process (e.g. perception, reasoning).

This cognitive structure presupposed by probability-matching behaviour is, however, not fully autonomous. It is always immediately linked to action.

In accordance with the nomenclature we have proposed, we might call the intuition of relative frequency a typical primary intuition, and, at the same time, an anticipatory intuition. It is not an affirmatory intuition. It is a pre-operational intuition in that, from the genetic point of view, as we shall soon see, it forms prior to the operational stage of the development of intelligence, and it acts, or is able to act, independently of any explicit reasoning.

The data to be presented now show the ontogenesis of this intuition, and will enable us, by extrapolation, to formulate a set of hypotheses concerning the nature and development of intuitions as a whole.

Before expounding these data on the ontogenesis of probability learning, it is necessary to consider the theoretical implications of the mathematical model of learning, which are important to the interpretation of the data.

THE MATHEMATICAL FRAMEWORK. THE STIMULUS
SAMPLING THEORY (SST)

Before dealing with the mathematical aspects of probability learning itself, we shall briefly discuss the more general outline provided by Estes' statistical theory of learning in the form of Stimulus Sampling Theory.

Mathematical learning theory has been developing since 1950. W.K. Estes published a fundamental study in 1950, and this was followed by Bush and Mosteller's paper describing a mathematical model for simple learning (Bush and Mosteller, 1951). Many papers and articles have since appeared on related subjects.

The most important contributions have been those of Estes and Straughan (1954), Burke *et al.* (1954), Bush and Mosteller (1955), Estes (1959a, 1959b, 1964), Estes and Suppes (1959), and Atkinson *et al.* (1964). Rouanet's book (1967) provides a good synthesis. Rumanian mathematicians have contributed to the generalisation of the theoretical model (Iosifescu, 1963; Iosifescu and Theodorescu, 1965, 1969).

Estes and Burke developed their statistical theory of learning as a formalisation of Guthrie's approach to stimulus-response associationism. It is a *stimulus sampling theory* (SST) in which the stimulus situation is represented as a set of independent elements. At any given trial, only a sample of the total population of elements (S) will be effective and will determine the subject's response. Let us assume two possible responses, A_1 and A_2 (for example pressing (A_1) or not pressing (A_2) a lever). Each stimulus element may be connected to one of the two responses. The theory assumes that the connection between an element of the stimulus situation and a given response does not vary in strength. From trial to trial, the stimulus elements will change their connections with the responses. The state of the system, i.e., the subject's tendency at any given moment to perform either of the two responses, is determined by the connections existing at that moment between the elements of the stimulus situation and each alternative response.

Estes uses a chemical analogy. In its simplest form, a chemical transformation develops across time according to the formula

$$\Delta x = q(S - x),$$

where x represents the concentration of the substance at a given moment,

S represents the maximum concentration, q is a proportionality constant, and Δx stands for the change in concentration during a unit of time (Estes, 1959a). The formula clearly expresses the fact that, over time, the changes in concentration (Δx) diminish, since $S - x$ decreases as x increases. In stimulus sampling theory, S can stand for the total number of elements in the stimulus situation, and q for the proportion of effective elements (that is, elements sampled by the subject on a given trial).

Let us introduce one more assumption, termed the *homogeneity hypothesis* (Bush and Mosteller, 1955). The ratio of the number of conditioned elements to the total number of elements in S is maintained by the sampling of the subject at any given moment of the stimulus situation. Bush and Mosteller use the following analogy to make this clear. If we have a homogeneous mixture of water and alcohol in a flask, and pour part of the mixture into a glass, the mixture in the glass is in the same ratio of water to alcohol as the mixture in the flask. Supposing, then, that not all the elements of the stimulus situation are effective for the subject at a given moment, but only some of them; according to the homogeneity hypothesis the given sample of the stimulus maintains the same proportion of elements connected respectively to A_1 and A_2 as that found in the stimulus situation as a whole.

Passing on now to probability, let us divide each side of the equation

$$\Delta x = q(S - x)$$

by S. We have, then

$$\frac{\Delta x}{S} = q\left(\frac{S}{S} - \frac{x}{S}\right)$$

x/S is the proportion of x elements connected to A_1 over the total of stimulus elements. Since the proportion of effective stimulus elements is the same in any sample of the stimulus situation, x/S is nothing other than the probability of the A_1 response.

Accordingly, $x/S = p$. Further on, we have

$$\Delta p = q(1 - p)$$

Estes replaces q by θ, which gives

$$\Delta p = \theta(1 - p).$$

Letting Δp stand for the *change in probability*, then

$$p_{n+1} = p_n + \Delta p,$$

that is,

$$p_{n+1} = p_n + \theta(1 - p_n).$$

We have thus obtained a formula which will enable us to predict the probability of a given response on a given trial, if we know its probability in the previous trial.

The symbol θ stands for the probability with which a given element of the stimulus population is included in the sample (independently of the total number comprised in the sample).

The extent to which the subject has 'learned' a response is determined by the total number of stimulus elements connected to that response. This represents the 'state of the system', and refers to a particular individual at a particular moment.

The 'state of the system' changes during the process of learning as a consequence of changes occurring in the connections established between stimulus elements and S responses.

"The probability of any given response is equal to the proportion of sampled elements on that trial that are connected to that response. If a sample of size 10 contains 5 elements connected to response A_1, 3 to A_2 and 2 to A_3, then the probabilities are 0.5, 0.3 and 0.2 respectively. If the number of elements is large, so that the statistical 'law of large numbers' applies, this performance rule has the effect of setting the probability of response A_1 equal to p, the proportion of A_1-connected elements in the population" (Hilgard and Bower, 1966, p. 340).

For each response elicited, all the elements of the given sample of a population of stimulus elements (including connected and unconnected elements) will be connected to that response. In this way, new elements, which were previously unbound, become connected to the response; and thus learning progresses. The theory assumes that if a trial ends with a reinforcing event E_k (the concordance between a sample of elements of the stimulus population and an A_k response), then *all* the elements of the sample are conditioned to the A_k response, regardless of the antecedent conditioning of these elements.

The equation

$$p_{n+1} = p_n + \theta(1 - p_n) \tag{1a}$$

refers to the situation in which there are two classes of possible responses, A_1 and A_2, their probabilities being respectively p_n and $1-p_n$, on trial n.

The equation can also be expressed as

$$p_{n+1} = (1 - \theta) p_n + \theta. \tag{1b}$$

Equation (1a) indicates that an event E_1 increases the probability of a response A_1 and p tends to a limit of unity. We therefore conclude that p_{n+1} is a linear function of p_n tending toward an asymptote equal to unity as E_1 reinforcements are repeated.

An E_2 reinforcing event increases the probability of an A_2 response, and reduces the probability of an A_1 response.

$$p_{n+1} = (1 - \theta) p_n + \theta \cdot 0 = (1 - \theta) p_n.$$

The product $(1 - \theta) p_n$ represents the probability of an element connected to A_1 not being included in the sample. Its position does not change at the next sampling. If *all the elements of the sample* are connected to A_2, then it appears that no more elements connected to A_1 are added, and so

$$p_{n+1} = (1 - \theta) p_n.$$

It is obvious that

$$p_{n+1} < p_n.$$

This is because some of the elements which were previously conditioned to A_1 have now, as a consequence of the event E_2, become connected to A_2 (i.e. all those included in the sample).

Briefly, the following results are possible with respect to the probability of an A_1 response at the nth trial (cf. Hilgard and Bower, 1966, p. 343):

$$p_{n+1} = \begin{cases} (1 - \theta) p_n + \theta & \text{if } E_{1,n} \\ (1 - \theta) p_n & \text{if } E_{2,n} \\ p_n & \text{if } E_{0,n} \end{cases} \tag{2}$$

E_0 refers to the absence of reinforcement, so that the situation does not change.

These equations show how the probability of a response is dependent on the events of the previous trial. We can also consider equations decribing the process as it develops across the whole set of trials. For a sequence of E_1 events, for example, the equation would take the following form

$$p_n = 1 - (1 - p_1)(1 - \theta)^{n-1}.$$ (3)

As n increases, p_n increases, but the function is negatively accelerated. When n takes very high values, $(1-\theta)^{n-1}$ tends to zero.

The symbol θ represents, as we have already said, the proportion of elements sampled at each trial, or the probability of an element being included in the sample. The 'rate of learning' is expressed by the value of θ, since θ indicates the degree to which new stimulus elements are connected to A_1 when an E_1 event takes place.

Probability Learning

The term *probability learning* refers to a situation in which the responses of the subject are not reinforced constantly, as in ordinary conditioning, but intermittently and randomly, with a particular relative frequency. For a very clear account of probability learning, see Millward (1971).

In its simplest form, an experiment of this kind proceeds as follows. In front of the subject, there are two different-coloured lights, and two keys. Above the two lights, there is a third one which is used as a 'ready' signal. When the signal lights, the subject is to press one of the two keys, corresponding to whichever of the coloured lights the subject predicts will come on next. After the subject has pressed the key, one of the two lights comes on, confirming or falsifying the prediction. And so the experiment continues. The subject makes another prediction, producing one of the two possible responses, A_1 or A_2, which will be followed by one of the two possible outcomes O_1 or O_2.

Let us assume that the probabilities of the outcomes are 70% for the right-hand light, and 30% for the left-hand light. The term 'probability learning' refers to the finding that the proportion of A_1 responses tends to match the proportion of E_1 events. In other words, the probability of a given response tends to equal the probability of the corresponding stimulus. In the above example there were two stimuli, i.e. the two possible outcomes O_1 and O_2, reinforcing the responses A_1 and A_2 respectively. E_1 is the reinforcing event constituted by the reinforcement of A_1 by O_1, and E_2 is the reinforcing event constituted by the reinforcement of A_2 by O_2.

The probability of E_1 on trial n is equal to π_n, and the probability of E_2 on trial n is equal to the complementary probability $1 - \pi_n$.

Since the probabilities of E_1 and E_2 on the preceding trial are known, the probability of the response A_1 on trial $n+1$ can be obtained from the following equation

$$p_{n+1} = \pi_n[(1 - \theta) p_n + \theta] + (1 - \pi_n) [(1 - \theta) p_n]. \qquad (4)$$

In (4) the two Equations (1a) and (1b) have been summed after weighting them with π_n and $1 - \pi_n$ respectively (corresponding to the probabilities of E_1 and E_2).

The above equation reduces to

$$p_{n+1} = (1 - \theta) p_n + \theta \pi_n . \qquad (5)$$

As in the previous case, it is possible to arrive inductively here also at a general equation expressing the probability of the response A_1 on trial n if p_1, θ and π are known.

$$p_n = \pi - (\pi - p_1)(1 - \theta)^{n-1}. \qquad (6)$$

This equation can in fact be obtained from Equation (3) by substituting π for 1. When n (number of trials) is very high, $(1 - \theta)^{n-1}$ tends to zero, and so

$$\lim p_n = \pi \qquad (7)$$

for $n \rightarrow \infty$.

The above equation therefore predicts that, over a large number of trials, the probability of the response A_1 tends to equal the probability of the event E_1 across trials. This is the 'probability matching' theorem. In fact, the experimenter has to compute the proportion of A_1 and A_2 responses in successive blocks of trials (per single individual and per group). In practice, the probability of a response can only be derived from proportions of responses per block of trials.

Probability learning experiments use a variety of experimental designs. In a noncontingent experiment, the outcome on a given trial (such as the lighting of a bulb, as in the preceding example) is not dependent on the subject's response, and thus the probability of each possible outcome (O_1, O_2, etc.) is not dependent on previous responses either.

A contingent probability learning experiment does involve such dependencies. The probability of each of the two reinforcing events E_1 and E_2 on any given trial depends on the responses of the subject on the previous trial.

π may be held constant, or may be increased or decreased according to a given rule. The outcome may depend on a series of previous responses.

The number of reinforcers used (i.e. outcomes O_1, O_2, etc.) depends on the various experimental models, and consequently the results obtained differ also. The effects of other variables, such as type of reward or punishment, form of instructions, etc. have also been investigated.

A basic theoretical problem is the extent to which probability learning results obtained from groups of individuals in the form of group averages accurately reflect the learning process which, of course, must be an individual phenomenon. Is the 'probability matching' predicted by Equation (3) confirmed in single-subject experiments? Does the superimposition of individual results produce curves which are mere artifacts?

The 'asymptotic probability matching' predicted by Equation (3) is, in fact, obtained much better in group curves than in individual curves. According to Estes (1964) it is a mistake to consider individual data. Direct inspection of individual data is, indeed, very little suggestive of the asymptotic tendency. They present irregularities, with successive increases and decreases which are not predicted by the model. The curves suggest individual differences in probability learning. Certain subjects seem to adopt a strategy resulting from the frequency of reinforements, but they later drop it in favour of random responding. Others adopt a maximising strategy, in which only the most frequently reinforced response is used. There are also subjects who, over many trials, manifest no systematic improvements.

According to Estes, the researcher should not rely on such data in drawing conclusions about individual learning. In fact, chance is a major variable in these individual results. Only statistical analysis of the data from groups of subjects – per block of trials – is able to give an accurate picture of the learning process.

Estes compared the data from an experiment on human subjects with simulated data generated by a computer.

In the second case, we are obviously no longer dealing with motivational phenomena and individual differences, but with the role of chance within the basic theoretical model.

"The artificial data give us an idea of how much variability to expect, both among individuals at any stage and over trial blocks for any individual, simply because of the probabilistic character of the choice behaviour, even when there are no individual differences in mode or rate of learning" (Estes, 1964, pp. 92–93).

The most striking fact is that data obtained in this way are very similar in every respect to those obtained from real subjects. Here too, 'individual' curves denote maximising strategies, long periods of uncertainty, and so on.

Comparison of the two sets of data is bound, according to Estes, to lead to the conclusion that one should be sceptical about individual data, for they are dependent on chance to the point where the tendencies of the true phenomenon are masked. It is only by averaging data from groups of individuals that a real picture of the basic trends can be obtained.

Recency effects are the effects that repetition of the same outcome on several trials has on the subject's responses. Following the theoretical model, after a run of exclusively O_1 outcomes, then the longer the run the higher the probability that the subject will predict the same outcome on the next trial. If, for instance, as in our example of a probability learning experiment, the red light comes on several times in succession, the probability of the subject predicting the red light on the following trial will be higher. This is what has been termed the *positive recency effect*.

In fact, experimental data do not accord with this prediction. As early as 1951, Jarvik showed that in probability learning experiments subjects tend to predict the O_2 outcome after a long run of O_1 outcomes. This has been termed the *negative recency effect* – the tendency to predict the outcome which has not appeared for some time.

Jarvik has explained the negative recency effect by what is called 'the gambler's fallacy'. After the repeated occurrence of a given outcome on several trials, the gambler is persuaded that the probability of the other outcome is increasing. In fact, in this type of experiment, each event is independent (such as, for example, the outcomes on successive tosses of a coin). The probability of a particular outcome on a given trial is not influenced by the outcome of the previous trials. The negative recency effect has been described by several authors (Anderson, 1960; Feldman, 1959; Nicks, 1959, etc.) (cf. Estes, 1964).

Estes claims that the negative recency effect does not contradict the

theoretical model. He says "... the negative recency function results largely from response tendencies the S's bring with them to the experiment,
via generalization from other situations, but which extinguish with experience in the experimental situation (Estes, 1964, p. 98).

Lindman and Edwards (1961) have indeed observed that the negative
recency effect is apparent on the early trials, but starts decreasing after
100 trials.

Jones and Myers (1966) have shown that the results of recency analyses
are dependent on the number of trials per block. Trials are usually ran-
domised in such a way that there are $N\pi$ O_1's per block of N amplitude.
In the case of relatively small blocks, the length of runs is also reduced.
Jones and Myers compared the results obtained on blocks ranging from
200 to 300 trials each, and found that the responses reflected the relative
probabilities within each size of block. Gambino and Myers (1966) have,
however, found that negative recency effects decrease as the variability of
runs increases.

Asymptotic behaviour depends on specific experimental conditions. Estes
(1964) has summarised as follows the dependence of asymptotic behaviour on certain experimental conditions:

"Probability matching behaviour manifests itself in those cases in which
the subject is required to make a prediction on each trial or to do his best
to answer correctly on each trial.

In the case in which the subject infers from the instruction that the
succession of reinforcing events is random or when the instruction stresses
that it is desirable to obtain as large a number of correct predictions as
possible, then the phenomenon of over-shooting appears, that is, the
subject's tendency is to predict the most frequent event with a probability
higher than the probability of the event itself."

As regards the role of reward or punishment, Estes believes that it does
not cause essential differences in the rate of learning. However, the following fact is noted. When differential reward or punishment are used,
the probability of predicting the most frequently rewarded alternative
tends to go above the matching value. The same tendency has been noted
in experiments with more than two possible outcomes. Estes quotes the
work of Cotton and Rechtschaffen (1958), Gardner (1957, 1958), and
McCormack (1959); cf. Estes, 1964.

NOTE

* The term 'action programme' recalls the 'Plan' of Miller, Galanter and Pribram (G. A. Miller, E. Galanter, and K. H. Pribram: *Plans and the Structure of Behavior*, Holt, Rinehart and Winston, 1967). These authors' use of the term 'Plan' is, however, much wider. A Plan is any hierarchical process in the organism that can control the order in which a sequence of operations is performed (Miller *et al.*, 1967, p. 16). Instincts, habits, and problem-solving procedures all presuppose Plans. Intuition, as we define it, therefore falls into this category of intervening variables. Yet, in addition, intuition presupposes a set of distinguishing features which confer specificity on it.

CHAPTER IV

PROBABILITY LEARNING IN CHILDREN

A number of studies of probability learning have been concerned with the developmental aspects of the problem. Several age-groups have been investigated, ranging from pre-school (aged 3) to adolescent children.

The principal aspects studied have been: (a) asymptotic and maximising behaviour as a function of age; (b) the role of reward and punishment; (c) the role of instructions; (d) recency effects and sequential analysis.

Probability matching and asymptotic behaviour. Experiments on probability learning are of prime importance to the study of the development of probabilistic intuitions in children. Probability matching behaviour does not presuppose any conceptual system proper, and it therefore serves as an index of the presence of behavioural schemas adapted to stochastic conditions at the early stages of development (that is, the preoperational stages).

The most important finding has been that even 3- to- 4 year-olds show a tendency to make predictions which match the probabilities of reinforcing stimuli.

Messik and Solley (1957) carried out a series of experiments with 7 children aged between 3 and 8 years. In the first experiment, the stimuli were cardboard figures representing human and animal figures which could take two size values, 'big' or 'small'. The following frequency pairs of these values were investigated: 1.00–0.00; 0.90–0.10; 0.75–0.25; 0.60–0.40. The second experiment varied the expression on the faces of the figures; 0.75 were 'happy', 0.25 were 'sad'. Each experiment ran for 200 trials, grouped in blocks of 20 trials.

Both experiments showed that the subjects' predictions reached an asymptote which was determined by the probabilities of the events. There were no differences in this respect among the different age-groups, even when the results were compared with those obtained from adults by other investigators. An asymptote was reached even in the case of the 0.60 frequency, differentiating behaviour at this frequency from when the frequency was at the 0.50 chance level.

Crandall *et al.* (1961) investigated probability matching in 6–8 year-old children and in adolescents (15–17 years old). The stimuli were a red and a green light, which were on with 80% and 20% frequencies, respectively. In 80 trials grouped into blocks of 10, these two outcomes occurred in the ratio 8:2. A further series of 80 trials followed, in which the 'light on' frequency was 50%–50%. The subjects were rewarded with one cent per four correct guesses. Two experimental variants were used. In the first, the outcomes randomly succeeded each other in a fixed proportion. In the second variant (run with the same subjects one year later) the outcomes occurred in a regular pattern; for the 80%–20% frequencies, the pattern was 4–1; 4–1 etc., while for the 50%–50% frequencies it was 5–5; 5–5, and so on.

Probability learning was assessed at both age levels. The predictions of the younger subjects did not reach the input probability levels on the 80%–20% schedule. On the same schedule, the older subjects' predictions matched the input probability levels. On the 50%–50% schedule, there were no differences among the age levels. In the second variant of the experiment, in which the order of reinforcing events was patterned, probability matching occurred faster in older subjects. The difference between older and younger subjects is much more salient in such circumstances. "The younger children more often employed molecular trial by trial expectations, the older children were likely to bring 'higher order' pattern expectations to the learning situation and to employ them effectively" (Crandall *et al.*, 1961, p. 36).

After each experimental session, the children were questioned about their predictions. It was observed that some of them believed in a fixed order, even in the unpatterned condition. This attitude is most frequently encountered in older children (30% of the 6–8 year-olds, and 90% of the 15–17 year-olds).

Craig and Myers (1963) worked with pre-school children and with fourth-grade (10–12) and eighth-grade (14–16) children. The reinforcing stimuli were two red lights. The subject had to predict which would light up by placing a card in a slot below the appropriate light. 60%–40% and 80%–20% schedules were used in 200 trials, grouped into blocks of 50.

In all six experimental groups, an increase in the number of A_1 responses (prediction of E_1, the most frequent event) was noted across the 200 trials. Children in the fourth and eighth grades were matching predictions to the input probabilities. Pre-school children produced an increasing number of A_1 responses over the series of trials, but their predictions were half-way between 50%–50% and the input probabilities.

Altogether, the pre-schoolers produced significantly fewer A_1 predictions than the other age levels.

"It appears that there is a developmental continuum with regard to asymptotic choice proportion and rate of acquisition, with the most marked change in approach to choice situations occurring between the ages of 5 and 9" (Craig and Myers, 1963, p. 491).

Siegel and Andrews (1962) worked with boys between 3:10 and 5 years. An object was hidden by the experimenter in one of two bottles placed in front of the child. The child had to guess where the object was hidden. Correct guesses were rewarded by giving the child the object. In a low-reward condition, the child received a button; in a high-reward condition, he was given a toy. Each child went through 100 trials in each condition, with one experimental group starting in the low-reward condition and the other in the high-reward condition. Trials were grouped in blocks of 20. With a 0.75–0.25 schedule, it was found that, even in the first hundred trials, the children's predictions approximated the π value (75%). Averaging asymptotic responses gave $\bar{p}_\infty(L) = 0.74$ for the low-reward condition, and $\bar{p}_\infty(H) = 0.84$ for the high-reward condition.

Siegel and Andrews have therefore demonstrated probability-matching behaviour in children as young as 3–5 years.

Offenbach (1964) worked with kindergarten children (4:5 to 6:5 years) and schoolchildren aged 9:3 to 11:10 years. The stimulus materials consisted of 100 cards, 75 with a red square and 25 with a blue square. The cards were shuffled, and the children predicted which colour square would come next as the cards were turned over. In the last 40 out of 100 trials in a non-rewarded variant of the experiment, a 58% prediction rate was obtained for the most frequent event (75%) in pre-school children, and a 62.5% rate was obtained in 10 year-old children. Offenbach thus confirmed the finding that approximation to the asymptotic value occurs faster in older children, but he believes that his data do not indicate probability matching *per se*.

Expectancy and the preference for complex solutions.
Stevenson and Weir (1959) started from the findings of a previous study

(Stevenson and Ziegler, 1958) in which probability learning data from normal and mentally retarded children, in one group, and from normal (high- or lowscoring) play-trained children, in a second group, were compared. The conclusion of both studies was that the discrepancies in responses between the groups were due to different degrees of expectancy concerning the proportions of reinforcing events. It had been hypothesised that subjects with a low level of expectancy would predict the most frequent stimulus most often, while subjects with a high level of expectancy would predict the most reinforced stimulus most often.

On the basis of this conclusion, it was further hypothesised that the percentage of predictions of the least frequent event would be higher in older children. To test this hypothesis, Stevenson and Weir carried out an experiment with children in the following age ranges: 3–3:11, 5–5:11, 7–7:11, and 8:9–10:2. There were 30 children in each age range. The apparatus was a board with three push-buttons on it. Only one of these buttons, when pressed, would release a marble. The child was instructed to press one of the buttons as soon as a light signal appeared. The 30 subjects were assigned to three groups corresponding to the following schedules: 100%, 66%, 33%. Reinforcement was contingent, and each subject went through 80 trials.

The essential finding was that older children chose the reinforced button less frequently, although on the 100% schedule there were no age differences in behaviour. According to Stevenson and Weir, the maximising strategy, which is in fact the most rational if the child intends to win, appears in young children and diminishes with age.

The results obtained by Stevenson and Weir differ from those of other studies mostly in that, in their experiment, the older subjects chose the reinforced response more rarely. This result could be due to the fact that only one of the three responses was reinforced (in contrast to the other studies, in which each response was reinforced with a given frequency). Older subjects are probably not satisfied with a completely stereotyped response, such as pressing always the same button out of three. It therefore seems that the main finding obtained by Stevenson and Weir is that *older subjects tend to resort to more complex solutions in their predictions.* In 1964, Weir published a report of his studies on developmental changes in probability learning. He had obtained data from 290 subjects, who ranged in age from 3 to 20 years. He reported a *U*-shaped relationship between age and asymptotic level of correct responses; adults (college students) and 3 to 5 year-old children showed a similar level of performance after 80 trials. Weir suggests that this similarity actually results from different tendencies. A detailed examination of the learning curves in the various age groups shows fundamentally different features. The performance of 3 and 5 year-old children shows a rapid rise to the asymptote, while in adults the rise is slower. It is Weir's opinion that the 3 and 5 year-olds choose the pay-off button most frequently "on the basis of a simple reinforcement notion only" (Weir, 1964, p. 477). In contrast, older subjects seek a more complex strategy which would enable them to reach 100% success in prediction. As for the maximising strategy itself, Weir reports the following: at age 3, 50% of subjects on the 33% schedule, and 70% of subjects on the 66% schedule display maximising behaviour. This tendency diminishes in older children (7 to 14 years old), and begins to rise again thereafter. In 18 year-olds, 17% of subjects on the 33% schedule, and 50% of subjects on the 66% schedule display a maximum gain strategy. Weir's data are consistent with those of Jones and Liverant (1960) who have reported that 4 to 6 year-old subjects show more maximisation on a two-choice task than older subjects (9 to 11 year-olds).

There is another possible explanation for Weir's finding that the maximising strategy diminishes with age. In his research, Weir only used rewards with children. This difference is likely to partly explain the difference in behaviour between children and adults.

In the main, however, it is possible to agree with Weir that the conflict in results obtained by other investigators has a more fundamental origin. What appears to be similar behaviour at different age levels is, in fact, determined by fundamentally different factors. In the case of the young child, the 'strategy' is merely the effect of conditioning, while in the case of older subjects the strategy reflects an authentic maximum gain rationale (the subject gradually recognises the advantage of choosing the pay-off button, or the most frequent outcome). But this rational behaviour is contradicted by the tendency to seek more complex strategies, more imaginative solutions than mere repetitions of the same response, as Weir suggests. Which of these two opposed tendencies will be elicited depends on the specific experimental conditions.

To summarise, then:

(1) All the above-mentioned authors report probability matching behaviour in children at age 5 or 6 at the latest.

(2) All of these authors – with the exception of Stevenson and Weir –
have noted that probability matching behaviour is a developmental phenomenon.

(3) Older children retain a belief in a determined order, even in conditions of a random succession of reinforcing stimuli.

The role of reward and punishment. One would expect that the introduction
of reward for correct guesses would improve the subject's probability
matching behaviour. Such an improvement would be expressed in maximising behaviour, i.e. the tendency to choose the most frequently-occurring reinforcing stimulus, even perhaps exceeding the input probability
level to the point of approximating 100% predictions of these stimuli.

Messik and Solley (1957), in the work reported above, used a reward
variant of their experiment in which the children received a sweet for
each correct guess. With the input probabilities at 0.75–0.25, their findings
were as follows. At 7 to 8 years of age, the prediction curves converge
toward 100% for the most frequent stimulus (in other words, at this age
level, reward induced a maximum gain behaviour). In 5 year-old children,
the curves maximised at 0.90, a value between the stimulus probability
and the 100% level. The predictions of 3 to 4 year-olds stabilise at 75%,
which is the probability value. Thus, according to Messik and Solley, the
*maximisation strategy is stimulated by reward, and its incidence increases
with the age of children.*

Stevenson and Weir (1959) used the apparatus described above (the
panel with 3 response buttons, only one of which produces reinforcement)
with 5 year-old children, in order to investigate the effects of two incentive conditions. In a high incentive condition, choice of the reinforcing
button resulted in the delivery of a small toy. In a low incentive condition,
the reward was a marble. The reinforcement schedules were 33%, 66%,
and 100%.

It had been hypothesised that the high incentive condition would induce
the subjects to try the non-reinforced buttons more frequently, in a search
for solutions which would maximise gain. The results confirmed this hypothesis: the high incentive condition induced subjects to choose the
reinforcing button less often. These results are in conflict with those ob-

tained by Messik and Solley (1957), who noted the reverse phenomenon, i.e. a tendency to overshoot under the influence of reward.

In 1959, Siegel and Goldstein described a model differing from that of Estes. As we have pointed out, equations based on the stimulus sampling theory do not explicitly include parameters dependent on the value of the reward. Siegel and Goldstein's equation takes the following form:

$$p = d(\pi - \tfrac{1}{2}) + \tfrac{1}{2},$$

where π is the probability of the most frequent event, p is the proportion of cases in which the subject predicts the most frequent event, and $d = a/b$, a being the marginal utility of a correct guess and b the marginal utility of alternating responses.

The model takes into account the fact that the response is dependent on the change in the amount of reinforcement (as it produces a change in marginal utiltiy). If $a = b$, the model predicts the same asymptotic behaviour as Estes' model; this is the situation in which the only source of reinforcement is knowledge of results.

Siegel and Andrews (1962) investigated high- and low-reward conditions in a probability learning experiment with boys aged from 3 to 5. They noted that, in the high-reward condition, the most frequently-occurring alternative was chosen most often. This contradicts the results of Stevenson and Weir, but confirms those of Messik and Solley.

The fact that the high-reward conditions reported in these experiments induce a maximisation strategy even at the age of 4 to 5 indicates, as Siegel and Andrews have pointed out, that children of this age are sensitive to the proportion of events, *which demonstrates that they have at least an elementary concept of probability.*

Brackbill *et al.* (1962) also started from the assumption that the maximum gain strategy is stimulated by reward. Their hypothesis, more precisely, was that on a typical noncontingent probability learning task, the maximum gain strategy is a function of the amount of reward following correct predictions.

Their subjects were 8 year-old children, 24 boys and 24 girls. The stimulus materials consisted of two packs of 200 cards, bearing pictures of either a dog or a cat in a 75%–25% proportion. The cards were divided into 20 blocks, each block maintaining the above proportion. The subject received a number of marbles for each correct guess. In order to vary the amount of reward, subjects were assigned to 4 groups, differing according to the number of marbles awarded for a correct guess, viz. 5, 3, 1, or 0 marbles. For every 100 marbles gained, the subject received a gift. It was observed that the maximising strategy increased with the amount of reward. The most important difference, however, was between rewarded and non-rewarded behaviour. This suggests, as Brackbill *et al.* point out, that the relationship between reward and performance is not linear.

Pubols (1960) has suggested, on the basis of his work with animals, that *the function relating performance to amount of reward is negatively accelerated, and may be logarithmic.*

Offenbach (1964) attempted to reduce the utility of guessing the less frequent event by punishing incorrect predictions. His subjects, as we have already indicated, were pre-school children and fourthgraders (10–12 years). They were divided into three groups as follows: (I) Group 0–0. No punishment and no reward. (II) Group 1–1. For each correct guess the subject received a marble, and for each incorrect guess returned a marble. (III) Group 3–3. For each correct guess the subject received 3 marbles, and for each incorrect guess returned 3 marbles. The marbles could be traded for toys; if all the marbles had been returned, then toys had to be returned. Counting only the proportion of predictions of the most frequent event ($\pi = 0.75$) over the last 40 trials, Offenbach obtained the following results:

	0–0	58.00
Preschool children	1–1	75.50
	3–3	70.75
	0–0	62.25
Fourth graders	1–1	72.25
	3–3	70.25

These data show that: (a) no age differences were found; (b) subjects in punishment – reward conditions were more likely than other subjects to predict the most frequent event; (c) the amount of reward did not produce significant differences in performance. Comparing his results with those of Brackbill *et al.* – who rewarded correct guesses, but did not punish incorrect ones – Offenbach concluded that *punishing incorrect predictions does not increase predictions of the most frequent event.*

Relationships between age, instructions, punishment, and patterns of response in probability learning. Flood (1954) has put forward the hypothesis that the maximising strategy is used only when subjects are convinced that the succession of reinforcing events is random, and that the 'mixed' strategy expresses the subject's belief in the existence of a fixed pattern of reinforcing events.

Goodnow (1955) carried out an experiment based on a two-choice task, in which one group of subjects were instructed so as to induce a 'gambling' set, while another group were instructed so as to induce a 'problem-solving' set. It was found that the 'gambling' set was more conductive to the maximising tendency (the predictions approximating 100%) than the 'problem-solving' set.

According to Siegel and Goldstein (1959), however, circumstances in which risk or punishment occur are most likely to induce a maximum gain strategy; since these elements were present in Goodnow's experiment, it is not possible to accept his interpretation of his results in terms of 'set' as being conclusive.

Gruen and Weir (1964) attempted to clarify the relationship between instruction set and punishment in probability learning. They designed a factorial experiment including age in addition to the cited variables. Reinforcement was non-contingent. Three instructional sets were used, as follows: (a) a 'problem-solving' set, in which it was suggested to the subjects that they find a correct solving procedure; (b) a 'gambling' set, in which it was suggested that the sequence of stimuli was random; and (c) no specific set was induced. In a punishment group, subjects had to return a marble if a prediction was incorrect. There were three age levels of subjects: 7 years, 13 years, and college students.

The apparatus resembled that used by Weir, described previously. The subject pressed one of three response buttons, and by pressing the correct button received a marble. This button was reinforced on a 66% schedule.

The results showed a significant difference between punishment and non-punishment conditions. The reinforced button was selected 82.8% of the time in the punishment condition, and 73.9% of the time in the non-punishment condition. Age differences were also significant; the average proportion of choices of the reinforcing stimulus increased with age: 65.8% at 7, 81.9% at 13, and 87.3% in students. Significant differences between instruction sets were found for the students only.

We may therefore conclude that *punishment changes behaviour in three-choice tasks when only one choice is reinforced.* As we know from Stevenson and Weir's (1959) experiment, prediction of the most frequent event decreases with age. Punishment can, therefore, change this situation in the case of the model using three potential responses, of which only one is reinforced.

Group behaviour and the effect of reward. Codirlă has studied the effect of reward on probability learning in groups of pre-school children aged 5 to 7 (1972a) and in groups of young school children aged from 6 to 9 (1972b).

In both experiments a pack of 150 cards was used, 70% of which were marked with a red circle, and 30% of which were marked with a blue circle. 15 blocks of 10 cards were presented, in which the 70%–30% proportion was maintained with few exceptions. The subjects were handed a block of cards, and asked to predict the colour of each successive card before it was turned face upwards. Reward was non-contingent.

In (1972a) reward and non-reward conditions were compared. In the reward condition, subjects were grouped 4 together, but each subject worked individually. Groups were told that the subject scoring the highest number of correct guesses in the group would receive a toy. In both reward and non-reward conditions, the prediction curve tended gradually toward the probability input level. Pre-school children, however, had failed to reach the input level on completion of the 150 trials. In the final blocks of trials, the proportion of responses to the 70% stimulus oscillated around 60%. In the reward condition, the number of predictions of the 70% stimulus was significantly higher than in the non-reward condition.

In (1972b), Codirlă used the following four experimental conditions, working with schoolchildren: (1) individual and non-rewarded; (2) individual, competitive, and rewarded (the subject with the highest number of correct guesses out of a group of 3 subjects received a prize); (3) group non-reward, in which groups of 3 subjects agreed on a single prediction; (4) group, rewarded, with competition, in which two groups of 3 subjects competed against each other, the group scoring the highest number of correct guesses receiving a prize.

The results showed that performance was better in the rewarded conditions, both per individual subject and per group. Group predictions, however, were inferior to individual predictions in respect of the A_1 response (the 70% prediction).

Comparing the results obtained by Codirlă on preschool (1972a) and school (1972b) children, it can be seen that the proportion of the latter's A_1 responses is the closest to π.

According to Codirlă, group organisation does not facilitate learning in this kind of experiment because group discussion interferes to some extent with correct frequency counting by the individual subject.

Social reinforcement. Some studies have reported findings concerning the role of social reinforcers in probabilistic tasks. McCullers and Stevenson (1960), using the three-button apparatus already described, found that the use of a verbal reinforcer such as 'good' or 'fine' would increase the number of choices of the verbally reinforced response.

Lewis (1965) has demonstrated that the proportion of choices of the most frequent stimulus is influenced by periods of isolation preceding the probabilistic task. Eight-year old children were left alone for periods of 0, 3, 6, 9, or 12 minutes before starting a two-choice card-guessing task (70%–30%). Correct guesses were reinforced by supportive comments from the experimenter.

Children left alone for either 3 or 12 minutes chose the 70% event more frequently than children who had been isolated for 6 or 9 minutes, or not isolated at all. Lewis explains this finding as follows. Children isolated for a short period of time become anxious about the task they are about to start, and therefore become more sensitive to praise from the experimenter. Children isolated for a longer period have time to become interested in their surroundings, and so their anxiety gradually diminishes. If, however, the period of isolation continues (12 minutes), they become habituated to the surroundings and the anxiety becomes dominant again.

If this explanation is correct, Lewis's findings support the idea that the higher the level of expectation, the more frequent the choices of the high-probability stimulus (in accordance with the findings of Siegel and Andrews (1962) and Brackbill *et al.* (1962)).

Another interesting finding was that of Gratch (1964) who found that independent children were more willing to gamble on their predictions than dependent children.

Summary

(1) Rewarding for correct guesses increases predictions of the most frequent event, regardless of age. Stevenson and Weir's data contain the only exception to this generalisation. Social reinforcement is equally effective.

(2) The maximisation strategy, if rewarded, becomes stronger with age.

(3) The effect of incorrect guesses is dependent on specific experimental conditions. In experiments in which more than one response is reinforced, punishment does not affect the results. When only one response is reinforced (e.g. Gruen and Weir, 1964) punishment results in an increase in the number of choices of the reinforced stimulus.

SEQUENTIAL EFFECTS

The analysis of sequential effects in probability learning tasks provides us with more information than simple inspection of prediction curves. *Sequential phenomena reveal the fundamental tendencies that are exhibited by subjects in interpreting sequences of stochastic events.*

Alternating predictions. In their previously cited experiment in which only one out of three responses was reinforced, Stevenson and Weir (1959) found that children produced structured sequences of responses in the pattern left-middle-right or right-middle-left. Such structured sequences appeared in children as young as 3, but the proportion increased over 5, 7, and 9 years. At these ages, about 50% of responses were patterned in this way. Stevenson and Weir infer from this that older subjects are more inclined to produce complex hypotheses.

The alternating-prediction tendency in children has been demonstrated by Ross (1966) in both hearing and deaf subjects. These subjects were hearing children at five age levels (7, 9, 11, 13, and 15) and deaf children at three age levels (11, 13, and 15). Although Ross's experiment was not concerned with probability learning, we are discussing his data because they confirm the sequential effects found by Stevenson and Weir.

In Ross's experiment, yellow and green balls were placed in a box in a given proportion. Subjects consecutively drew balls without replacement (except on some trials). Before each draw, the subject predicted the colour of the ball. It was observed that 7 and 9 year-olds were frequently wrong in their predictions, even with widely differing numbers of yellow and green balls (e.g. 5 to 1). Ross suggests that subjects' *unawareness of the great number of wrong guesses was the result of a strong tendency toward alternating predictions at these age levels*. Table I reproduced below, after Ross, shows the mean percentages of inappropriate alternating predictions at initial uneven odds.

TABLE I

Mean per cent inappropriate alternating predictions at
initial uneven odds (after Ross, 1966, p. 924)

Group	Age				
	7	9	11	13	15
Hearing					
Boys	59.4	62.5	43.8	31.2	21.9
Girls	53.1	50.0	59.0	37.5	34.4
Deaf					
Boys			55.0	32.5	32.5
Girls			72.5	55.0	27.5

Alternation behaviour also appears when odds are even. It is particularly marked at the start of a trial, but decreases as the trial progresses. According to Ross, it is therefore possible to conclude that "...alternating predictions at the beginning of a series is a strong pre-experimentally determined habit" (Ross, 1966, p. 925).

From the above table, it also appears that: (a) the alternation tendency is greater in girls than in boys; (b) the alternation tendency is greater in deaf than in hearing children.

The effects of instructions and penalty on alternating predictions. Gruen and Weir (1964) using the same apparatus as Stevenson and Weir (1959), with one response button reinforced out of three in 66% of the cases, studied the effects of different instructions and of penalising incorrect predictions on response sequence patterns. Three sets of instructions were investigated: (a) the subject was instructed to seek a correct guessing procedure; (b) the subject was instructed that there was no correct guessing procedure; (c) no instructions were given regarding any correct guessing procedure.

Analysis of the proportion of sterotyped sequences relative to the total number of varying responses showed the following facts.

Instruction differences did not result in significant differences in the number of stereotyped sequences. Instead, significant differences appeared as a function of age and penalty. The proportion of stereotyped series relative to the total number of varying responses was related to age as follows: in 7 year-olds 0.37; in 13 year-olds 0.26; and in students 0.29. Therefore, *in 7 year-olds there was a higher proportion of stereotyped response patterns than in older children.*

Penalty reduced the number of stereotyped response patterns (over all subjects). The proportions were 0.22 for the penalty group, and 0.33 for the non-penalty group. This indicates that penalty, by increasing expectancy, can induce, even in 7 year-olds, increased effort toward finding an efficient procedure.

A number of significant interactions appeared also. In 7 year-olds, instructions which suggested that there would be a random succession of stimuli were more likely to induce patterned response sequences, whereas the reverse was true for the older children, for whom the other types of instruction produced patterned responses.

These interactions might be explained as follows. In older children, the notion of a random sequence quite naturally induces a tendency to predict almost exclusively the only reinforced stimulus (especially if there are no instructions to search for a more complex procedure). This would certainly reduce the amount of stereotyped alternation. In 7 year-old children, the maximisation strategy (which is in fact the most rational) is not yet firmly established, and therefore, when there has been no instruction that the succession of stimuli will be random, the children will conclude (less efficiently) that they can resort to simple alternation of predictions.

Gruen and Weir also observed a strong negative recency effect, especially in 7 year-old children, thus confirming results reported by Stevenson and Weir (1959), Jones and Liverant (1960), and Kessen and Kessen (1961).

Dependence of predictions on antecedent events. Recency effects. Craig and

Myers (1963) paid particular attention to sequential effects in their study of probability learning. Their subjects were pre-schoolers, nine year-olds, and 13 year-olds, performing a two-choice task with 80:20 and 60:40 frequencies.

The mean number of predictions of the E_1 event was observed in runs reiterating E_1 at least four times (on the 60:40 schedule) or five times (on the 80:20 schedule). Information was thus obtained on the prediction of E_1 after repeated occurrences of this stimulus.

In 13 year-olds, both curves showed an increase on the first five trials, followed by a slight decrease (marking a negative recency effect) and a recovery tendency, with fluctuations. In nine year-olds, the initial increase appears only in the case of the 80:20 proportion. There is no such initial increase in either pre-school children or 9 year-olds for the 60:40 proportion.

The number of A_1 responses following the possible pairs A_1E_1, A_2E_1, A_1E_2, and A_2E_2 was also noted (i.e. the prediction of E_1 as a function of confirmation or falsification of the E_1 or E_2 prediction on the preceding trial). In pre-school children, a marked tendency to alternate predictions was noted, regardless of the preceding event, especially on the 60:40 schedule. In 13 year-olds, however, perseveration was observed after a correct response, most often when it concerned the most frequent event. In other words, a correct guess tended to be repeated immediately. 9 year-olds were much more like 13 year-olds than pre-schoolers; in them, the alternation tendency was weaker than in the pre-school children. On the other hand, the 9 year-olds did not perseverate on correct responses so markedly as the older children. In general, *9 and 13 year-olds are influenced by preceding stimulus patterns.* Pre-school children seem to need more information before being able to detect a pattern of events.

Weir (1967), confirming these findings, reports however that younger children (3 to 6 years) "are much more affected by their prior responses than prior events.... Children in this age range seem to pay more attention to what they just did than to what actually happened (what stimulus event occurred)." (Weir, 1967, p. 147).

Comparing their findings with those obtained from adults (Jarvik, 1951; Anderson, 1960; Myers and Fort, 1961), Craig and Myers (1963) have found that negative recency effects are less marked in children than in adults.

Learning of fixed regularities within probability learning. Offenbach (1964), observing pre-school and 9–11 year-old children on a two-choice probability learning task (75% cards with a red sign, and 25% with a blue sign) found that the children were able to detect certain regularities within the overall random string of stimuli which was relevant to their predictions. Each blue-sign card was followed by a red-sign card, except for two cases when blue was followed by blue. Thus, the probability learning task included an extra learning task. Offenbach's data show that some progress is made during the experimental session by both age groups in correct predictions of red following blue, but this progress is faster and significantly better in the older children.

These findings therefore confirm those of Craig and Myers (1963). Pre-school children appear little, if at all, responsive to sequential properties of the stimuli. Their predictions are therefore much less dependent on antecedent sequences of stimuli than the predictions of older children.

As Offenbach points out, the comments of older children on their performance during the experimental session indicate that they are attempting to discover whether the sequences of the two events could be accounted for by some rule.

Summary. The following sequential features have been found in children's probability learning:

(a) Most investigators have found that the alternation tendency is most strong between the ages of 7 and 9. Comparison of the data reported by several authors shows variation in the changes with age of this tendency. Such variation can be accounted for by the fact that different experimental paradigms have been used.

Stimulating factors (in particular, punishment of incorrect responses) reduce the tendency to alternate responses.

(b) In the case of runs of events, the prediction curve in older subjects shows an initial increase. This indicates that these subjects make more use of information derived from preceding trials.

(c) Further evidence in favour of the conclusion that older children make fuller use of information from preceding sequences of events is provided by the finding that older children can detect regularities in patterned sequences of stimuli, and make use of these regularities in their predictions.

(d) Some investigators have found that negative recency effects are very marked in children older than 7. According to other authors, these effects are less marked in children than in adults.

THE RELATIONSHIP BETWEEN TYPE OF REINFORCEMENT (CONTINGENT OR NON-CONTINGENT) AND STIMULUS SET SIZE

There is some disagreement concerning the dependence of asymptotic behaviour on the size of the stimulus set in probability learning.

Neimark (1956) in a three-choice experiment found that the final response proportions very closely matched the input probabilities. Gardner (1957) has suggested however that this may merely have been a chance result of having the cut-off point after 100 trials. Had the trials continued the values may have kept changing. Gardner concluded that the probability of predicting the most frequent event increases with the size of the stimulus set. A similar finding is reported by MacCormack (1959).

In an unpublished manuscript, Estes *et al.* (1964) report data similar to those obtained by Neimark (c.f. Estes, 1964). For the most frequently reinforced choices, i.e. 0.60, 0.50, and 0.40, Estes *et al.* obtained in the last 40 out of 240 trials the following values: 0.593, 0.480, and 0.382.

Results in the opposite direction have been obtained by Detambel (1959) from children, and Weir and Gruen from (1965) adults – they found that as the number of choices increased, the frequency of choosing the most probable event decreased.

Wittig and Weir (1971) reviewed these findings and suggested that the discrepancy among them may result from the different types of reinforcement used – i.e. contingent or non-contingent. *In non-contingent reinforcement experiments, the proportion of predictions of the most probable stimulus increases as the stimulus set size increases, while in contingent reinforcement experiments an inverse relation holds.*

Wittig and Weir devised the following experiment in order to test this hypothesis. The subject was placed before a vertical panel with 4 response buttons. Two of these buttons could be concealed from view. When a red light, also mounted on the panel, came on, the child was to press one of the response buttons. In the contingent condition, the subject was instructed that if the correct button had been pressed, it would light up, and at the same time a bell would ring. If the wrong button had been pressed, neither of these events would occur.

In the non-contingent condition, the subject was instructed that if the correct button had been pressed, it would light up and a bell would ring. If the wrong button had been pressed, the correct button would light up, but there would be no bell. Thus, the reinforcing event (lighting of the correct button) was independent of the subject's performance.

Two sizes of stimulus set were used, 4-choice and 2-choice. After some practice trials, each child was run through 80 trials.

In the 2-choice variant, the high probability stimulus (HPS) was present 0.64% of the time, and the low probability stimulus was present 0.36% of the time. In the 4-choice variant, the value of HPS was 0.64%, and the value of the remaining three was 0.12% each.

The subjects were boys and girls at two age levels; one group had a mean age of 4.5 years, and the other 5.5 years. Altogether, 16 experimental groups were included in a factorial design.

The following results were obtained. Except for group 4C (4-choice, contingent reinforcement), *all groups showed a clear tendency to match the proportion of responses to the reinforcement probability.*

The number of HPS responses (over all 80 trials) in the 2-choice variant was twice as high as in the 4-choice variant. The number of HPS responses in the non-contingent condition was significantly higher than in the contingent condition. With regard to the age variable, the mean number of HPS responses in 4.5 year-olds was 38.2; and in 5.5 year-olds it was 43.6, which, according to Wittig and Weir indicates that *the maximisation tendency increases with age* (in line with previous findings).

The dependence of the number of choices of the HPS on type of reinforcement and stimulus set size has been confirmed by Weir (1972) in a later study on adults. In a contingent condition, there were fewer choices of the HPS in the 4-choice than in the 2-choice variant. In a non-contingent condition, the reverse was true.

These findings of Wittig and Weir, showing that *the effect of increasing the stimulus set size is dependent on the type of reinforcement,* confirm those of Weir and Gruen (1965) for children, and of Detambel (1955) and Neimark (1956) for adults.

There is a possible explanation for the fact that *the number of HPS choices decreases with an increasing stimulus set size only with contingent reinforce-*

ment. With non-contingent reinforcement, the subject learns the correct response after each guess, and this leads to probability matching and even to the maximising tendency. An increase in the number of possible choices does not affect this tendency, since the HPS continues to polarise the subject's responses – the subject is continuously acquiring information about the HPS, since reinforcement is non-contingent. Moreover, as Wittig and Weir (1971) have pointed out, an increase in the number of choices available will increase the discrepancy between the proportion of the HPS and the proportions of the other stimuli. In their research, for instance, Wittig and Weir used the frequencies 0.64, 0.12, 0.12, and 0.12 in the 4-choice variant, and the frequencies 0.64 and 0.36 in the 2-choice variant.

With contingent reinforcement, the subject does not receive information about the correct response after each choice. This means that the subject does not have a sufficiently immediate concept of the HPS to polarise his responses. The result is that, as the stimulus set size increases, the subject's responses become more widely scattered, and the proportion of HPS predictions becomes lower.

This phenomenon does not occur when there are only two choices, as Wittig and Weir have demonstrated, for in this case the subject can easily infer which is the correct button from the non-reinforcement of the other button.

This dependency of the number of choices of the HPS on the type of reinforcement and the stimulus set size is present even in 4 to 5 year-old children. This is a most important finding, since it demonstrates that the maturation of complex probabilistic intuitions takes place relatively early in intellectual development.

The effect of preliminary instruction on probability matching behaviour. Ojemann *et al.* (1965a, 1965b, 1966) and Keller (1971) have investigated the effects of preliminary instruction in the theory of probability on performance in probability learning tasks.

Ojemann *et al.* carried out experiments with 8 year-old (1965a) and 10 year-old (1965b) children, in which the experimental subjects underwent an instruction programme supervised by a teacher. The experiment was later replicated on another group of 10 year-olds, who underwent a self-instruction programme (1966).

In 8 year-olds, there were no significant differences in the proportion of choices of the HPS between the experimental and the control group. However, there was a tendency toward maximisation in the children of the experimental group. The experiment was therefore replicated with 10 year-olds, who first underwent a series of self-instruction exercises. It was believed that children of this age would benefit more from the experience gained in self-instruction.

The instruction programme consisted of 5 sessions of 30 minutes each, with one session daily for five days. The content of the 5 sessions was, briefly, as follows:

(1) The concepts of risk, chance, prediction, and maximisation. The concept of equal and unequal chances was presented through experimentation.

(2) Predicting the colour of marbles on successive draws, with and without replacement. Forecasting temperature and rainfall on the basis of known data.

(3) Predicting the contents of a scoopful of sand from a jar of sand in which marbles and coins are mixed in known proportions.

(4) Predicting scores from throws of two dice. The point was made that, where outcomes are uncertain, predictions are more reliable the more information is available.

(5) Revision of the basic points of the preceding four sessions.

Three of the experimental tests consisted of a number of prediction tasks in which the proportions of elements were known, and on these tests the experimental group subjects had generally higher scores.

Another of the experimental tests was a probability learning task. Three black and nine white marbles were placed in a box. The subjects, without knowing these proportions, were to predict 'black' or 'white' before each draw in 15 blocks of 6 draws each. Draws were made with replacement. Control subjects' predictions reached the input probabilities on the last four trials, after a gradual approximation over all 15 blocks. Given that there are 6 predictions per block, and that white occurs with a probability of 0.75, the number of predictions of white which should be made in order to match the input probabilities should be $6 \times 0.75 = 4.5$. The number of 'white' predictions on the last four trials were: 4.54, 4.33, 4.43, and 4.64; while the initial numbers had been 2.79, 2.95, etc. These figures fit Estes' model. Experimental subjects, on the other hand, attained and exceeded the input level as early as the third trial (4.68), arriving at 5.27 and 5.21 on the last two trials.

The remarkable conclusion of this piece of research is that the experimental subjects' familiarisation with the concepts of chance, risk, and so on, not only *increased the accuracy of predictions (on trials with known proportions)* but also resulted in *maximisation behaviour in a typical probability learning situation* (i.e. where the proportions were not known in advance).

Maximisation, therefore, is not only increased by reward reinforcement – as the experiments of Messik and Solley (1957) *show – but also by enhancement of the subject's knowledge of the concept and the measurement of chance.* It seems, then, that an interaction or interchange takes place, during probability learning, between the conceptual level and the level of elementary intuitive response.

This finding of Ojemann *et al.* is crucial to the interpretation of behaviour in probability learning tasks. As we have already pointed out, probability matching behaviour can be demonstrated even in pre-school children.

The finding is important, also, in that *it makes it possible to hypothesise that the teaching of probability theory in the elementary school will not only contribute to the extension of knowledge in this field, but may also enhance the day-to-day practical existence of the individual, who is frequently required to make rapid decisions in uncertain situations on the basis merely of global intuitive appraisals of odds.*

Ojemann *et al.* (1966) have replicated this investigation also with 10 year-olds on a self-instruction programme, consisting of 365 frames spread over 7 sessions of 30 minutes each. In the experimental probability learning task with a 75–25 proportion, control subjects failed to reach the input probability (though drawing close) even by the final (20th) block of trials (4.11, 4.07, 4.14). In the experimental group, the input probability was reached and exceeded as early as the 3rd or 4th block of trials, after which maximisation behaviour was attained, exceeding 80% predictions for the 75% alternative. This indicates that the effect of instruction on maximisation behaviour is mainly a result of individual practice, rather than an effect of teaching done by the instructor.

Keller (1971) has carried out a more complex experiment on the effects of prior instruction on probability learning. In addition to the instruction variable, the variables of locus of control and schedule of reinforcement were investigated. The subjects were schoolchildren with ages ranging from 10 to 14 years.

The instruction was of the programmed learning type, in which was used a modified version of Ojemann's booklet, designed for teaching probability concepts to 10 year-olds. There were also sets of materials such as dice, marbles, etc.

Half of the subjects received this programmed instruction, in 6 half-hour sessions. The other subjects attended 6 sessions of comparatively general, non-specific instruction in probability.

'Locus of control' is a personality dimension. Subjects with an internal locus of control are said to feel that they are capable, through their actions, of influencing events. Subjects with an external locus of control consider that events are beyond their personal control, i.e. that events are the result of chance. In this experiment, the locus of control dimension was measured with a pencil-and-paper test (the Children's Locus of Control Scale).

The experimental apparatus was essentially similar to that used by Weir *et al.* (1959). There were three response buttons on a panel, only one of which was reinforced. Correct predictions were rewarded with a marble, and marbles could be traded for a variety of other articles when a sufficient number of them had been earned. The experiment had two stages. During the first stage, the reinforced button was reinforced in the proportions 33%, 66%, or 100% during the first 80 trials. For the last 60 trials (second stage) a different button was reinforced, on a 90% schedule. Reinforcement was contingent.

No significant differences were found between the programmed-instruction group and the non-specific instruction group in performance on the probability learning tasks. There were significant differences between these two groups, however, in their performance on two post-experimental pencil-and-paper tests which included problems on probability. Subjects did, therefore, benefit from the preliminary programmed instruction, but not in a way that was manifested in probability learning.

This result is in the opposite direction, then, to that obtained by Ojemann *et al.* (1965b, 1966) who found a significant effect of prior instruction on probability matching in children of the same age. According to Keller, his result indicates that there was no transfer from the instructional sessions, which involved binary choices, to the probability learning situation, which involved choices between three responses.

There are, however, other possible explanations for Keller's result. Keller used reward, while Ojemann *et al.* did not, and it is possible that the effect of reward in inducing probability matching was strong enough to mask any effects of instruction.

Furthermore, the subjects who received non-specific instruction nevertheless received generalised information about probability during their instruction sessions, and this alone may have been sufficient to equalise their performance with that of the other group in probability learning.

Keller had hypothesised that programmed instruction would be more effective with the external locus of control subjects than with the internal locus of control subjects. Subjects who at first believe that predictions cannot be improved by certain procedures may discover that instruction can in fact provide effective procedures. In other words, instruction may induce in external locus of control subjects an attitude close to that of internal locus of control subjects. If this is the case, there should have been a significant interaction between the instruction variable and the locus of control variable. There was in fact such an interaction: external locus of control subjects benefited most from instruction. A significant interaction was found between the 'instruction', 'locus of control', and 'trial' variables.

Keller's data showed that the number of correct predictions according to the three schedules of reinforcement increased across trials, but in such a way that the relative proportions were always maintained; thus the highest rate of increase was for the 100%-reinforced response. On the last 60 trials, after the reinforced button had been changed, and the schedule of reinforcement had been changed to 90%, predictions improved and came closer to 90%, but still maintained the order established in the first part of the experiment. The subjects who were in the 100%-reinforcement group for the first part of the experiment actually attained 90% correct prediction in the second part; the other subjects attained about 80%.

The subjects who had undergone programmed instruction developed better probability matching on the 90% schedule than the other subjects, who were less sensitive to the change of schedule. This fact confirms, though somewhat indirectly, *the effect of prior conceptual instruction on probability matching behaviour.*

It is important to note that scores on the locus of control scale correlate positively with I.Q.

There are two important facts about the learning of probability concepts to be derived from Keller's research. Firstly, there are individual differences between subjects in the extent to which it is believed possible to control random sequences of events. These may be differences in the intuitive substrate of probabilistic thinking itself, and such differences would result in different effects of prior instruction on probability matching behaviour. Secondly, prior conceptual instruction in probability results in a more flexible performance in probability matching. In other words, subjects who have received this type of prior instruction are better able to adapt their predictions to changes in the reinforcement schedule.

Generalisation in Probability Learning Tasks

Does the phenomenon of generalisation that appears in classical conditioning also appear in probability learning tasks? In order to answer this question, Le Ny (1961) carried out the following experiments with 10–12 year-old children. The experiments were presented as a game involving four hunters named (A) Kavazu, (B) Kavaju, (C) Kasiro, and (D) Melene. It was hypothesised that the proportion of predictions of each stimulus would be higher the more the given stimulus (the hunter's name) resembled the most frequently reinforced stimulus (A). The name of each hunter appeared on a screen with a given frequency, and on each trial the subject predicted whether or not the hunter whose name flashed on the screen would hit his target. After each trial, the subject was informed whether the prediction had been correct or not.

In all, there were three experiments. In the first part of Experiment I, the word Kavazu only was presented (90 times in succession). 80% of these presentations were reinforced (by the word 'plus', indicating target hit. The word 'zero' indicated target missed). It was found that the subjects approached a level of 80% 'target hit' predictions (as in a customary probability learning experiment).

In the second part of Experiment I, all four stimuli were presented. Kavazu was still reinforced on 80% of its appearances, while Kavaju, Kasiro, and Melene were only reinforced on 20% of their appearances. In the last block of 30 trials (there were 90 trials in all) the following proportions of 'plus' (target hit) predictions were obtained: (A) 75.7, (B) 52.0, (C) 39.2, (D) 47.2.

In Experiment II, the procedure was the same except for two modifications: from the outset, the subjects were informed that there were four hunters in all, and the number of trials was doubled to make two sessions of 90 trials. This time, in the last block of 15 trials the following proportions of predictions of 'plus' were obtained: (A) 82.1, (B) 53.6, (C) 30.4, (D) 21.6.

Experiment III was the same as Experiment II, except in the percentages of reinforced stimuli, which were 80% for (A), and 40% for (B), (C), and (D). In the last block of 15 trials, the proportions of 'plus' predictions were: (A) 75.7, (B) 46.4, (C) 30.4, (D) 39.2.

It was observed that, for the most frequently reinforced stimulus, subjects adjusted the frequency of their predictions to that of the stimulus. There was no such matching to the other three stimuli. The hypothesis was upheld in that the frequency of prediction of 'plus' for the other three stimuli was higher the closer the stimulus name was to the most frequently reinforced name.

Probability Learning in Children–Summary

(1) A tendency to match input probabilities in probability learning tasks is manifest at all age levels studied, down to three years of age.

(2) The rate at which the proportion of choices reaches the input probability level across trials increases with age. The input level is reached, at the latest, by 5–6 years.

(3) Reward induces a maximisation tendency which becomes stronger with age.

(4) Between the ages of 7 and 9 there is a tendency toward stereotyped responses, particularly alternating responses. After the age of 11, however, predictions are determined more by patterns extrapolated from antecedent sequences of events.

(5) Older children increasingly seek more sophisticated strategies, based on the conviction that there are rules determining random sequences.

(6) Probability matching behaviour in children is subject to generalisation in the same way as classical conditioning.

(7) Prior instruction in the concepts of chance and probability – as well as in some simple procedures of probability computation – improve prob-

ability matching performance in probability learning tasks. This finding supports the hypothesis that there is a rudimentary conceptual organisation underlying probability matching behaviour and spontaneous probabilistic behaviour in general.

CHAPTER V

THE INTUITION OF RELATIVE FREQUENCY

We have defined an intuition as an action programme which is partially autonomous within cognition, and which is a synthesis of individual experience in a given domain. Its global, immediate nature enables it to control action instantaneously. According to this view, probability matching is the expression of a particular intuition, the *intuition of relative frequency*.

The experimental data to be presented in this chapter underline the following aspects of this and other probabilistic intuitions:

(a) The intuition of relative frequency develops naturally during the ontogenesis of behaviour, as a consequence of the fact that the individual lives in an environment characterised by stochastic processes.

(b) Probability matching is not confined to motor behaviour established by conditioning, since it can also occur when there is no reward other than 'cognitive reinforcement'.

The subject acts according to a given schedule of proportions, and not in terms of a one-to-one correspondence between stimuli and responses. This fact implies a partially autonomous (and comparatively polyvalent) schema related to the action proper, in other words, a characteristic cognitive schema.

(c) The intuition of relative frequency develops with age, but the major development has occurred by the age of 14–15, or earlier. Is this fact merely a necessary consequence of general intellectual development, or is it the result of learning in a stochastic environment?

Practice effects in probability learning are demonstrated by the fact that matching the probability of a given event takes time. The phenomenon is revealed by a curve which, within an experimental session with hundreds of trials, gradually draws closer to the input probability level.

The view that the development of the intuition of relative frequency is a function of general intellectual development is supported by the fact that the two develop in parallel, and that probability matching behaviour stabilises with the completion of general intellectual development.

(d) Maximisation behaviour, as we have already pointed out, increases with age – at least under certain experimental conditions, which include reward. With adequate reinforcement conditions, therefore, the intuition of relative frequency can lead to a more effective adaptive solution than simple probability matching, i.e. to a *maximisation strategy* which uses *feedback from previous choices*.

The intuition of relative frequency can therefore be considered as a basic cognitive mechanism which can be adapted to cope with a variety of environmental conditions. This adaptive flexibility is evidenced also in the number of experimental conditions which have been found to modify probability matching behaviour – stimulus set size, type of instructions, changes in the proportions of reinforcing events. *We are dealing, then with a stochastic category of adaptive schemas, which has more general functions than simple adjustment to the probability of stimuli. These are schemas which are able to generate, according to specific circumstances, a variety of predictive responses within the same basic grammar that governs behaviour in a stochastic environment.* A hierarchical organisation of this kind, with generative capacities, is likely to characterise any structural acquisition of intelligence.

(e) Experiments of the *probability learning type* also demonstrate secondary effects of the intuition of relative frequency which lead to *fallacies*, in particular the *negative recency effect*. This effect is seen in the decreasing probability of predicting an event as a consequence of the event having occurred repeatedly on previous trials (although no such dependency in fact occurs in experiments with non-contingent reinforcement).

This is an important effect, for it reveals some of the mechanisms whereby erroneous primary intuitions are set up during the ontogenesis of the intellect. There is, in the first place, what might be called *the sampling intuition*. Suppose we draw successive random samples from a homogeneous mixture of elements. In each sample, different proportions of the elements are possible, but the probability that a given proportion will be drawn is higher the closer this proportion is to the actual proportion of elements in the parent population. This is a correct intuition which corresponds to a mathematical truth and which, no doubt, develops over time in the course of the individual's daily experience. Now suppose that a box contains an equal number of black and white beads, and we draw 6 beads at random (replacing each bead after it has been drawn, so as not to change the original proportions). The probability of drawing three white and three black beads is higher than the probability of drawing, say, five white beads and one black bead. *But this truth has nothing to do with the order of appearance. It refers to a situation in which the order of elements is ignored.* Consequently, after a run of three black beads, a white bead has exactly the same probability of being drawn as a black bead (i.e. $\frac{1}{2}$). The WWWBBB *sequence* is no more, and no less, likely to occur than the BBBWWW sequence, or the BBBBBB, WWWWWW sequences, *as sequences.* BBBBBW has the same probability of occurrence as BBBBBB. The probability of occurrence of any particular sequence (sequence *with imposed order*) is, in the experiment in question, equal to $(\frac{1}{2})^6$.

In probability learning experiments, events occur successively and on each trial the subject predicts the next event. Order cannot be ignored in such a situation. Subjects tend to match their predictions, as we have seen, to the proportions of events; but at the same time they feel the need to put to use the other intuition which seems relevant in this situation, i.e. the *sampling intuition*. In memory, antecedent trials are roughly grouped in 'chunks', in which prediction rates should approximate the probabilities learned during the course of the experiment. This is, of course, a fallacious extrapolation: the subject is referring, in a situation in which order cannot be ignored (because of the nature of the experiment) to a truth which only holds when order *is* ignored.

The above interpretation presupposes that subjects predict on the basis of 'chunks' of past events, within the frame of which they intuitively estimate the proportions of events overall.

There are some findings in support of this interpretation. Vitz and Hazan (1969) asked their subjects at intervals during an experiment to record all that they could remember of the preceding strings of events. The most striking finding was the 'chunked' structure of the memory data. "That is, S would recall a short string or chunk of events, then leave a gap and recall another chunk" (Vitz and Hazan, 1969, p. 54).

This suggests that *the subject actually organises information in memory in the form of structures or configurations* which facilitate the estimation of the probability schedule of reinforcing events. An important fact is that the schedule of the most recent chunks actually corresponds to the objective schedule of events.

It is fallacious extrapolations such as these which are frequently the cause of faulty intuitive interpretations. From intuitions which are valid only in the world of medium dimensions, we fallaciously extrapolate to the cosmic and sub-atomic worlds; from intuitions about the finite domain, we fallaciously extrapolate to the non-finite domain, and so on.

In probabilistic thinking, the problem is still more complex. We have to take into account the tendency toward rationalisation of events. This tendency, which becomes stronger with age, is fostered by school and by the whole social environment in which human development takes place in modern society.

Recency effects are an expression of this rationalising tendency. Reason is the ability to predict; the capacity to discover, by means of induction, certain rules beyond chance which enable the subject to control – at least partially – the course of events. In the case of independent events, reason implicitly and fallaciously borrows a computation rule from the intuitive level. Thus, after a black marble has been drawn five times in succession, it seems reasonable to suppose that the chances of drawing a white marble have increased. The need for rationalisation, the need for prediction, and the need of human beings to rely on regularity lead them, in this case, to the use of an inappropriate deductive procedure.

In the case of unequal probabilities, of course, the subject can make a justifiable choice. But in this case also, research has shown that the negative recency effect manifests itself, suggesting that the subject tends toward alternating predictions which are not motivated by the proportions of the stimuli.

The fact that older subjects tend primarily to repeat confirmed predictions (positive recency effect), and that it is only subsequently that the negative recency effect occurs, is a clear indication of an attitude which is generated at this level by rational considerations (Craig and Myers, 1963). Thus the subject begins by reproducing the reinforced response but, since the same outcome is being repeated, the belief develops that the alternative outcome must soon appear.

Weir (1964) pointed out the fact that adult subjects expect to find a rational procedure which will enable them to attain 100% reinforcements, or at least 100% correct predictions with regard to the occurrence or non-occurrence of the reinforcing event. Adult subjects use complex strategies based on complex hypotheses concerning the nature of the task and the reinforcing schedule (Stevenson and Weir, 1963). Hyman and Jenkins have shown that it is much harder to convince adult subjects that a sequence of events is random, and not programmed.

The fact that the negative recency effect appears after 6–7 years of age, and is stronger in adults, is a further argument in support of the hypothesis that we are dealing with the manifestations of a phenomenon which is part of the overall intellectual development of the individual.

The increasing tendency, with age, to resort to deductive procedures is also revealed in the results of the investigations we have already discussed in the preceding pages: the alternation of responses in the child between 7 and 9 (Stevenson and Weir, 1959; Weir, 1962; Ross, 1966); the search for and the utilisation of regularities (Matalon, 1959; Brackbill *et al.*, 1962; Offenbach, 1965). The fact that the negative recency effect and the alternation tendency emerge at the same time suggests that they have a common origin. The recency effect is stronger in adults, while the alternation tendency diminishes after the age of 10–11, which indicates the more sophisticated nature of the recency effect.

In both cases, however, we are dealing with a rationalising tendency which, enconraged by the cultural environment of the individual, assumes regularities and dependencies beyond the evidence afforded by the sequence of events.

(f) In some recent papers, Tversky and Kahneman (1972, 1973) have described two heuristics by which people subjectively evaluate the frequencies of classes and the likelihood of events.

One of these heuristics is *availability*. "A person is said to employ the availability heuristic whenever he estimates frequency or probability by the ease with which instances or associations could be brought to mind" (Tversky and Kahneman, 1973, p. 208).

Suppose we sample a word containing the letter *k* from an English text. Considering words beginning with a *k* and words in which *k* is the third letter, is it more likely that the word we have sampled belongs to the first or the second category? The majority of subjects will answer that words beginning with a *k* are more frequent than words having *k* as the third letter. In fact, the reverse is true: a typical text contains twice as many words with *k* as the third letter than words beginning with *k*.

The explanation of this bias of the intuition of frequency is that the subject, when searching for instances of the two categories, will more easily (and therefore more frequently) find instances of words beginning with a certain letter, than instances of words containing it as a third letter. Being more available, the words from the first category appear to be more frequent, more probable.

A second heuristic described by Tversky and Kahneman is *representativeness*. An event seems to be more probable the more representative it is of the parent population from which it is drawn. Let us consider some examples.

"The average heights of adult males and females in the U.S. are respectively 5ft 10in and 5ft 4in. Both distributions are approximately normal with a standard deviation of about 2.5in.

An investigator has selected one population by chance and has drawn from it a random sample. What do you think are the odds that he has selected the male population if

(I)   the sample consists of a single person whose height is 5ft 10in
(II)   the sample consists of 6 persons whose average height is 5ft 8in?"

The majority of subjects consider that the former case is more probable than the latter, although the opposite answer is objectively correct. The reason for selecting the first case is that a single person 5ft 10in in height is more 'representative' of the given population, being of the same height as the average for the population. The authors conclude: "Here again it appears that S's base their judgements on sample mean with insufficient concern for sample size" (Kahneman and Tversky, 1972, p. 449).

A second example concerning representativeness:

"On each round of a game 20 marbles are distributed at random among five children: Alan, Ben, Carl, Dan and Ed. Consider the following distributions:

	I	II
Alan	4	4
Ben	4	4
Carl	5	4
Dan	4	4
Ed	3	4

In many rounds of the game, will there be more results of type I or of type II?

A significant majority of S's considered the first distribution to be more probable, though the uniform distribution (II) is objectively more probable. In fact this second distribution appears too 'lawful' for a random process" (Kahneman and Tversky, 1972, p. 134).

This line of research is of very great importance in shedding light on the intuitive substrate of probabilistic thinking. The intuition of relative frequency, though correct in many situations, especially in the 'pure' form of probability learning tasks, is in fact influenced and biased by a variety of conditions.

We suggest that two categories of such disturbing factors should be distinguished. In the first category, there are factors which are extrinsic to the psychological mechanisms of statistical evaluations. Availability is an example. The errors in this case are not due to an incorrect probability judgement as such, but to the initial information on which the judgement is based. In the same category may be placed the biases due to affective influences (considering a fact which is very desirable to be very likely, for instance).

The second category contains errors which are due to the mechanisms of evaluation *per se*. The examples given by Kahneman and Tversky to illustrate the heuristic of representativeness belong to this category.

From the point of view of the development of probabilistic intuitions, it is the second category which seems to be the more important. The errors in this category are due primarily, of course, to insufficient knowledge of the theory of probability. This is a trivial statement. But what is more significant is the fact that *the errors are not blind errors*. They are generally determined by the subject's tendency to interpret randomness as though it were rationally governed.

The theory of probability as a branch of mathematics originates from the same essential human tendency. Representativeness, the search for clear interpretable patterns, the transformation of the law of large numbers into a 'law of small numbers' ('local representativeness', as Kahneman and Tversky call it), the recency effects – all of these biases of the intuition of relative frequency may be explained as being caused by the effort of human intelligence to make the random more reasonable, in the absence of sufficient mathematical knowledge.

(g) We would like to stress, therefore, that the structure of intuitions cannot be accounted for outside of the mechanisms and tendencies of intelligence as a whole. *Intuitions themselves become more 'rational' with age, in that they adopt strategies and solutions which are based on rational grounds.*

It is possible, as we have seen, that an intuition originating from an operational process should nonetheless fail to express a rationally valid conclusion (the most telling example of this is the negative recency phenomenon).

CHAPTER VI

ESTIMATING ODDS AND THE CONCEPT
OF PROBABILITY

The first part of this book has presented data on the behaviour of the child in probability learning tasks.

These data have enabled us to observe in detail the spontaneous responses of the child to a stochastic sequence of stimuli with fixed frequencies. The matching of predictions to the frequencies of stimuli, the tendency toward maximising predictions in the context of reward or specific instructions, the fine adjustment of the frequency of predictions after a small change in the relative frequencies of the stimuli – all these behaviours lead to the conclusion that it is possible to postulate the existence of certain pre-operational intuitive mechanisms for the estimation of odds, even in pre-school children.

The data we have considered concern behaviour only, without the introduction of any explicit conceptual constructs, but we will now go on to consider data concerning the *conceptual organisation* relevant to the ontogenesis of thinking, of the notion of chance and the estimation of odds, and of the notion of probability.

From a discussion of experiments on the global estimation of odds, we will go on to consider experiments in which the elements of explicit computation appear, based on the intuitive comparison or estimation of certain relationships.

1. CHANCE AND NECESSITY

According to Piaget and Inhelder (1951) the concepts of chance and necessity develop in a complementary manner: "The discovery of chance is made gradually, as some operations fail; and it is by referring to the structure of these operations that the child grasps the notion of chance, which eventually gives rise to a system of probabilities" (Piaget and Inhelder, 1951, p. 225).

For this reason, before the age of 7–8, children do not distinguish between the possible and the necessary. Their expectations are coloured by subjective tendencies, which still express "a lack of differentiation between notions which would be, in practice, either intuitive foresight or whim" (*ibid.*, p. 227).

The understanding that certain relations are objectively necessary, and can be thought about in a deductive manner, requires a grouped organisation of thought, characterised by commutation, reversibility, and mobility. These qualities of operational thought do not, however, appear before the age of 7–8.

Piaget and Inhelder relate the notion of chance to that of *mixture*. Before the age of 7, children do not understand the irreversibility of the operation of mixing. If, for instance, a number of red and white beads are mixed in a box, many children believe that shaking the box is an operation which will separate the beads into distinct sets of red and white. The *irreversibility* characteristic of a fortuitous mixture is not understood at this age, since the child does not have an understanding of the notion of *reversibility* (the understanding of reversibility is an essential characteristic of operational thought). The irreversibility of a fortuitous mixture can only be understood by a subject who realises that each stage of the mixture is only one among many which could be obtained with the same elements. The chances of separating a mixture into sets of elements by shaking it are very small. The idea of chance implies, therefore, according to Piaget and Inhelder, the existence of combinatorial mechanisms which the child does not possess before the age of 7.

After 7 years, children begin to accept the idea of a real and changing mixture (as the result of successively shaking the box). Not yet possessing the operational schema of permutation, however, these children still do not (before the level of formal operations) understand a mixture as only one of many possible permutations, but simply as the result of individual and isolated displacements of elements (the interaction of which displacements they do not recognise).

At the level of formal operations (after the age of 12) the child begins to assimilate the process of mixing to the schema of a set of permutations, and therefore is able to understand the interaction of individual displacements of elements (since the displacement of every individual bead can now be conceived of simultaneously). The child can now understand also that the mixture progresses as a result of successively shaking it. Thus the child comes to an intuitive understanding of the law of large numbers.

The development of the notion of chance has also been considered under other experimental paradigms by Piaget and Inhelder (1951).

Throwing counters. A number of white counters have a cross on one face, and a circle on the other. 10 to 20 counters are thrown one after the other, and the child is to guess which face will land uppermost each time. Subsequently, without the child's knowledge, counters are thrown which have crosses on both faces.

From a bag containing red and blue marbles, single marbles are drawn at random. The child guesses in advance the colour of each marble to be drawn. In the second phase of this experimental paradigm, a switch is made, as above, and blue marbles only are used. Finally, the child is told that there is a 'trick', and the experimenter waits for the moment when the child realises that all the marbles are coming from a homogeneous population.

In Piaget's first stage of development, the following kinds of behaviour have been shown in children (Piaget and Inhelder, 1951, p. 112–114): (a) *Phenomenalism* – acceptance of immediate experience, whether real or apparent; (b) *passive induction* or empirical induction (as opposed to experimental induction), which is a tendency derived directly from phenomenalism: children do not approach objective facts in a deductive manner (in this case, with a combinatorial schema). This is why they are unable to evaluate facts as being essentially either acceptable or unacceptable. They approach them from the point of view of the immediately previous experience (if there has been one), in relation to which the new phenomenon may appear natural, or perhaps merely 'odd', since it represents something new (repeated appearances of the 'cross' face of the counter). There seems, therefore, to be *an intuition of frequency and rarity*, but which has a totally empirical character. (c) A tendency to compensate, manifested in the positive and negative recency effects which, as we have seen, also occur in probability learning. (d) Belief in the personal power of whoever throws the counters. Although the children observe the random movements of the counters in the air, they believe that the final result can be controlled by the thrower.

All this demonstrates that, although preschool children possess the intuition of chance (see Chapter I) and are capable of matching behaviour, these do not derive from a conceptual schema.

After the age of 6–7 (the second developmental stage) children do not accept that the repeated appearance of the 'same' face of the counter is due to chance, and they conclude that both faces of the counter have the same sign. This is no longer a case of the purely empirical estimation of relative frequency, as in the younger children. These children judge the results with reference to a schema – even though not a very explicit one – in which 'mixture' fulfills a combinatorial role. One child explained: "The counters can't all fall on the same side because they are too mixed up" (Piaget and Inhelder, 1951, p. 115).

The superiority of children in the third stage of development consists in the fact that these children are capable of a finer estimation of odds: "...probability, instead of remaining global, as in stage II, is analysed in terms of graduated judgements which indicate the existence of implicit computation" (Piaget and Inhelder, 1951, p. 121). "'If you go on you can know...you are more and more certain...because with small numbers the chance is less'" (*ibid.*, p. 119).

In Piaget and Inhelder's interpretation of the concept of chance, the following aspects seem to us to be open to further discussion.

A chance result is not always the same thing as a result with a small probability of occurrence. A chance result does have a small probability of occurrence in cases where the number of possible results is great. But if, for instance, a coin is tossed, there are only two possible results. Whether heads or tails lands uppermost is still a matter of chance. Chance is equivalent to the unforeseeable, or the non-deducible. The 'unforeseeability' quantum increases as the difference between the chances of either alternative occurring decreases. For any given number of possibilities, the uncertainty – and consequently the information value – is greatest when all the possibilities are equiprobable. A coin-toss, from which there are only two possible outcomes, is still a matter of chance, even though the probability of each outcome is $\frac{1}{2}$.

The problem is therefore to know whether, in a situation where the number of possible states is not in itself a difficulty, the responses of the child express the same lack of understanding of chance.

Permutation, like the other combinatorial operations, does not develop until much later (after 14–15) in the stage of formal thought, according to Piaget and Inhelder (see p. 101–103).

In cases where the design of the experiment is such that the response to a probability problem depends on correctly – or at least intuitively –

solving a permutation problem, there is a risk of masking those difficulties which are specific to the concept of chance.

There is another aspect which complicates things still further. The data we have discussed (see the chapter on combinatorial operations) have demonstrated that there is a strong natural tendency towards minimisation in the subjective estimate of the number of possible permutations which can be obtained with a given number of elements, even at the stage of formal operations. Thus, for example, with 5 objects (from which 120 permutations are actually possible) the mean subjective estimate of the number of possible permutations is only 16. Intuition is unable to grasp the rapid increase in the number of permutations which become possible as the number of objects increases.

These considerations lead us to doubt Piaget and Inhelder's conclusion that the idea of chance is formed only after the age of 7, i.e. after the establishment of concrete operations.

It is necessary to distinguish between the *primary intuition* of chance and the *concept* of chance. Understanding of the concept of chance clearly presupposes an evolved conceptual system (and primarily that operational thought has been attained) and also a certain amount of familiarity with the notions of necessity, laws, causality, etc. However, if we are considering, not the scientific concept of chance, but rather the intuition of chance, in the sense in which the child arrives at the distinction between stochastic and determined phenomena, the situation is rather different.

In situations where combinatorial operations are not required, it has been observed, as we shall presently see, that the intuition of chance (in the sense of the opposite of 'determined') emerges much earlier than the previously discussed experiments of Piaget and Inhelder would indicate.

Further more, it is evident from the protocols cited by Piaget and Inhelder themselves that the intuition of chance emerges at the pre-operational level:

"Mon. (4.10). 'Where will the marble go?' *'Perhaps there, or there'* (pointing to the two possible exits). (The trial is run, and the marble rolls toward the right-hand exit). 'And the next?' *'There'* (Trial: left-hand exit.) 'What about the rest of the marbles?' *'I don't know...'*" (Piaget and Inhelder, 1951, p. 44.) (The experimental apparatus consisted of five rectangular boxes placed on a slope, with a number of exits at the bottom.)

Roulette experiment: "Mon. (4.11). 'Can we tell where it will stop?'

'*No, because if we say it will stop at blue, and then it goes past blue, we won't know.*'" (*ibid.*, p. 74.)

It is therefore possible to suggest that the intuition of chance is present even before the age of 6–7 years. There certainly exists a primary, pre-operational intuition constructed out of the day-to-day experience of the child and complementary to the intuition of necessity.

This polar pair of intuitions, chance-necessity, is largely a part of the adaptive behaviour of the child, whose cognitive reasoning is still vague and uncertain. Since they are not constrained by the coordinates which characterise the operational level, these pre-operational intuitions can be influenced by subjective or perceptual considerations.

At the concrete-operational level, the tendency to favour univocal solutions (the expression of deductive thinking) is intensified. The result is not, as might be expected, a compromise between these two possible inter-pretations (chance-necessity) but an oscillation between them. The growing tendency to give univocal responses leads the child into errors by invoking causal dependencies where none exist in reality.

This preference for univocal solutions is not generated by the operational structure of thought, but by the influence of the social environment, in particular that of the school. The child is taught that explanation consists in specifying a cause; that a scientific prediction must be a certainty; that ambiguity and uncertainty are not acceptable in scientific reasoning, and so on. Even if all this is not explicitly stated, it is implied in all that is taught in schools.

We have returned to the problem of determining the child's idea of chance by setting up situations in which chance operates in the simplest possible manner, starting with situations with two equiprobable alternatives (for a complete description of methods and results, see E. Fischbein, Ileana Pampu, and I. Mînzat 'The Child's Intuition of Probability', reprinted in Appendix II).

The subjects were children aged from 6 to 14, grouped in five age levels. The experimental apparatus consisted of inclined boards on which a set of progressively forked channels had been constructed, using thin wooden strips. The children were asked to imagine that marbles had been released in the main channel, and to say whether or not the marbles would follow any particular route in preference to the other possible ones, and, if so, to indicate the expected route. There were five different layouts of channels.

For the first three layouts, the correct response was that any route was equally probable.

Layout 1 contained two equiprobable routes, layout 2 eight, and layout 3 four equiprobable routes. In addition, layout 3 was asymmetrical. Layouts 4 and 5 contained routes which were not equiprobable.

The most surprising finding was that, for the layouts with equiprobable routes, it was the youngest children (pre-school) who gave the greatest number of *correct* responses (i.e. responses indicating the equality of chances). Older children opted more frequently for a determined route, and it was they who were most misled by the asymmetry of layout 3. They offered obviously confabulated causal explanations to justify their choices. For layouts 4 and 5, the proportion of correct responses increased with age.

The following conclusions can be drawn from these results:

(a) Well before the operational stage, the child possesses an intuition of chance, and carries out intuitive estimation of odds, although the absence of operationally structured thought precludes the conceptual structuring of this intuition, which is complementary to the intuition of necessity.

The existence of subjective interpretations, the relative lack of differentiation between chance and caprice, and between the arbitrary and the possible at this age do not, in our view, oppose the hypothesis of an intuition of chance and probability in pre-school children.

As we have seen earlier, in *probability learning tasks* the pre-school child also demonstrates the possibility of an intuitive computation of stochastic outcomes, in the form of an intuition of relative frequencies. This is a further argument in favour of the hypothesis we are putting forward.

(b) At the level of formal operations, according to Piaget and Inhelder, there will be an improvement in the estimation of probabilities. In fact, however, as our experiments have shown, with increasing age *the estimations become poorer: pre-school children give the highest percentage of correct responses, when compared with 12–13 year-olds, in situations with equiprobable outcomes.* With increasing age, the responses become more erratic, more hesitant, and more frequently incorrect.

The explanation of these results would seem to lie in the fact that, as we have already mentioned, schools inculcate the notion of univocal determinism. At the operational level, the child looks for causal relations which will permit univocal predictions, even when the objective situation provides no evidence of such relations. The most revealing of our results, in this respect, were those obtained with layout 3, in which a geometric modification to the apparatus, having no effect on the probabilities of the situation, misled particularly the older children. Evidently, chance implies to these children nothing but ambiguity and uncertainty, and thus denotes the failure of cognitive efforts. The pre-school child is less disturbed by ambiguity. The child approaching adolescence is in the habit (inculcated by instruction in physics, chemistry, mathematics, and even history and geography) of seeking causal relations which can justify univocal explanations.

This is why the intuition of chance remains outside of intellectual development, and does not benefit sufficiently from the development of operational schemas of thought, which instead are harnessed solely to the service of deductive reasoning.

2. Estimation and Comparison of Odds. the Concept of Probability

The essential difference between the experiments carried out by Piaget and Inhelder, described above, and other experiments of the probability learning type, is that in the former case the subject makes predictions while *knowing the structure of the conditions* (for example, the composition of the urn). This involves going beyond simple conditioning (although of a different type to classical conditioning) to processes of conceptual organisation which call into play specific operational schemas.

The experiments which we shall now discuss also call into play intellectual schemas, but in addition they throw light on *the ability of the subject to compare odds*, and therefore, in the first place, *to order them according to processes of estimation*.

Experiments by Piaget and Inhelder. Piaget and Inhelder report some experiments of this type (1951, pp. 144–172).

The child is shown two sets of white counters, some of which are marked with a cross. The child is fully aware of the composition of the sets. The counters are mixed in each set, and the subject is to decide which set has the greater probability of having a marked counter drawn from it.

Several kinds of questions are put to the subject: (1) Double impossibility. Neither of the two sets contains a marked counter; nevertheless the child is asked to indicate whether a marked counter can be drawn. (2) Double certainty. All the counters are marked (the sets differing in size). (3) Certainty-impossibility. (4) Possibility-certainty. (5) Possibility – impossibility. (6) Identical sets. (7) Proportionality (the sets are numerically unequal, but the proportion of marked and unmarked counters within each is the same). (8) Inequality of marked counters and equality of total counters. (9) Equality of marked counters and inequality of total counters. (10) Inequality of marked and of total counters, without proportionality.

Stage I. Children aged 4–5 frequently give incorrect responses to these questions, even in cases where the solution appears obvious – as in situations where the total number of counters is equal $(\frac{3}{3}:\frac{2}{3})$ or the number of marked counters is equal $(\frac{1}{2}:\frac{1}{3})$, and so on.

In order to respond correctly, subjects had to consider, simultaneously, both the number of marked counters and the total number of counters in each set. According to Piaget and Inhelder, they did not succeed in making this double comparison, and their responses were determined by inessential features. For example, when comparing $\frac{1}{2}:\frac{2}{4}$, children preferred the first set, since the uniqueness of the marked counter made them believe that it would be found more easily (in fact, the probabilities are equal). When comparing $\frac{1}{2}:\frac{1}{3}$ they estimated that the odds were equal, since the number of marked counters is the same – without taking into account, therefore, the total number of counters.

Piaget and Inhelder's explanation of these failures is as follows. At this age, the child cannot yet reason correctly on the relationships between part and whole – a difficulty which is, in turn, due to the absence of reversibility. The child does not yet understand the reciprocity between the union $(A+A'=B)$ and the partitions $(B-A=A')$ and $(B-A'=A)$. If a whole is analysed into parts, it ceases to exist for the child as the potential result of a union (1951, pp. 156–157).

In consequence, the logical operation of disjunction cannot be carried out, since disjunction presupposes the possibility of alternation (either A or A') and also of remembering the whole of which the two classes are parts.

Lacking the support structure of logical precedures, the child of 4–6 is unable to perform the comparisons necessary for estimating odds. Such comparisons require analysis and disjunction and, in general, the correct understanding of whole-part relationships.

Stage IB (6–7 years). At this stage, children are not yet able to resolve problems in which both the number of favourable outcomes and the number of total possible outcomes are varied together (questions 7 and 10). They can cope, though only partially, with problems in which there is only one variable. The fact that correct responses are sometimes given (though only sometimes) is explained, according to Piaget and Inhelder, by the fact that these responses are not based on operational reasoning, but purely and simply on intuitive rules (pp. 159–160).

Piaget and Inhelder therefore attribute these cases to intuition, since the responses are based solely on the perceptual configuration of the sets.

Stage IIA (7–10 years). Responses to questions involving a single variable are systematically correct, and the arguments used show cognizance of favourable outcomes, unfavourable outcomes, and total possible outcomes to an equal extent.

In contrast, problems in which the number of favourable outcomes and the total number of possible outcomes are both varied are not generally solved, although the comments of the children show concern with both aspects simultaneously.

The difficulty with two-variable problems (questions 7 and 10) is explained by the intellectual requirements of this type of problem. A comparison of two ratios is called for. It is, in fact, a double comparison which requires the ability to think about two systems at the same time – an ability which does not emerge, according to Piaget and Inhelder, before the stage of formal operations.

Stage IIB (9–12 years). At this stage, subjects are beginning to give correct solutions to two-variable questions (7 and 10). But these problems are still solved by empirical methods, and not from a base of formal reasoning. The child considers the favourable outcomes and the unfavourable outcomes alternately, and then attempts to determine the differences between them.

In the case of equal ratios (and therefore equal odds) – for example $\frac{2}{6}:\frac{1}{3}$, if the larger set is broken down in such a way that its subsets which are each equal to the smaller set become evident, the child recognises the proportionality. But when the larger set is reconstituted, the child forgets the solution. "...as a double relationship, proportion therefore requires formal operations, but before these are possible, intuitive solutions are adopted which are comparable to those which precede concrete operations" (p. 169).

In stage III, children respond correctly in estimating proportions, although they are not yet able to perform explicit calculations with fractions.

The conclusion of Piaget and Inhelder is that "fundamental probabilistic notions are not constructed until the level of formal operations" (*ibid.*, p. 172) for the reason that proportions require 'second-order operations', 'operations on operations', which are not available until the level of formal operations.

Comparison of odds in pre-school children. The research by Piaget and Inhelder on the concepts of chance and probability has inspired other research which has been directed mainly at the question: is it possible to speak of a concept, even a rudimentary concept, of probability in the pre-school child?

Some research work has not confined itself to the pre-school level, but has also considered older children in order to outline the evolution of the concept as well as its ontogenesis.

The data available so far from this research seem to be contradictory. On the one hand, there are data from experiments of the probability learning type which indicate that something like an intuition of probability is already beginning to manifest itself in pre-school children – an indication which is particularly strongly supported by the phenomenon of adaptation to the probability of the stimulus (probability matching behaviour). On the other hand, data obtained by Piaget and Inhelder (and also by Offenbach from a probability learning experiment, 1964, 1965) indicate that the idea of probability is not systematically established until the level of formal operations, and that, before the age of 7, the child does not even possess the concepts of mixture and chance, much less the concept of comparing odds and probability.

Yost, Siegel and Andrews (1962) and later Davies (1965) and Goldberg (1966) have followed up the experiments of Piaget and Inhelder in this field in trying to replicate them more rigorously by eliminating possible artefacts (stemming from preferences, positions, etc.) and by using statistical analysis.

Yost *et al.* (1962) took as their point of departure an article by Piaget on the concept of probability (1950). From their list of references, it is evident that they were not aware of the book *La genèse de l'idée de hasard chez l'enfant*, which was published by Piaget and Inhelder in 1951.

The main problem to which they addressed themselves was that of whether pre-school children possess the concept of probability. They began by criticising Piaget's procedure, and proposed to eliminate its deficiencies by the use of more rigorous techniques.

A résumé of this critical analysis is important at this point for the purposes of the discussion as a whole.

– Piaget's method was based, in large part, on verbal responses. The absence of such responses could obscure the presence of certain real possibilities of responding correctly in the situations considered.

– Piaget's method also confounded subjective preference with the estimation of odds. For example, by asking the child to predict a colour which would be drawn at random, it is possible that the prediction was confounded with colour preference. (It does in fact emerge from the data reported by Piaget and Inhelder that subjective considerations were operating in the children's responses.)

– The fact that sets of counters were first displayed to the subjects before being placed in containers, so that the subject would remember the contents of the container, may have influenced responses with perceptual factors having no bearing on the estimation of odds.

– There was no reward for correct responses.

– The data were not analysed statistically.

Yost *et al.* proposed to overcome these faults by using a procedure which they call 'a non-verbal decision-making technique'.

In fact, this type of procedure had already been used by Piaget and Inhelder, and described in their book *La genèse de l'idée de hasard chez l'enfant*, which, as we have pointed out, Yost and his co-workers seem to have been unaware of.

Piaget and Inhelder used a set of counters, some of which were marked on one side by a cross. In the 'decision-making' type of experiment, the subject was shown two piles containing marked counters in different proportions. The subject knew these proportions, and was asked to say which pile had the greatest probability of yielding a marked counter.

Yost *et al.* used two plastic boxes containing counters of two different colours in different proportions. Since the boxes were transparent, the counters were visible and their proportions could be estimated. The subject was asked to indicate which box was most likely to yield a counter of a given colour, if a counter was drawn at random and without looking at the contents of the boxes.

The experiment carried out by Yost *et al.* compared this latter procedure (labelled DM in the following table) with Piaget's procedure (labelled P) involving a single set of counters. Half the subjects underwent both procedures in the order: session I: P, session II: DM, and the other half of the subjects underwent the same procedures in the reverse order. There were 10 subjects in each half, composed of 5 boys and 5 girls. Each subject underwent 24 trials, which were preceded by preliminary exercises. The subject's final score consisted of the number of correct responses given to the 24 items.

The results are shown in the following table (adapted from Yost *et al.*, 1962), indicating the mean number of correct responses:

Session I	Session II
Cond. P_1: 12	Cond. DM_2: 19
Cond. DM_1: 18	Cond. P_2: 18

It is clear that the result in condition P_1 (12 correct out of 24 trials) is no better than would be expected by chance.

There were, however, significant differences between the P and DM conditions in the first session, and also overall. Yost *et al.* draw the following conclusions from these results:

– Children of 4 do have some understanding of probability, contrary to Piaget's conclusion.

– Children are able to improve their estimates of probability as a result of experience. Thus the P condition produced better responses when it was in the second session, when it had been preceded by the DM condition, than when it was in the first session, and there had been no prior experience of this kind.

– There is a significant correlation between the understanding of the idea of probability (condition DM) and developmental level.

It seems to us that these conclusions call for some qualification. As we have seen, it is necessary to distinguish between the *concept* of probability as an explicit, correct computation of odds and the *intuition* of probability as a subjective, global evaluation of odds. The notion of chance implies nothing more than global estimation of odds, although in this case also there is at least what could be called an *ordinal scale* according to the terminology proposed by Stevens (1951, p. 26).

The experiments of Yost *et al.*, therefore, are revealing not so much about the concept of probability, but about *the intuitive estimation of odds*.

Secondly, in the two sets of counters used by Yost *et al.*, one of the two colours was always represented by the same number of counters (e.g. 4 blue, 1 white; 4 blue, 16 white). It is possible that the correct responses actually did express intuitive estimations of odds; but there is also a possibility that the responses were simple quantitative comparisons of the unequal numbers of counters. Hoemann and Ross (1971) have in fact concluded that this is exactly what is done by pre-school children.

Continuing this point, there are in fact two somewhat different situations in the tasks used by Yost *et al.* In some of the trials, there were two boxes to choose between, which had an equal number of non-winning counters and an unequal number of winning counters. The example mentioned above with the blue and white counters is such a case, if the white counter is winning. In such a situation, it is evident that the correct response could be determined simply by counting the number of white counters in each box. In the second situation, the winning counters are equal in number and the non-winning counters unequal. This would be the case if, in the example cited, the blue counters are winning. It may be supposed that, in this situation, estimation is made by comparing ratios, since the number of winning counters is equal. Yost *et al.* make no distinction between these two different situations.

Thirdly, reinforcement was used only in the DM condition. It is possible that the superior results obtained in this condition were partly due to this factor. Reward alone cannot explain the results, since the correct responses have to be effectively found – however, reward may have enhanced the effect. It is not possible to isolate the effect of this factor from the data as reported.

Fourthly and finally, Flavell (1963, p. 393) referring to an earlier report of studies by Yost and her co-workers (Yost *et al.*, 1961) suggests that the superiority of responses in the *DM* condition can be explained by the fact that this procedure "was simply a more effective training procedure for inculcating response patterns (and perhaps concepts as well) which the child did not have in his repertoire when he walked into the experimental room." According to Flavell, therefore, it is possible that the child of 4–5 does not possess the concept of probability, as Yost *et al.* maintain, but rather *the capacity to acquire it under suitable conditions of instruction.* However, an hypothesis such as this requires careful consideration, since according to Piaget: (1) the concept of probability presupposes structural cognitive schemas which the child of 4–5 years does not possess. (2) Cognitive schemas are not acquired in a short time. Their acquisition involves a profound reorganisation of mental processes, which takes time of the order of months or years.

Goldberg (1966) has followed the same line of research, concentrating, like Yost *et al.*, on pre-school children, and using a technique essentially similar to theirs. Conditions P and DM were compared, with certain modifications in order to exclude extraneous variables more adequately. The only reinforcement used was knowledge of results, and the experimental items were constructed in such a way that it was possible to independently control the effects of the following factors: probability, the absolute numbers of counters, and the structure of the items (i.e. equal numbers of winning or non-winning counters were used; see the earlier discussion of the failure of Yost *et al.* to control for unequal numbers of winning and non-winning counters).

The proportions used were: 0.66, 0.75, and 0.80. In condition P, each proportion was represented by four different-sized sets of counters, for expample $\frac{1}{4}$, $\frac{2}{8}$, $\frac{4}{16}$, and $\frac{8}{32}$. In the DM condition, each test included two out of the four possible set sizes.

Of the 24 trials in each condition, in twelve the correct box was on the left side, and in twelve it was on the right side.

This is an example of condition P:

	Number of *m* counters	Number of *l* counters	Correct response
A	4	1	*m*
A	1	4	*l*
C	4	16	*l*
C	16	4	*m*

(*m* = preferred colour; *l* = non-preferred colour)

This is an example of condition DM:

Number of *m* counters in each box	Added counters		Winning colour	Correct response
	left	right		
4	16	1	*m*	left
4	1	16	*m*	right
4	16	1	*l*	left
4	1	16	*l*	right

In condition P, the 24 tests were constructed in such a way that they used all possible combinations of the 3 probabilities, the 2 colours, and the 4 set sizes.

Condition DM used all combinations of the 3 probabilities, two set-sizes, and two positions (left or right). There were 32 subjects (16 boys and 16 girls).

Taking the subject's score as the total number of correct responses out of the 24 possible, the following results (tabulated as mean values) were obtained:

	Session I	Session II
I: P; II: DM	P: 13.4	DM: 16.6
I: DM; II: P	DM: 15.4	P: 15.5

(1) It is clear that condition DM produced a greater number of correct responses, even though there was no difference in reinforcement between the two conditions.

(2) Subjects made significantly more errors when the winning counters were equal in number, and the non-winning counters were unequal in number. This result is very important, since it supports the view that *pre-school children do not choose the correct box on the criterion of proportion, but by comparing absolute numbers* (giving correct responses especially when the non-winning counters are equal in number, and the winning counters unequal in number).

Goldberg's procedure is still, however, open to a criticism which may throw doubt on this conclusion. On the occasions when the winning counters were equal in number, they were also of the non-preferred colour. It is therefore possible that it was this attitudinal factor which led to the increase of errors on these occasions. Even if this interpretation is not very plausible, it cannot be eliminated.

(3) There were no significant differences in the estimations of odds as a function of the absolute number of counters.

(4) Errors increased as the probability approached 50%. This result was not unexpected, since the discrimination becomes more difficult in the region of 50% probability. The effect was statistically significant in condition P, but in condition DM it was significant only in the case of subjects whose scores were better than 17 out of 24 ($p < 0.05$). Among the 32 subjects, 12 were in this category.

(5) If the results from the first 12 and the last 12 tests are compared within each experimental session, it appears, in condition P as well as in condition DM, that the responses were better in the second part of the session. Goldberg concludes from this that there was a learning effect. Since this learning effect occurred in both conditions, Flavell's hypothesis, according to which the DM condition in Yost's experiments produced better responses because it stimulated learning, is disconfirmed. These learning effects are small in Goldberg's experiment, but they are of the same order for both P and DM conditions.

Developmental aspects. The role of verbal and perceptual factors. Davies (1965) has also attacked the problem of the concept of probability in children, but she has used a rather different approach from that of Yost *et al.* (1962).

Davies set out to test the following hypotheses:

(1) The acquisition of the concept of probability is a progressive phenomenon. As we have seen, Yost *et al.* did not consider children beyond the pre-school level. Davies used six age levels in her experiments, based on yearly divisions between subjects aged from 3 to 9 years, with 16 subjects in each age level.

(2) Non-verbal probabilistic behaviour appears before verbalisation of the concept of probability. This hypothesis is suggested both by data reported in the literature (especially probability matching behaviour) and

by the naturalistically observed behaviour of children at the pre-operational level, which indicates that their responses are frequently adapted to the probabilities of events (Messik and Solley, 1957).

(3) Pire (1958) has claimed that, for all age levels, boys have a superior concept of probability to that of girls. Davies set out to test this hypothesis also.

The investigation of non-verbal behaviour was carried out in the following manner. Two glass jars were filled with red and white beads. In one of the jars, the proportion of white to red beads was $\frac{4}{5}$, and in the other jar the proportion was reversed. By pressing on a lever, the subject could release a single bead. The subjects were told that they could make ten lever-presses, and for each bead of a specified colour they would receive a reward; four trials of ten lever-presses were run.

The subject could choose either jar for the ten lever-presses. The apparatus was set up in such a way that the beads were not in fact delivered from the jars which could be seen, but from one which was hidden from view, and which contained 5 red and 5 white beads, the proportion of delivered beads therefore being 50%–50%. The last bead delivered was always of the rewarded colour, so that the total of 5 rewarded beads had not been delivered until the end of the trial.

This experimental arrangement tested simultaneously:

(a) non-verbal behaviour in probabilistic situations; and

(b) the relationship between direct, perceived information and information obtained by counting the frequencies of stimuli.

The results showed that subjects responded according to the perceived proportions – that is to say, they preferred the jar in which the proportion of rewarded beads was $\frac{4}{5}$. This preference was maintained throughout the experiment, even though the proportions of beads actually delivered pointed to a different conclusion, and should, eventually, have led to an equalisation of preference between the two jars.

The verbal test. Davies used the following procedure. Five small boxes were filled with coloured beads in the same proportions as in the non-verbal test $(\frac{4}{5}, \frac{1}{5})$, though the colours were different. The child was asked to draw a bead from each of the five boxes in turn, with eyes closed, and to name the colour of the bead drawn, together with a reason for naming that particular colour. After the five draws, the child was asked which colour would be drawn if each bead was returned to its box, and again to give reasons for the answer. Scores between 1 and 10 were awarded on the basis of overall test performance (considering the correctness both of responses and explanations); if the subject had named the less numerous colour, but in explanation had said that "sometimes" this colour could be drawn, the response was counted correct.

The following results were obtained: (1) Confirming the hypothesis that the concept of probability is a progressive phenomenon, the percentage of correct responses increased with age. The mean ages at which subjects (a) failed both tests (b) passed only the non-verbal test (c) passed both tests, are respectively for (a) 3.11, for (b) 4.5, and for (c) 7.4 (Davies, 1966. p. 788). (2) The non-verbal behaviour of the pre-school child proves that the child behaves in conformity with the probabilities of events. (3) Non-verbal behaviour reflecting objective probability (event probability) appears earlier than the corresponding verbal behaviour. This conclusion is based on the comparison between the percentages of correct responses on the verbal and non-verbal tests for each age group, and the fact that no subject responded correctly on the verbal test, but incorrectly on the non-verbal test. (4) The hypothesis that there would be a sex difference was not confirmed.

The result which seems to us to have particular importance is that, in the non-verbal test, children responded throughout the session in accordance with the *perceived proportions*, and not according to the frequency of reinforcement.

From data discussed previously, we know that the child adapts its responses to the frequency of reinforcement.

In Davies' experiments, we have a situation of conflict between a directly perceived proportion and a frequency which must be computed. In such a situation, the *probability of reinforcement no longer controls the responses of the child, which come instead under the control of the directly perceived proportion.*

Comparing her results with those of Piaget and Inhelder, Davies suggests that they have based their conclusions exclusively on the verbal behaviour of the child, in so far as they claim that the concept of probability is established during the period of formal operations. (In fact, Piaget and Inhelder indicate that the concept of probability is not established as a generalised modality of thought until the level of formal operations, thereby implicating operations on proportions and combinations.)

Davies' experiments have established the fact that, in estimating odds, the child uses predominantly information which is directly perceived. If there is conflict between this and information which is obtained by computing frequencies, it is the perceptual information which will determine the child's prediction. This fact leads us to wonder whether in fact the responses of the child, at least until the age of 6–7, are only *apparently* judgements of probability, and may be reduced to comparative evaluations of sizes alone, which would be quite a different process.

Taking the experiments of Yost *et al.* (1962), Davies (1965), and Goldberg (1966) as their starting-point, Hoemann and Ross (1971) have tried to settle this question of whether 'probabilistic' judgements by children really are probabilistic. Their hypothesis was that pre-school children do not make probabilistic judgements; their responses only *appear* to be probabilistic, because of the experimental context in which they are made, and they are in reality nothing more than perceptual comparisons.

It was therefore necessary to set up experiments which would differentiate probabilistic judgments from perceptual comparisons. Certain details of the experimental procedure will be described below, since they are crucial to a correct interpretation of the results. In all, four experiments were carried out.

Subjects in the first experiment were aged 4, 6, 7, and 10, and were divided into sets of two groups within each age level, corresponding to two experimental conditions.

On a series of paper discs were drawn circles which were segmented in black and white to differing proportions. In the probability condition, two such discs were attached to two spinners. The subject was asked to choose the spinner which would give the best chance of winning on the colour designated by the experimenter. In the proportionality condition, the subject simply had to choose the disc which contained more white (or black). In some cases, the discs had only two segments, one black and one white; in other cases the segments of black and white alternated.

The rationale behind this experiment was as follows. If there were approximately the same number of errors in both experimental conditions, it could be supposed that the judgements which were being made were not probabilistic, but perceptual. If there were fewer correct responses in the probability condition, it could be supposed that the difference was due to some probabilistic judgement, over and above perceptual judgement.

Three odds difference levels between discs were used $\frac{1}{2}$, $\frac{1}{4}$, and $\frac{1}{8}$. (i.e. differences between proportions in which the desired colour covered the two discs which the subject had to compare. For instance: $\frac{7}{8} - \frac{3}{8} = \frac{4}{8} = \frac{1}{2}$).

The main finding was that there were no significant differences between the two conditions at any age level. (In fact, the data show a slightly lower percentage of correct responses in the probability condition, particularly in the case of the younger subjects.)

Hoemann and Ross conclude from this experiment that the experimental design used could not differentiate between perceptual comparisons and probability judgements. The correct responses of subjects showed only their ability to perceptually compare two different sizes.

The second experiment used seven age levels, with subjects aged between 4 and 13. This time, the task involved comparisons on a single disc. In the probability condition, the subject was asked to say on which colour the pointer would stop after the spinner had been started. In the proportionality condition, the subject was asked simply to compare the amounts of black and white, and say which was the greater.

The results showed significant differences between the two conditions; there were more errors in the probability judgement task. The authors conclude that this is a task which is capable of testing the ability to make probability judgements (in contrast to the two spinners task). It also emerged from the results that 4 year-old subjects are not capable of probability judgements, since the number of correct responses given by these children (56%) did not differ significantly from the chance level. Between the ages of 5 and 8, there is a clear improvement in performance on the proportionality task, but performance on the probability task is still very poor.

Hoemann and Ross claim that these findings contradict the view of Yost et al. (1962), Davies (1965), and Goldberg (1966) that pre-school children are capable of probability judgement, and that they confirm the view of Piaget and Inhelder, which is that it is impossible to speak of a concept of chance and probability before the stage of concrete operations.

Hoemann and Ross's third experiment used the same conditions as the first experiment, with the difference that the subjects were asked to compare several colours on the two discs. There were two groups of 7 year-old children, each group corresponding to one experimental condition. The results were very close to those obtained in the experiment using only one spinner.

Instead of the spinners, experiment four used draws of coloured (red and green) ping-pong balls from transparent urns. The procedure was essentially the same as in similar experiments by Yost *et al.* (1962), Goldberg (1966) and others, in which the subject, knowing the composition of the urns, must estimate which urn offers the greatest chances of drawing an item of a specified colour. The subjects were normal children at two age levels (7 and 11) and deaf children of 11 years. The same odds difference levels were used ($\frac{1}{2}$, $\frac{1}{4}$, and $\frac{1}{8}$).

The results of experiment four were similar to those of experiment three, showing that a task requiring comparisons of sets of discrete elements (ping-pong balls) can differentiate probabilistic from perceptual judgements. The similarity of results leads to the conclusion that the different tasks used in these two experiments are in fact analogous.

Hoemann and Ross come to the overal conclusion that their experiments two, three, and four confirm the view of Piaget and Inhelder that pre-school children do not possess concepts of chance and probability.

It also emerges from all the experiments by Hoemann and Ross that performance improves with age.

Hoemann and Ross posed the fundamental problem of differentiating between true probabilistic judgements and judgements which are simply perceptual size comparisons, which have been mistaken for true probabilistic judgements by other investigators.

Their central argument is that, in certain tasks, the results which could be obtained from estimating odds could just as easily be obtained by direct comparison of sizes, while in other tasks the difference between these two processes is made apparent.

This reasoning is vulnerable at several points. It is clear, in the first place, that size comparison enters into probabilistic judgement, since odds are represented in size relationships. This underlying comparison may be made in either perceptual or numerical terms, and in either case can be more or less complex. The transition from this initial comparison to actual estimation of odds may be direct, or it may be complicated by the nature of the problem itself.

The fact that a child asked to compare certain probabilities on two discs segmented into two colours obtains the same result for the probabilistic task and for the perceptual comparison does not necessarily prove that probabilistic judgement has not taken place. In such a task, the estimation of odds proceeds directly from the perceptual comparison, but this does not show that it can be completely reduced to this perceptual comparison. The actual wording of the test used by Hoemann and Ross was as follows: "I want you to look at the two spinners very carefully and show me which one you will spin to make the pointer point to black (white)" (Hoemann-Ross, p. 244).

The problem as posed is in terms of estimating odds, and a correct response indicates that the child really does (although no doubt implicitly) make use of the idea of chance. Otherwise the child could not respond to this question as it is posed! The use of perceptual comparison *mediates* the response. Nothing in the formulation of the question *directly* suggests a perceptual comparison. The child is simply asked to show the spot where the spinner will stop. Without an intuition of probability, nothing suggests a quantitaitve comparison of the two colours. It could equally well be maintained that, in more difficult problems, where the estimation of proportions must be carried out, correct responses do not depend on probability judgements, but can be reduced to comparing proportions – whether perceptual or numerical.

It seems therefore to be the nature of the problem, including the way in which it is formulated, which will show whether the task – and the respective response – involves a probabilistic judgement or not.

There is still the problem of why, in some cases, responses to probabilistic tasks are poorer than responses to perceptual or the corresponding numerical comparisons (c.f. Hoemann and Ross' second experiment). The most plausible explanation is that given by Piaget and Inhelder for an analogous situation. They found that, when sets of beads are used, better responses are obtained if two sets of beads are compared for probabilities than if two colours are compared within a single set "...in the case of a single set... the combination of elements in a single intuitive unit prevents the subject from thinking simultaneously of the whole and of the parts" (Piaget and Inhelder, 1951, p. 161).

Direct perceptual comparison is straightforward. The child simply has to show the colour which is present in larger quantity. But in order to estimate odds, the child has to relate each of the colours in turn to the total area of the disc. In the condition with *two* spinners, *there are two equal total areas* which are simultaneously perceived. In the single spinner condition, the *same total area* must serve simultaneously for both comparisons. The degree of abstraction required is greater.

Things are complicated still more when the two colours are divided into several alternating segments (as in Hoemann and Ross' experiments). In this situation, the child tends to respond at random.

The fact that inadequacy of response in probabilistic tasks can be caused by the specific nature of the task itself, i.e. by the way in which the estimation of proportions is to be carried out, rather than by the probabilistic aspect of the problem, is demonstrated also by the following result described by Hoemann and Ross. When two spinners were used, and subjects were asked to estimate chances *in a situation where several colours were winning* (third experiment), poorer responses were obtained, analogous to the responses obtained with a single disc in the first experiment.

Now, from the point of view of strict probability judgement, there is no difference between situations in which the winning elements are all of the same colour, and situations in which they are of more than one colour. *The difficulty consists in the perceptual comparison itself.*

Our conclusion is that the similarity of results obtained from probabilistic tasks and from tasks requiring numerical or perceptual comparisons does not constitute a sufficient argument for the view that there is no probabilistic judgement in these tasks. *Furthermore, the fact that subjects respond well to problems whose formulation implies the estimation of chances seems to us to constitute the proof that they are operating with the concept of chance, even if the estimation is carried out on the basis of simple perceptual comparisons.*

3. THE EFFECT OF INSTRUCTION ON THE QUANTITATIVE ESTIMATION OF ODDS

The results obtained by Piaget and Inhelder (1951), Yost *et al.* (1962), Davies (1965), and Goldberg (1966) have been from naive, unpractised subjects.

Together with Mânzat and Pampu, we have approached the problem of the concept of probability in children from the point of view of the results which can be obtained by means of systematic instruction.

It will be recalled that Ojemann *et al.* (1965a, b, 1966) also used a programme of systematic instruction in order to develop probabilistic concepts, and they obtained significant improvements in children aged 11 and upwards.

We have used a similar approach (1970), but working with children aged 5, 9, and 12, in order to observe the interaction of instruction with age. A complete description of this work will be found in the article reprinted in the Appendix: E. Fischbein, Ileana Pampu, and I. Mînzat, Comparison of ratios and the chance concept in children. We made use of a *decision-making* technique similar to that used by Yost *et al.*

From two plastic boxes containing black and white marbles (for example 6 white and 2 black marbles in one box, 10 white and 5 black in the other) the child was asked to select the box which, because of its content, favoured the *chance* extraction of a marble of a specified colour.

We asked the subjects 18 questions, divided into three categories. In category C_1, the ratios between the two sets of marbles were arranged in such a way that the black and white marbles in one box were equal in number, or that the number of marbles of one colour were the same in both boxes (for example, 1 white, 2 black; 5 white, 2 black– an arrangement which clearly facilitates the choice). In C_2, no restrictions were placed on the arrangement of the marbles. C_3 consisted of 'equal' ratios, i.e. proportions. The experiments comprised three variants:

Condition I_1: the subjects received only a brief explanation of the nature of the experiment, and of the three possible responses with regard to the choice of box with the most probable favourable outcome (right, left, indifferent).

Condition I_2: the subjects received a short, but systematic explanation of how the problems could be solved. This had two stages: (a) two boxes containing, for example, 4B, 1W and 8B, 2W were presented, and after 20 draws from each box it was pointed out that the relative frequencies of black marbles which were drawn were equal (this result was arranged in advance, in order not to have to complicate the explanation); (b) the child was shown a technique of grouping which would permit the practical solution of the problems; for example, 4B, 1W and 8B, 2W become 4B, 1W and 4B, 1W + 4B, 1W – i.e. the probabilities are equal, since out of 5 marbles 4 are black, in each box.

If there are, for example, 4B, 1W and 9B, 2W, this shows the excess of black in the second box. We used this technique for two reasons: (a) it requires no knowledge of fractions, (b) it clearly demonstrates the concept of proportionality and relative frequency.

Condition I_3: in this variant, the subjects received only explanations concerning the technique of grouping described for I_2, but with a larger number of examples.

In I_2 and I_3, subjects were taught essentially that chances cannot be estimated only by considering the number of possible favourable outcomes, but that it is necessary to relate this number to the total composition of the box.

The experiment was designed as a factorial experiment with three factors: 3 age levels $\times$ 3 instruction types $\times$ 3 question categories, with repeated measures (the same subjects) on the last factor. Twenty different subjects were assigned to each experimental condition (I_1, I_2, I_3). There was a total of 180 subjects.

In condition I_1, there were nearly as many pre-school as 9–10 year-old children who correctly solved *only* C_1 *tests* (which were reducible to a comparison of two terms). In contrast, 12–13 year-old subjects were able to deal with all three categories of problem, without special instruction.

In conditions I_2 and I_3, with prior instruction, there were no essential differences from condition I_1 as far as the pre-school and the older children were concerned. The pre-school children could not be induced to carry out a double comparison, or to understand the idea of proportionality, which is an essential component of the concept of probability, while the 12–13 year-old subjects gave good responses from the outset. *There were striking improvements in the responses of 9–10 year-olds, who, after brief instruction, were able to carry out the double comparison required for the evaluation of chances, and in general to operate correctly with the concept of probability.*

According to Piaget and Inhelder, such concepts are not available until the level of formal operations (after 12 years); but their data have been based exclusively on spontaneous responses of subjects. The finding that the mental mechanisms necessary for the active understanding of proportionality are already present at the level of concrete operations and can be brought into play by means of brief instruction, is of central importance to the teaching of probability.

EXPERIMENTAL LESSONS

As a result of the findings detailed above, we proceeded, during the school year 1972–73, to investigate the effects of some experimental lessons on notions of probability and statistics with children aged 9, 10, 11, 12, and 13.

We judged that the best learning conditions could be created by pointing out simultaneously the combinatorial, statistical, and probabilistic aspects of certain practical situations.

In our view, these notions must be learned, in the first place, from concrete experiences which demonstrate the dynamics of stochastic phenomena which are subject to statistical laws (a similar approach is taken in the excellent book by A. J. Malpas *Experiments in statistics*, 1969).

We began by teaching, with the aid of examples, the notion of an *event*, and the notions of a possible event, a certain event, and an impossible event. The concept of probability was presented as a measure of the foreseeable chances in a given situation (passing from the intuitive estimation of odds by the children, as described in the experiments above, to the classical definition). The fundamental notion to be conveyed by these lessons was that of *the stability of relative frequencies*, and this was attempted by means of a dual approach.

First procedure: the children were shown an urn containing beads of two colours, and the probabilities were determined by referring to the composition of the contents of the urn. One colour was designated as 'winning'. Each child drew a bead, which was thus either winning or losing. The bead was then replaced, and the result of the draw was recorded on a blackboard. The relative frequencies were indicated in blocks of 10 draws, and the children were able to follow the oscillations of frequencies. This procedure included: (a) a theoretical prediction, (b) an experiment verifying the prediction, (c) a demonstration of the oscillating frequencies, with their convergence towards a theoretical point, which is the probability.

This type of instruction is doubly attractive. The children observe with great interest the result of each draw, since it scores a loss or gain for the child concerned. They also follow the oscillations of the results very closely, to see whether or not the prediction will be borne out.

Second procedure: An urn was filled with beans, of which a few were coloured. Some of the beans were scooped out, and counted. This operation was repeated several times, and the relationship between the number of coloured beans drawn and the total drawn was commented upon each time. It was pointed out that the values expressing this relationship oscillate around the value deduced from the composition of the total contents of the urn.

From this procedure, the children acquire the important concept of the *sample*. They realise its practical significance, the way in which a sample is obtained, they begin to understand statistical inference, and they begin to grasp the inductive steps of scientific investigation. It would be possible to outline a variety of procedures which could achieve this, but it is not the teaching methods as such we wish to emphasise. What seems to us most important is that *practical experience with probabilities provides an ideal way of familiarising children with the fundamental concepts of science, such as prediction, experiment and verification, chance and necessity, laws and statistical laws, knowledge through induction, and so on.* Children show great interest in this type of activity, which has all the characteristics of a game (since it is the children themselves who make the draws, and who 'lose' or 'win') but is at the same time a true scientific experiment.

All of these lessons made use of the children's knowledge of fractions, which was in turn enhanced by relating to a multiplicity of possible situations.

Finally, a varied range of phenomena were discussed from a probabilistic perspective (physical, meteorological, biological, demographic, and sociological phenomena, and the practical and scientific usefulness of sampling).

With the 11 year-old children (who had already had experimental instruction from us in previous years), the emphasis was on using combinatory ability by means of tree diagrams. Diagrams were constructed which corresponded, for instance, to two, three, four, or five draws of two or three letters (or numbers) from an urn.

A diagram like this permits us to (a) represent the concept of equiprobability (which is quite difficult for children to understand) in visual terms; (b) attach probabilities to some possible results (for example, 'what is the probability of drawing A four times in a row?' or 'what is the probability of drawing B twice in a row in four draws?', and so on); (c) show that extreme cases are rare, and that 'mixed' cases are far more frequent;

(d) prepare the intuitive ground for theorems concerning the addition and multiplication of probabilities.

We have also used tree diagrams for experiments with sampling without replacement, in which the probabilities change with each draw. The children were easily able to construct the corresponding diagrams. The main aim of the exercises was to induce the essential mental skills of combinatory thinking. If this step is omitted, and the pupils exposed too suddenly to formulae and schemas, they may be able to solve standard exercises, but will not be so capable of independent and productive thought in this domain.

We also judged it necessary to introduce the *statistical dimension of probability* in this context. At the end of the second lesson, the children were given the following piece of practical homework: to write the capital letters A and B on individual slips of paper, fold them, and put them in a container; then to make four successive draws, mixing the slips of paper well each time, and to make a note of each letter drawn. This was to be done five times.

During the next lesson, a diagram of the sample space was drawn on the blackboard, and for each event in this sample space (each event being one of the 16 possible sets of letters) the number of times it had occurred during the homework assignment was noted. If 32 children each drew 5 sets of letters, this meant that there was a total of 160 sets which must be distributed across the 16 cells of the diagram. This indicated that, in theory, each set should occur 10 times $(160/16=10)$. The children were able to see that, in fact, the frequency of occurrence of each set did oscillate around this number, and that this was due purely to chance – since each child had independently drawn five sets of letters.

An experiment like this is another way of demonstrating the empirical tendency of relative frequencies to oscillate around the theoretically calculated probability, and of consolidating the children's understanding of the relationship between the empirical and theoretical components of the concept of probability. Such an experiment also has the following advantages: (a) the concept of an event is amplified; the unitary event, irreducible from the point of view of the definition of the experiment, is not, in this case, the result of a single draw, but the result of 4 draws (a set of 4 letters). (b) The children acquire an understanding of what is meant by 'possible case', 'equally possible cases', and 'total number of equally possible cases'. The sequence ABBA, for instance, is a possible case – it could occur at any time. But, in fact, *every sequence is logically possible.* They are equally possible for reasons of symmetry, since, all other things being equal, there is no reason to believe that any one sequence will occur more often than any other. The draws prove that chance operates in such a way that each event does occur the same number of times. This is, again, a way of seeing a theoretically deduced prediction confirmed. Understanding of the fundamental concept of 'equally possible cases' requires the fusion, within the effective experimental context, of the logical and the empirical view, as described above. (c) Finally, there is the advantage that, in familiarising the children with such an inventory of all possible outcomes within a given situation, one has in fact given them the concept of a sample space.

The most surprising finding was that even those children who had previously been weak in mathematics were attracted by this type of activity. Furthermore, this produced an improvement in all their mathematical abilities. We were able to confirm that these experimental lessons in statistics and probability stimulated the imagination of young adolescents, who participated naturally and enthusiastically in this game of setting up an inventory of possibilities and making predictions from it.

In order to give a more detailed picture of the content of the lessons (for the 11-year-olds) and of the results obtained, we will give below the questions in the final written test, and the percentages of correct responses.

(1) There are 3 white beads, 2 black beads, and 5 red beads in a jar. What is the probability that the following will be drawn by chance? (a) a white bead? (b) a white bead after another white bead has been drawn? (c) either a black bead or a white bead?

(2) A jar contains identical counters on which the numbers 1 or 2 have been marked. 4 successive draws are made, and each time the drawn counter is replaced. Draw a diagram representing the sample space. What is the probability of drawing (a) the number 2 four times in succession? (b) a set whose numbers total 6? (c) a set in which the first two numbers are 2? (d) a set in which the number 2 occurs exactly twice? (e) a set containing the number 1 at least twice?

(3) A jar contains the letters A, E, and R marked on identical counters. What is the probability of drawing: (a) a meaningful word? (b) an ad-

jective? (c) a verb? Write down the words you have thought of in answering these questions.

(4) How many combinations of three numbers can be formed, using the numbers from 1 to 9, if (a) the numbers can be repeated? (b) the numbers cannot be repeated?

(5) The Ionescu family have three children. What is the probability that: (a) they are all boys? (b) there are just two boys? (c) there are at least two boys?

(6) The numbers from 1 to 9 are placed in a jar. Four successive draws are made, replacing the drawn number each time. What is the probability of drawing a set in which none of the numbers are repeated?

The following percentages of correct responses to these questions were obtained:

(1) (a) 93.7; (b) 77.5; (c) 81.9.
(2) (a) 93.3; (b) 84.6; (c) 83.8; (d) 80.8; (e) 75.8.
(3) (a) 53.9; (b) 55.8; (c) 53.7; (d) 66.2.
(4) (a) 78.5; (b) 75.8.
(5) (a) 81.7; (b) 76.0; (c) 72.4.
(6) 31.6. ·

Many children gave erroneous responses to question (3), since they had thought that letters could be repeated. A small investigation, however, led us to the discovery that it was their teachers who had wrongly advised them! We have in fact found more difficulty in making teachers understand the concepts of probability than in making their pupils understand them. The teachers had wrongly corrected the tests on several occasions; the children had given the correct reponses, but the teachers had interpreted the questions wrongly. This is in fact an important finding, since it demonstrates the loss with age of certain intuitive faculties. An adolescent has better chances of rebuilding an intuitive structure than an adult.

THE INTUITIVE FOUNDATION OF ELEMENTARY PROBABILISTIC OPERATIONS

During the experimental lessons we have described, we became aware of certain intuitive deficiencies when we attempted to teach the probabilities of mutually exclusive and independent events. We carried out a research project with Ileana Bărbat and Ion Mînzat (1971) in order to specify the details of these deficiencies. The subjects were adolescents aged 13, 15, and 17. (For full details, see the article reprinted in Appendix I: E. Fischbein, Ileana Bărbat, and I. Mînzat, 'Primary and Secondary Intuitions in the Introduction of Probability').

The technique we devised (and called *learning by programmed discovery*) consisted of asking subjects successive standardised questions which could be reduced to smaller items. For each problem, we started with a specialised question, depending on the field, and if the correct response was not obtained, we asked progressively more general, elementary questions which were closer to the relevant intuition. With this technique, the subjects revealed their difficulties and abilities, and in fact the whole range of mental and intuitive mechanisms, whether correct or erroneous, available to them in attempting to solve any given problem.

We were interested in the following aspects: probability as a metric of chance, the multiplication law of probabilities, the addition law (particularly in the case of mutually exclusive events) and the use of these laws, once learned.

We found, as we had done in previous investigations, that the concepts of chance and probability could be built on a natural intuitive foundation. This primary intuition also facilitated the acquisition of the basic axioms of the theory of probability. In the case of independent events, primary intuition facilitates understanding of the multiplication law (chances are reduced as more conditions are imposed), but the final calculation cannot be found intuitively.

In the case of mutually exclusive events, the probability is naturally deduced by the addition of the probabilities of the elementary events. There is, however, a difficulty in the operation of making an inventory of these elementary, equiprobable events, and, prior to this, in understanding that such a complete inventory is necessary in the first place. Generally speaking, intuition contributes nothing to these two steps.

Within the age limits investigated (13–17) there was no improvement in the primary intuitive base relevant to probability. If specific instructional procedures are not used, the intuitive base remains unchanged from the period of formal operations onward.

The Estimation of Odds: Summary

Pre-school children possess a natural intuition of chance and the quantification of chance, but, at this age, only estimations based on binary comparisons are possible. Instruction does not bring about any significant improvement in this respect.

If appropriate instruction is given at the level of concrete operations, children can learn to compare odds by means of a quantitative comparison of ratios.

At the level of formal operations, these estimations are carried out directly. The difficulties encountered by the intelligence in acquiring and using probabilistic concepts are explained in part by certain fundamental lacunae within the set of intuitions relevant to probability, and in part by an increasing tendency of maturing intelligence to seek univocal causal explanations.

CHAPTER VII

COMBINATORIAL ANALYSIS

Suggestive data. The inventory of possible cases cannot be reduced to an enumeration of elements, except in some very simple experiments. Such an inventory generally presupposes a rational, constructive process which, on the basis of existing information, sets up a sample space of all possible outcomes. (More accurately, of all *equally* possible outcomes. Without this equality of probability of all possible cases, established by rational, objective considerations, the classical definition loses its meaning.)

An inventory of possible outcomes is constructed, usually, by means of combinatorial analysis. This means that, if the subject does not possess combinatory ability, the concept of probability can only be used in the very restricted case where the possible outcomes can be directly enumerated (the case of 'concrete probability' in the terminology of Piaget and Inhelder, 1955, p. 287).

From the findings of their own research, Piaget and Inhelder (1951, 1954) have concluded that combinatorial operations are not available until the level of formal thought. In their book *La genèse de l'idée de hasard chez l'enfant*, Piaget and Inhelder have described experiments concerned with combinations, permutations, and arrangements.

In their book *De la logique de l'enfant à la logique de l'adolescent* (1951) they also considered the problems of the concepts of the possible and the necessary, of chance and probability, and combinatorial operations.

According to Piaget and Inhelder, even the logic of propositions – which is established in adolescents – is based on "a combinatorial synthesis of elements" (Piaget and Inhelder, 1955, p. 95). At the level of concrete operations, there are only simple 'hook-ups' of the classes and relations of concrete logic.

Hypothetico-deductive reasoning does not operate by establishing closer and closer relations, collapsing classes together, from the starting point of certain facts expressed in the premises. On the contrary, the reasoning operates with possibilities which are discovered, formulated, evaluated, and articulated together by means of the 'combinatorial synthesis' of which Piaget and Inhelder have written.

Combinatorial operations therefore represent something much more important than a branch of mathematics. They represent a schema with a character as general as that of the schemas of proportionality and correlation, which emerge simultaneously after the age of 12–13.

The close relationship between combinatory ability and logical thought has suggested to some authors the possibility of using combinatorial tasks to test intellectual development (Claparède, c.f. Dubosson, 1957; Langeot, 1968). The use of such tests with children of different ages (Dubosson, 5–9 years; Langeot, 9–16 years) has shown an improvement in performance with age.

Langeot (1968) has also studied the transfer effect of mathematical instruction (in the concept of the Cartesian product) on combinatory ability (permutations) in adolescents.

In 1951, Piaget and Inhelder carried out the following series of experiments on combinations, permutations, and arrangements.

Combinations. The subjects were shown several piles of coloured counters; one white pile, one red pile, and so on. They were asked to make as many as possible different pairs of colours.

Children at the first developmental stage (6–7) succeeded in finding some of the possible pairs. These were arrived at by trial and error, and not by means of a systematic procedure including an inventory of all possible pairs.

Children at the second stage (8–11) tried several methods but they still did not arrive at an exhaustive procedure. The reason for this failure lay in the fact that these subjects still tended to limit themselves to juxtapositions (AB, CD, or AB, BC, CD) and symmetries (A and F, etc.)

At the third stage (after 11-12) some subjects discovered the method. by which they could obtain all possible pairs. For example, a subject first of all makes a line of five yellow (A) counters (there being six piles in all) and associates each counter with one of the other colours, B, C, D, E, F. Subsequently a line of five blue counters is made, and so on.

How can we explain the fact that, at the second stage, the children are still unable to find all possible pairs, although they do by this stage possess the operation of placing items in correspondence? According to

Piaget and Inhelder (1951) the explanation is that combination is not juxtaposition of correspondences, but a unique operation which involves the coordination of two other operations – seriation and correspondence. Combination is, therefore, *an operation on operations*, and is therefore characteristic of the level of formal thought.

In 1955, Piaget and Inhelder described another experiment on combinatorial operations. Four bottles, labelled 1 to 4, contained colourless and odourless substances: (1) dilute sulphuric acid, (2) water, (3) hydrogen peroxide, (4) thiosulphate. A fifth bottle (g) contained drops of potassium iodide. If the liquids in bottles 1, 3, and g were combined, this gave a yellow-coloured mixture. If water was then added, there was no change; but if thiosulphate from bottle 4 was added, the mixture became colourless. The experimenter produced two glasses. One contained a mixture of dilute sulphuric acid and hydrogen peroxide, and the other contained water. The subject added drops of potassium iodide to the two glasses (not knowing their contents) and was asked to note the different reactions.

The subject was then asked to reproduce the yellow colour, using any of the five bottles.

At level IIA, the subjects did nothing more than add drops of liquid g to other four bottles. At level IIB, the children tried several combinations, but did not use a systematic approach. It was only at level IIIA, and then only just (note that this is the stage of formal operations) that what Piaget and Inhelder call 'une combinatoire systématique' emerges – i.e. a systematic method of finding all the different possible combinations of the five liquids (Inhelder and Piaget, 1955, pp. 97–98).

Experiments on permutations (Piaget and Inhelder, 1951). The child is given two counters, A and B, of different colours, and asked to show in how many different ways they can be arranged. The child is then asked to place two pairs of counters, AB and BA, so that one pair is in a row below the other. Three piles of counters, in colours A, B, C are then presented, and the child asked to form permutations with the elements A, B, C, selecting one counter at a time, and making up rows of permutations one below the other. If this is done successfully with three elements, the task progresses to four elements.

At level IA (before 7–8), the child has difficulty in understanding the problem, and in realising that different permutations can be obtained with the same elements. At level IB, the child succeeds in making some permutations, and even discovers some regularities (for example reversing the positions of two of the elements) but does not progress to a general strategy. The subject who does not yet possess operational mobility, in order to find all possible permutations, would have to make use of decentrations which are characteristic of 'articulated intuitions' (p. 191). Without such intuitive mobility, the initial order of the elements is seen as the only possible one.

At level IIB, the child finds several possible permutations, but still does not make the discovery of a method. In fact, of course, the permutations are all derivable from each other, and this entails reference to the principle of reversibility, among others.

Lack of knowledge of reversibility prevents the child from discovering a systematic method for making all possible permutations. Each change of position must be understood to be reversible, otherwise there can be no concept of permutation, or any understanding that the permutations are derived from each other, and that the point of departure can always be returned to.

In the second stage, children make the empirical discovery of a procedure, first of all for three elements (at level IIA) and later for four elements (at level IIB) i.e. after the age of 10, when they generalise the procedure used with three elements. However, children at this age (10–12) still do not arrive at a truly general procedure for making permutations.

By the end of level IIB, but only just, children can generalise the procedure for 2 and 3 elements to permutations with 4, 5, and 6 elements. They are now able to carry out the calculation $2 \times 3 \times 4 \times 5$ directly. Piaget and Inhelder insist on the point that there is a gap of several years between the acquisition of combinations and the acquisition of permutations. Children of 11–12 can systematically solve combination problems, but it is only at the age of 14–15 that permutation problems begin to be dealt with successfully.

Their explanation is as follows: "... Combinations consist simply of all possible associations, whereas permutations, which are much more numerous, imply an arrangement according to a mobile and reversible system of reference..." (Piaget and Inhelder, 1951, p. 207).

In fact, however, the design of the experiment they carried out does not permit such a comparison. In the case of combinations, they did not ask subjects to do more than form combinations of *n* elements (with a maximum of 6) *which were always presented in pairs,* which represents a rather special case and is much simplified. A true comparison between combinations and permutations would have required passing on to combinations of n elements, taken 2 by 2, 3 by 3, and so on. If the question really is, whether the process of acquisition of these operations is completed during the stage of formal operations, a valid comparison should address itself to the generalised *acquisition* of the respective operations.

Furthermore, Piaget and Inhelder demonstrated combinations only in some, not all, of their subjects (*ibid.*, p. 183) which also reduces the validity of their comparison.

It cannot, therefore, be finally concluded that combinations are acquired earlier than permutations.

One final criticism of Piaget and Inhelder's experiment is important, in view of points which we shall make later: in the case of permutations, the method of investigation itself introduced a learning factor. The method began with two elements, and progressed to three, four, and so on. After the two permutations possible with A and B (AB and BA) have been worked out, the third element, C, can be placed in three possible positions (at the beginning, the middle, or the end) in relation to the two original permutations – thus CAB, ACB, ABC; CBA, BCA, BAC. Permutations with a greater number of elements are obtained by generalising this procedure. It is our contention that, by progressing from a few to a larger number of elements, the method used by Piaget and Inhelder was bound to involve a learning effect. This means that their experimental paradigm is unable to determine the *initial* extent of acquisition of permutations.

Permutations, like combinations, represent for Piaget and Inhelder operations of the second order – operations on operations – which explains why they are not acquired until the stage of formal operations. If changing order is, in itself, an elementary (or 'concrete') operation, the multiplication of order changes is no longer a simple operation, since it is an operation on other operations, i.e. an operation of the second order ("à la seconde puissance") (*ibid.*, p. 206).

Arrangements (Piaget and Inhelder, 1951). In this experiment, the experimental material consisted of cards with the numbers 1, 2, or 3 printed on them; or, for the smaller children, pictures of railway engines (f), passenger wagons (w), or goods wagons (m). The task was to form all possible arrangements of two elements out of the three elements given.

The experiment had three stages: (a) The child had to make up the arrangements by selecting cards from three separate packs. (b) All the cards were piled haphazard in front of the child, who was asked to take two, and predict the third. Each arrangement thus obtained was recorded. (c) The table of recorded arrangements was analysed, and the child was asked to say whether, if the number of cards was increased, the irregularity of the distribution of the arrangements would decrease or increase.

Children in developmental stage I used a random procedure, without trying to find a systematic method. They took two cards at random, and eliminated any pairs which had already been obtained. In the case of the haphazard pile of cards, they showed a belief in a continuing order of emergence of cards, which was based either on repeated occurrences of the same card, or on some moral consideration. Predictions conformed to the pattern which has been found in previous experiments; perseveration, recency effects, and so on. The law of large numbers, apparently, did not affect judgements. Multiplying the number of elements led to some curious effects, involving regularities of the type 11, 22, 33, etc.

Children in developmental stage II did look for a systematic procedure, as in the case of combinations and permutations. The protocols show different progressive stages in the acquisition of arrangements. Through trial and error, the children discover some empirical procedures of limited efficiency for constructing arrangements. The idea of mixture is better understood in terms of the operation of chance. The law of large numbers, with its 'standardising' effect on distributions, seems to operate only for small sets. When large sets of elements are used, as in the preceding experiments, children are unable to predict that the distribution will become more balanced.

Two levels must be distinguished within developmental stage III. At level IIIA (11–12 years) children can complete the inventory of all arrangements of 3 and 4 elements, taken 2 by 2, and even arrive at the result n^2, although they are unable to give an explicit account of this result. At level IIIB (12–13 years) children understand the principle of constructing arrangements with repetitions, and operate with the formula n^2.

THE EFFECT OF INSTRUCTION ON COMBINATORY CAPACITY

General Problems

In general terms, then, Piaget and Inhelder's account is that during the pre-operational period children try out different random associations of elements without searching for a system; during the period of concrete operations, children begin to look for a systematic method of setting up the inventory of all possible groupings, but they do not progress beyond empirical procedures with limited outcomes. It is not until the period of formal operations that children arrive at systematic procedures of constructing all possible groupings of elements obtained by permutations, arrangements, or combinations.

A more detailed analysis of the results obtained by Piaget and Inhelder brings out the following aspects of performance at the level of formal operations.

Firstly, not all subjects at this age are able to discover the method of constructing combinations. We do not know what percentage of the total these subjects represent. Subjects are not able to deal satisfactorily with arrangements until the age of 13, and they do not find a method for dealing with permutations, although this would appear to be a simpler operation, until the age of 14–15 years. All this indicates that, during the stage of formal operations (12–15 years) the intellectual capacities required for combinatorial operations are continuing gradually to develop, and this development is not, in fact, completed during this stage.

Secondly, as we have seen, the experimental design used by Piaget and Inhelder incorporated a learning factor, since the gradual increase in the set size of elements suggested a particular method to the subjects.

It is therefore quite natural to wonder what would happen if one intervened in the developmental process (which, in its natural form, seems to be quite slow and laborious) by offering the adolescent a systematic combination technique.

This problem has several theoretical aspects.

Mathematical induction. In the first place, combinatorial techniques require, as we have seen in previous discussions, a number of very general schemas. Inductive thinking is the most important of these, but this is not meant in the sense of empirical induction, which proceeds by closer and closer approximations and only arrives at a restricted set of results, but rather in the sense of complete, or mathematical, induction.

In mathematical induction, the end product is an integral part of a demonstration, and is therefore characterised by the rigour of deductive reasoning.

In reality, there are not two separate and distinct modes of thought, one succeeding the other, as the text-books would have us believe.

Let us consider for the moment permutations. The formula for constructing permutations is first discovered empirically, through successive approximations to it. It is clear that, with only one element, one can have only one permutation. With two elements, two permutations are possible (1,2 and 2,1), and with three elements there are six possible permutations, since the third element can occupy three different positions in each of the two preceding permutations, and so on. Reasoning in this way, one generalises by empirical induction and obtains the formula $p_n = 1.2.3.4...n$.

Since the generalisation has been carried out by empirical induction, the formula has not been demonstrated. The demonstration is carried out by mathematical induction. First of all, it is shown that the proposition $P(n)$, $(n \in N)$, is true for $n = 1$. It is then demonstrated that, in the case where it is true for $P(n)$ it is also true for $P(n+1)$. Therefore if the proposition is true for $n = 1$, it is equally true for $n = 2$, and if it is true for $n = 2$, it is true for $n = 3$, and so on.

In fact, induction has not disappeared from this demonstrative reasoning; but each step is legitimised by explicit deductive demonstration.

Recursive reasoning is basically nothing more, in the expression of Poincaré, than a sequence of 'cascading' syllogisms (Poincaré 1906, p. 20). It is, in fact, a sequence of hypothetical syllogisms which, from the genetic point of view, is very material to this discussion.

The strength and creativity of this type of reasoning does not, however, consist – at least not primarily – in the justification of steps, but rather in the non-finite character of the inductive process, in the infinity of the area it can cover. "This rule" (the rule of recursive reasoning) writes Poincaré "(which is) incapable of either analytic or empirical demonstration, is the veritable type of synthetic *a priori* judgement" (Poincaré, 1906. p. 23).

We shall not enter into the details of the discussion of Kantian apriorism, with which Poincaré is concerned, except to refer to a point of view which we have already mentioned in previous discussion. The source of our conviction concerning certain truths is not their *a priori* character, but the objective universality of certain laws or properties, which creates an illusion of apriorism (in the sense that we cannot make abstractions of the respective relations or properties).

"The power of the mind" which Poincaré writes of in relation to recursive reasoning, the creative capacity *par excellence*, is not innate – otherwise it would not depend on intellectual development (and its dependence on intellectual development has been amply demonstrated by studies of genetic epistemology).

The limitless generality of mathematical induction is the expression of the adequacy of mind (i.e. of the constructive capacity of mind) to the infinite potentiality of nature. Clearly, non-finiteness as such cannot be realised in human experience, and it cannot be derived from experience. But the non-finiteness of nature is an axiom which the economy of the normal mind obliges it to accept, just as it is obliged to accept the objective reality of the material world.

Consequently, it is the essence of recursive reasoning that it consists of a potentially infinite sequence of hypothetical syllogisms, which is deductively guaranteed, and which, *at the same time, has the full creative capacity of induction.*

The child who is to acquire a combinatorial technique must, therefore, already possess such a set of intellectual schemas, namely hypothetico-deductive reasoning, inductive generalisation, and the ability to combine these two approaches in a unique iterative procedure – an infinitely recursive method of generating a limitless sequence of results from a given set, which is subject to rigorous control.

From what age is the child capable of such operations?

Theoretically, these operations imply an architectonic of operational schemas which is not available until the level of formal operations. We have seen that this conceptual architectonic is acquired over a period of several years, after the age of 12.

We were interested, therefore, in the following problem: is it possible that systematic instruction could accelerate this acquisition? An important aspect of this process would be that it would require the acquisition of structures, and not of specific information or particular procedures.

In this case, it is possible also to ask whether a 9–10 year-old child (who, according to Piaget and Inhelder, can only transcend the concrete by successive empirical approximations) could assimilate the intellectual structures required for generalised induction and sequences of hypothetico-deductive reasoning?

We have already seen that, at the level of concrete operations, children are not necessarily content with random associations of elements, but will try to discover procedures for forming all possible combinations. They are indeed sometimes successful in discovering procedures, though of limited efficiency. Would they be capable of assimilating, through instruction, the general procedures which they do not manage to discover for themselves?

This question has some bearing also on the problem of the formation of the concept of probability. If such combinatorial procedures cannot be assimilated, it would mean also that the child could not be induced through instruction to apply rational structures to the solution of simple probability problems involving an inventory, obtained by combinatorial procedures, of all possible outcomes.

On the other hand, if a child of 9–10 *can* assimilate such procedures, it is possible that operations involving the concept of probability would begin to be acquired during the stage of concrete operations.

Prefiguration of structures. We have seen in the previous chapter that if adequate figural means are available, children of 9 years can learn to operate with the concept of proportion in comparing ratios – something which Piaget and Inhelder consider to be possible only after the age of 12.

Essentially, this is a matter of accelerating development to a higher intellectual level by prefiguration of the characteristics of this higher level at the previous level of development.

Bruner's hypothesis is primarily relevant here. This is the hypothesis that a structure can be concretised in each of three fundamental modes of representation – the enactive, the iconic, and the symbolic – without changing the essential features of the structure in any way (Bruner, 1966, pp. 1–67).

If children learn a game in which concrete objects are used (such as coloured counters, geometric forms, etc.) they can, at the same time, assimilate a mathematical group structure, or a vector space, and also certain logical operations, if the rules of the game incorporate the corresponding properties.

In reality, however, things are not so simple. In the first place, a concrete embodiment of a structure can be a vehicle for this structure – but it does not necessarily communicate it, since there may be 'noise' present from the other objective properties of the representing object (particular colour, size, and so on) which may interfere with the perception of its structural aspects. This is why, in general, it is necessary to present the same structure in several different concretisations. Dienes has called this 'the principle of perceptual variability' or, more generally, 'the principle of multiple concretisations' (Dienes, 1963). With multiple concretisations of the same structure, whether in a single modality, such as the iconic, or in all the modalities – enactive, iconic, and symbolic – the intellect extracts the common feature, i.e. the logico-mathematical structure over and above the 'perceptual variability'.

The multiple concretisations used in teaching certain concepts thus acquire a significance which goes far beyond the ancient notion of intuition.

Firstly, we can see that this is not a simple one-way method of teaching the structure – from intuition to abstraction – but that the interaction of the three modalities of representation has to be taken into account. Secondly, it is not a local, tactical method in which the structure is abstracted from concrete examples, but rather a very general teaching strategy which covers entire periods of intellectual development. The *prefiguration of structures* is a general teaching strategy, which expresses the necessity (not merely the possibility) of preparing for the assimilation of abstract structures by prefiguring these structures in the previous stage of intellectual development to that in which they are normally assimilated, but which uses the methods appropriate to this prior stage. Each successive stage of development begins by consolidating the acquisitions of the previous stages, which are then integrated with the specific resources of the new stage (Piaget, 1956).

What Bruner adds to this account is that, by using adequate methods of prefiguration, it is possible not only to prepare for the next stage of development, but to accelerate development toward the new stage (a point of view which it is well known that Piaget disagrees with).

Schemas. As has already been mentioned, there are three principal ways of representing a structure. In fact, human experience in general and teaching experience in particular have evolved mixed forms of representation. The most important of these mixed forms is the schema.

According to Gonseth, a schema has the following essential characteristics: (a) it consists of a minimal description, (b) it is perfectible, (c) it possesses its own intrinsic structure, and (d) it has an external referent or denotation (Gonseth, 1936, p. 14).

"To operate with a schema" writes Servais "is in fact to use the structure which the schema represents in any given situation. The schema is thus a concrete system with an abstract use" (Servais, 1970, p. 436).

The schema performs an essential function in productive thinking, which is to cross-fertilise the abstract with the concrete. The schema, which is a simplification and distillation of the concrete, prepares the ground for conceptualisation by giving to abstract relations a spatial representation, dynamic meaning, and consequently a constructive and creative potential.

Generative models. We have already discussed the ability of different concrete models to represent and transmit the same abstract structure.

A good model is always a *generative* model. The term 'generative' in this context has a similar meaning to that suggested by Chomsky's use of the term in his writings on generative grammar. By *generative*, we mean to express the following properties:

– By analogy with grammatical competence, which permits us to construct an unlimited number of sentences with a finite number of rules, a model is genuinely useful in productive thinking if, with a limited number of elements and rules for their combination, it can correctly represent an unlimited number of different situations. In fact, a model which does not fulfill this condition is not, strictly speaking, a model, but simply an impoverished and distorted representation of some particular reality.

– Secondly, a model must be heuristic; that is to say, it must, by itself, lead to solutions which must be valid for the original as a result of the genuine isomorphism between the two realities involved (i.e. the model and the original).

– Thirdly, in order for a model to be generative, it must be capable of self-reproduction, in that its image-concept coding is sufficiently general for it to be able to suggest new models. This means that a model adapted to represent a certain class of situations must be able to suggest transitions to further models which represent more general classes of situations.

The system of rules permitting a model to uniquely specify the structure of the original represent what may be called *the syntax of the model.*

The code for translation either way (from model to original, and from original to model) and the construction rules must be automatised to the degree that they confer the character of *intuitions* on decisions of the model concerning interpretations and approaches to solutions.

A good example of such a model is the tree diagram used in combinatorial analysis and probability theory. For example, how many different arrangements, including repetitions, can be made with three numbers, using only the numbers 1 and 2?

The diagram below shows the solution. But a diagram like this also possesses a number of the qualities which are essential to productive thinking. Once the correspondence between the elements of the diagram and the operation of forming groups is understood, i.e. once the rationale

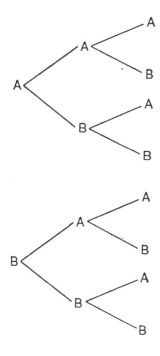

of construction of the diagram is seen, it can be generalised without limit, no matter how large the number of elements. This quality might be called *iterative generalisation* (which, in mathematics, would take the form of mathematical induction). Furthermore – and this is essential – when the problem changes and another method of constructing a diagram is required, it is possible that the new technique will be spontaneously suggested by experience with the previous one – this would be *constructive generalisation*.

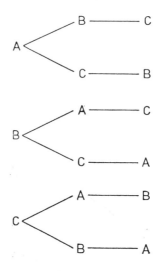

The problem, for example, is to find the number of permutations possible with three elements. The method of constructing the diagram is different, but the general principle is the same. Children of 10, with whom we have experimented, understood the principle of construction of the first diagram, and were also able to construct the second. The principle of the tree diagram had, therefore, been assimilated as a generative model, since it did not simply illustrate a particular operation, but also permitted: (a) by means of *iterative generalisation*, the solution of problems similar in nature to the first, but with a different number of elements; (b) by means of *constructive generalisation*, the construction of new models capable of solving previously unmet problems, different in nature from the first, but related. The mathematical formulae derived from such models (a^n in the case of arrangements with repetition; $n!$ in the case of permutations) must therefore incorporate something much more than a working scheme for a particular task. They incorporate a constructive principle which, on the one hand gives them a very close relevance to real situations, and on the other hand gives them the possibility of very easy transfer to new situations.

The basic notion which we would like to put across is that *a generative model, in the sense that we have used this phrase, possesses even at the figural level the capacity to suggest and to inculcate the constructive generality which is characteristic of recursive reasoning.*

In learning to make use of a tree diagram, children are in fact assimilating *a law of construction.* The inductive resources of the model are evident: the successive steps of reasoning within the model take place inductively, and almost directly.

It could be objected that the demonstrative aspect is absent; the subjects arrive at the principle of construction by induction, and by progressive approximations from this point eventually discover the calculation rule, but they are not strictly speaking using recursive demonstration.

Our view, however, is that even if deductive control is not explicit, it does occur in the constructive process, and is fully evident in the symbolic modality.

When children have understood how the diagram works in the construction of permutations, they must necessarily have understood that the step from $k-1$ objects to k objects is made by multiplying by k. Recursive demonstration cannot, in fact, do more than this, since even recursive demonstration does not eliminate, but must incorporate, the intuition of an inductive genesis (the intuition of the universal applicability of such a genesis).

No deductive construction can completely dispense with an appeal to intuition, since intuition is involved in the selection of axioms and of directions of reasoning. There are even intuitions of rigour, generality, and of the non-contradiction of a conceptual system (intuitions which may be true or false).

In educating children in mathematical thinking, these intuitions must be systematically formed before the conceptual support structure of the corresponding reasoning can be assimilated.

The figurative generative models which we have discussed can fulfill precisely this function. Their usefulness lies not simply in transmitting a particular procedure (which is what would happen if children only learned the calculation formula) but in communicating at the intuitive level an essentially mathematical method of construction. This is then understood and assimilated as both a rigorous and infinitely productive technique.

We have carried out research on the extent to which children's assimilation of such generative models can accelerate their acquisition of combinatorial operations (see E. Fischbein, Ileana Pampu, and I. Mînzat: 'Effects of Age and Instruction on Combinatory Ability in Children', reprinted in the Appendix).

Our subjects were schoolchildren aged 10, 12, and 14. The first stage of the investigation obtained subjective estimates from the children of how many permutations were possible with 3, 4, and 5 elements. The results showed a strong tendency to underestimate at all ages.

Children of 14, for example, estimated that with 5 objects one could have (on average) 16 permutations (120 being the correct number). These underestimations become more striking as the number of elements is increased.

In the second part of the investigation, we tried to teach these same children the tree diagram technique for making inventories of arrangements (with repetition) of two objects, taken 3 by 3 and 4 by 4, and of permutations of 3, 4, and 5 objects.

At the beginning of the experiment, we found differences between the three age levels. But as the session advanced, these differences diminished and even the 10-year-olds were able to understand and use the diagrams and thus respond correctly to combinatorial problems. The essential proof of the structurality of this acquisition is the fact that, *at all age levels, there was evidence of transfer by iterative generalisation, and even of transfer by constructive generalisation.* A child (even as young as 10) who had learned the technique of setting up an inventory of the arrangements of 2 objects taken 3 by 3 with the help of the tree diagram was immediately able to solve the same problem for 4 objects, and so on. When we then went on to permutations, although the method of constructing the diagram is different, the children immediately succeeded in tackling the new problem.

These results are especially important in relation to the level of concrete operations (10 years of age) because they demonstrate that an adequate instructional method, in particular the use of an adapted generative model, can succeed in bringing about a spectacular leap in intellectual development.

In the context of this work, the following facts seem to us to be specially interesting. (a) Even at the level of formal operations, combinatorial techniques are not spontaneously acquired. Instruction is necessary. (b) Even at the level of concrete operations, it is possible to induce children to assimilate combinatorial techniques quite readily with figurative aids.

The fact that a good generative model can rapidly advance genuine understanding of a conceptual procedure (as is shown by transfer) leads us to the heart of the problem of how an intuition is formed. For the adolescent, the fundamental discovery concerning combinatorial operations is that different collections (arrangements, permutations, etc.) are generated *by successively multiplying possibilities*. This is a new intuition, and it is not acquired spontaneously (in its generalised form) even at the stage of formal operations.

We base this assertion on the results of some recent research on the learning of logical operations by adolescents (Fischbein *et al.*, 1974).

The subject is seated at a console on which is mounted an electric circuit, composed of a battery, a light bulb, and two or three switches. The connections are not visible. By trying out the switches and observing the effect on the bulb, the subject has to determine whether the circuit is connected in series, in parallel, or in a mixed system.

We shall not enter into the details of this research here, but what was striking was the difficulty which children had, even the 14 year-olds, in reasoning on conjoint causes in order to work out the number of possible situations. The fact that the three switches (each one with two possible positions) contributed to eight possible combinations was not easily seen. The spontaneous decision was 3×2 (or $2+2+2)=6$. The normal type of reasoning in such situations (which continues in fact throughout life unless specific instruction is given) is *additive reasoning*. If, however, a diagram was introduced into the experiment, performance changed. The subject began to *visualise* the multiplicative operation. A new intuition was being formed. What the diagram provided was a principle of construction which synthesised induction and deduction in a single operation – a *working formula* which was at the same time a conceptual, cognitive schema. Extrapolation follows naturally from such a schema; it follows from the working formula itself, but not from the mathematical formula which derives from it, and which only formalises an accepted truth.

The principle of constructing the diagram is therefore an action programme which serves action directly, but is at the same time a distinct cognitive acquisition, relatively autonomous in relation to action. It is a flexible programme, because it can easily be adapted to all kinds of combinatorial operations. It is therefore adaptable to any particular situation, without having to modify in any way the principle from which it derives. *Visualisation* and *spatialisation* are the sources of its constructive qualities. *The acquisition of such a programme is therefore equivalent to the acquisition of an intuition.* The intuition which derives from it possesses the hierarchical structure, the flexibility, the immediate coherence, the rapidity of solution, and the extrapolative capacity, combined with spontaneous conviction, which characterise all intuition. But at the foundation of such an intuition will be found a generative model.

The construction of secondary intuitions by pedagogical methods may ultimately be reduced to a matter of creating and using adequate generative models. It could, in fact, be argued that a model is generative only in so far as it meets the requirements of an intuition. This may be especially true in the domain of probabilities and combinatorial operations.

CHAPTER VIII

SUMMARY AND CONCLUSIONS

The Concept of Intuition

Intuitions are an integral part of intelligent behaviour. They are cognitive acquisitions which intervene directly in practical or mental action, by virtue of their characteristic immediacy, globality, extrapolative capacity, structurality, and self-evidentness.

Primary intuitions are cognitive acquisitions which are derived from the experience of the individual, without the need for any systematic instruction.

Secondary intuitions are acquisitions which have all the characteristics of intuitions, but they are formed by scientific education, mainly in school.

Intuitions can also be classified as *affirmatory* or as *anticipatory* intuitions. Affirmatory intuitions embody the knowledge of the external world which we accept as evident. *Anticipatory* intuitions are mental constructs which globally anticipate the solution to a problem before the detailed steps of the solution have been found.

In an environment characterised by probabilistic events, behaviour requires specific intuitions. The future course of events has to be 'guessed at', and predictions and responses selected accordingly. In what follows, we will summarise the main aspects of the development of probabilistic intuitions in children.

THE DEVELOPMENT OF PROBABILISTIC INTUITIONS IN THE CHILD

The Pre-School Child

The intuition of chance. Pre-school children can distinguish the random, in the sense of the unpredictable, from the deducible, but their interpretations are distorted by some general features of their intelligence:

(a) subjectivism – the child confuses the random with the arbitrary (interpreting the objectively random as the manifestation of the 'will' of the object concerned);

(b) passive induction (Piaget): the child judges facts on the basis of the immediately preceding facts, and not on the basis of a deductive schema (a combinatory schema, for example). This explains the inability of the pre-school child to correctly interpret random phenomena when the number of possible events is large;

(c) the belief that random events can be controlled by the person who triggers the events (Piaget) when, objectively, any such control is absent (the throwing of dice, for instance);

(d) the distinction between the random and the necessary is unstable in the absence of an operational deductive system. Inessential changes in the experimental conditions (subjective preference, preceding outcomes, etc.) can easily influence the decisions of the child as to whether events are random or determined.

Basing themselves on such facts, Piaget and Inhelder have maintained that the idea of chance is not acquired before the stage of concrete operations (i.e. before the age of 7). According to them, the understanding of chance presupposes an understanding of the irreversibility of a mixture, and therefore requires the possession of a combinatory schema.

In fact, the conceptual schema of chance can only exist as a function of the relevant operational resources. But the *primary intuition* of chance is present in the everyday behaviour of the child, even before the age of 7. Chance is equivalent to unpredictability, and not necessarily to the smallness of odds.

When the number of possibilities, and correspondingly of possible combinations, is small, the pre-school child reasons correctly – and sometimes more correctly than the child at the stage of formal operations.

The intuition of relative frequency. The results of probability learning experiments argue strongly in favour of the view that pre-school children adapt their predictions to the probabilities of events. According to some investigators, however, these children do not attain the input frequencies. But this point is not crucial. What is important is *the tendency of the response curve over trials to approach the probability level of the reinforcing stimuli.* Our view is that this adaptation is the typical expression of a primary intuition. The apparent role of experience results from the fact that this phenomenon is more marked with age. The fact that this behaviour can also be obtained without the use of material reward (i.e. with reinforcement from knowledge of results only) shows that this is not a matter of simple motor conditioning, but of a cognitive mental formation, i.e. of a relatively automatised and polyvalent action programme which shares the characteristics of all cognitive processes.

The phenomenon of over-shooting (in which the frequency of predictions of the most frequent event is greater than the actual frequency, and tends toward 100%) has been found more commonly even in pre-school children than adults, in some investigations.

There are two possible interpretations of this:

– the pre-school child grasps more readily than the adult that the maximum of correct predictions can be obtained by adopting the 'pure' strategy, i.e. constant prediction of the most frequent event. This is not a far-fetched explanation; it accords with results we have obtained which demonstrate the superior ability of small children to estimate odds (in certain experimental conditions).

– The over-shooting phenomenon is the direct result of a conditioning process. The pre-school child is bound to the most frequently reinforced stimulus (in fact, to the only reinforced stimulus, in certain experimental paradigms such as that of Weir) and does not progress to a more complex strategy (according to Weir).

It is possible that both of these interpretations are correct. It may be precisely because they do not yet possess certain intellectual mechanisms stimulating them to look for more complex strategies that pre-school children sometimes more easily discover the response strategy which is most profitable (and, apparently, the most rudimentary).

The estimation of odds. Some authors have hypothesised that the pre-school child would be incapable of correctly estimating the odds of random events. Their main argument has been that the child of this age does not possess the necessary resources: (a) the ability to distinguish between the random and the deducible on the basis of operational procedures, (b) the concept of proportion or, in more general terms, of comparing ratios, (c) the combinatorial procedures by which it is possible to set up an inventory of all equally possible outcomes in a given situation. None of these specific resources appears until the level of formal operations (though they may be present in incipient form, closely tied to the concrete, during the period of concrete operations).

According to these authors, even if the pre-school child appears to estimate chances correctly in a given situation, this does not indicate a true probabilistic judgement in the sense of an intuitive estimation of odds. The child's estimate could, in fact, be reduced to a perceptual comparison of two sizes (areas, sets of marbles, etc.) Odds are only estimated correctly in situations where, when several different sets of objects are used, either the favoured or the non-favoured objects are present in equal numbers in each set, and the operation can thus be reduced to a binary comparison.

In our view, these facts do not prove that the pre-school child is not capable of probabilistic judgement (in the previously-defined sense of an intuitive estimation of odds). There are at least two aspects of the performance of pre-school children which must not be overlooked:

(a) the phenomenon of probability-matching, which has been amply demonstrated in the pre-school child, indicates the existence of primary, intuitive, pre-operational mechanisms of chance estimation;

(b) the fact that the pre-school child responds correctly to questions concerning the evaluation of chances (when the problem has been specifically and unambiguously posed in these terms) shows that the child has correctly grasped the problem, and that the response truly expresses a probabilistic judgement. In order for such a response to be correct, it is clearly necessary that the auxiliary procedures needed (enumeration of possible outcomes, comparison of ratios, etc.) should not be beyond the intellectual resources of the child.

The probabilistic judgement of pre-school children is precarious because they do not yet have an adequate conceptual framework. Their responses can only express intuitive, pre-operational estimates. The play of influences at the cognitive level can easily mislead the child in making decisions, because of the absence of any relevant conceptual control. In particular, the influence of perceptual configurations on the estimation of odds in pre-school children has been shown. Children estimate odds and make predictions primarily on the basis of what they perceive. If there is a discrepancy between directly perceived and stored information, the directly perceived information will govern responses, even in situations where predictions should be made on the basis of stored information (Piaget, 1951; Davies, 1965). Estimates are also influenced, in pre-school children, by colour preferences and the position of objects in space.

However, if such effects are removed, by adequate experimental control, and the auxiliary operations of comparison and calculation required are simple, the pre-school child is capable of correctly estimating odds in a truly probabilistic manner.

The effect of instruction. Using an elementary instruction procedure, we have attempted to improve children's responses to questions involving the comparison of odds in situations where the ratios do not have equal terms (Fischbein *et al.*, 1970). This attempt was not successful. It is possible that, at this age, children cannot assimilate a schema involving a double comparison.

Combinatorial operations. Piaget and Inhelder have shown that the pre-school child can make some combinations, permutations, and arrangements only in an empirical manner, and does not even attempt to find a method of setting up exhaustive inventories.

THE PERIOD OF CONCRETE OPERATIONS

The intuition of chance. Through the acquisition of spatio-temporal and logico-mathematical operational schemas, the child becomes able to distinguish between the random and the deducible, even at the conceptual level. Clearly, this process is not completed during this period, since thinking is still largely tied to the concrete level. Nevertheless, the representation of chance, which is nothing more than a primary intuition in the pre-school child, becomes a distinct, organised, conceptual structure after the age of 7. Chance in the sense of the non-determined is explicitly understood in opposition to the deducible (Piaget). The child begins to understand the interaction of causal chains which lead to unpredictable events, and the irreversibility of random phenomena (simultaneously with understanding reversibility).

The intuition of relative frequency. Most investigators have found that probability matching improves with age. After the age of 7–8, matching is more rapid over the experimental session than in the pre-school years. This no doubt indicates development in the primary intuition of relative frequency.

Such a development could be explained in several different ways. If intuition is seen as the cognitively fixed outcome of accumulated experience, it could be supposed that the intuition of relative frequency develops naturally as a result of the child's experience with situations involving probabilistic events, in which responses must express a correct estimation of the objective frequency of phenomena. On the other hand, the schemas of developing intelligence – which in turn imply a better coordination of operations – may ensure a more correct interpretation of data concerning the relative frequencies of experienced events. At this age, the child is no longer so dominated by perceptual data as the pre-school child, and representations are more consistent and efficient than in the pre-school child. The intuition of relative frequency presupposes an ability to 'chunk' runs of events in such a way that global estimates of proportions can be made. All this indicates that *the intuition of relative frequency, while primary and pre-operational (analogous to a classically-conditioned response) nevertheless benefits from the general acquisitions of intelligence during the operational stages.*

This interaction between the intuitive and the conceptual, shown particularly by the experiments of Ojemann *et al.*, seems to us to have important implications for the theory of intuition.

The estimation of odds and the concept of probability. If they have not received appropriate instruction, 9–10 year-old children can only solve problems involving comparisons of odds in situations where either the number of favourable cases or the number of unfavourable cases are equal (their estimation being based on a binary comparison). For this type of problem, the percentage of correct responses is greater in 9–10 year-olds than in pre-school children. In situations which cannot be reduced to binary comparisons, the number of correct responses does not exceed the chance level. As we have indicated, these findings were obtained from children who had not had relevant instruction.

For situations involving equal probabilities, two types of experimental paradigm have been used. In problems where the odds are referable to proportions of discrete elements (marbles in a jar) the responses of 9–10 year-old-children are no better than would be expected by chance, and are not significantly better than the responses of pre-school children. In problems where the odds have to be determined from a geometric configuration (forked channels down which marbles can travel at random) the percentage of correct responses decreases with age.

The effect of instruction. With instruction, the responses of 9–10 year-olds can be significantly improved (though not the responses of pre-school children), in problems which cannot be reduced to binary comparisons. This finding is important, since it must throw doubt on the claim of Piaget and Inhelder that establishing proportionality is a characteristically formal operation. We have demonstrated that, through the use of figural procedures, schemas considered by Piaget and Inhelder to be accessible only at the level of formal operations can be constructed at the level of concrete operations. At the least, we have shown that the absence of proportionality is not an obstacle to learning the concept of probability. Even before the age of 10, the child is capable of assimilating this schema with the help of elementary instruction.

Sequential effects, recency effects, stereotypies. In probability learning experiments, children of 6–7 and older show response patterns which are superimposed on probability matching behaviour. Some of these sequential phenomena are:

(a) Stereotyped response sequences, for example left-centre-right when there are three possible responses. The frequency of stereotyped responses decreases toward the end of the period of concrete operations.

(b) Positive recency, the tendency to predict the outcome O_1 after a string of O_1 outcomes, is followed by the negative recency effect, the tendency to predict O_2 after a string of O_1 outcomes.

(c) The tendency to base predictions on patterns which have been discovered on previous trials.

(d) In experiments where only one response is reinforced, children of 9–10 do not adopt the maximum gain strategy, which is common in small children, but attempt other strategies which permit greater variability of prediction.

Combinatorial procedures. During the period of concrete operations, children look for ways of setting up inventories of all permutations, arrangements, and combinations possible with a given set of elements, and arrive at rudimentary procedures by trial and error.

Our experiments have shown that, at the end of this period (10–11 years) children can, with the help of instruction, assimilate the enumerative procedures used in constructing tree diagrams. This is a structural acquisition, since it is capable of transfer – both close transfer (by iterative generalisation) and more distant transfer (by constructive generalisation).

Chance and determinism. What we have said so far indicates contradictory trends in the development of probabilistic thinking. On the one hand, there are progressive tendencies, such as matching behaviour, and on the other hand there are apparently retrograde tendencies, such as stereotypies, and difficulty in recognising equal probabilities in certain circumstances. These contradictory tendencies can, however, be explained. The intuitions of chance, relative frequency, and probability develop with age as a function of intellectual development and the day to day experience of the child. At the same time, however, and particularly under the influence of instruction received at school, a tendency develops toward deterministic, univocal interpretations of phenomena. It is generally true that contemporary education oversimplifies the rational, scientific interpretation of phenomena by representing it as a pursuit of *univocal* causal or logical dependencies. Whatever does not conform to strict determinism, whatever is associated with uncertainty, surprise, or randomness is seen as being outside the possibility of a consistent, rational, scientific, explanation.

In Piaget and Inhelder's theory, the necessary and the possible become distinct at the level of concrete operations. After a phase in which the random and the determined are seen as absolute opposites, the child arrives, during the stage of formal operations, at a synthesis of these two complementary aspects in a unique interpretation – the probabilistic interpretation. In fact, however, these two modes of interpretation become fused only in a rather unstable manner, since our present type of education is such that only one of them is systematically cultivated. The two schemas continue to coexist in the mind of the child, and later the adult, either without fusing at all, or perhaps partially fusing in certain cases. There may be a vacillation between the two interpretations, together with a profound sense of failure to understand the phenomena in question.

The supremacy of deterministic schemas in thinking (in univocal determinism) is manifested in over-rationalisation. The intuitions of chance and probability are influenced, and ultimately deformed, by this excessive tendency toward univocal prediction.

The most primitive method of rationalising randomness is to respond in a stereotyped pattern. Finding themselves unable to predict the pattern of events, children settle for a pattern of responses which is intelligible to them. These stereotypies could be described as the simplest possible strategies for attributing a rational structure to events; they are, however, vitiated by their maladaptive character.

The negative recency effect is a more subtle strategy expressing the same maladaptive rationalising tendency. Even when events are strictly independent, the probability of each event being independent of preceding events, the child looks for sequential dependencies which would reduce the uncertainty. This is an invalid extrapolation from what we have called the *sampling intuition*. The subject understands intuitively that the proportion of elements in the sample tends toward the proportion in the total number of elements. Random samples which deviate far from the proportion in the total number of elements are correspondingly rare. In this type of reasoning, the order of elements (i.e. events) is not important, only the proportion of events. But subjects extrapolate illicitly from these intuitive estimations to situations in which they have to predict events one by one. Long sequences of repeated elements seem to occur with a lower probability than short, alternating sequences of different elements. The result is the negative recency effect, which becomes stronger with age, since the intellectual mechanisms on which it depends develop with age.

We have dealt with the negative recency effect at some length, because it throws light on the fundamental mechanisms of intuitions. Intuitions are not the rigid, invariant schemas, independent of experience, that Kantian apriorism and, to some extent, the Einsicht concept of Gestalt psychology would suggest. Nor are they cognitive modalities which stem from irrational motivations, as in Jung's psychology (Jung, 1962, pp. 120–123) or instinctual in origin, as in Bergson's philosophy. Intuitions are cognitive components of intelligent behaviour which are adapted, in their function and properties, to ensure the efficiency of behaviour. They are stable, structural schemas which select, assimilate and store everything in the experience of the individual which has been found to enhance rapidity, adaptibility, and efficiency of action. Their essential characteristic in intelligent behaviour is to serve as a base for extrapolations.

An extrapolation, by definition, is a leap into the unknown; the conclusion goes beyond what was rigourously deducible from the premises. The feeling of confidence and conviction which accompanies an intuition is designed to compensate for (and perhaps mask) the gap which separates the strictly available information from the final interpretation.

Intuitions therefore develop as a function of whatever enhances the capacity to extrapolate, among other things as a function of the mechanisms of logical inference, to the extent that they can be condensed into mental habits.

In the absence of systematic control from the conceptual system, primary intuitions can lead, by way of illicit extrapolations, to errors of interpretation and prediction. However these errors are not, in general, aberrant. They stem from the inappropriate use of certain acquisitions of intelligence, proper to the particular stage of development. Such inappropriate applications are seen in extrapolating from the perceptual to the abstract, from the particular to the general, from the finite to the non-finite, from the model to the original, and so on.

In saying that intuitions are formed by experience, we do not mean to imply that they are constructed out of experiences which are linked exclusively to intuition, and vice versa. This point leads us to the second important conclusion which can be drawn from the negative recency effect. Clearly, experience does not conform to the expectations of the gambler who behaves as though chance had a memory. The intuition which results in the recency effect is, in fact, based on confirmed experience (expressed in the sampling intuition); but it is an illicit borrowing which was meant to serve the major need of intelligence at the operational level (i.e. the need for quantifiable predictions). Experience which is confirmed and fixed in an intuition can thus confer a false validity on an erroneous interpretation or prediction, by illicit extrapolation.

Erroneous intuitions can therefore arise from fusions, shortcircuits, transfers, and illicit extrapolations within the schemas of general intelligence at any particular stage of development. On the other hand, if correct intuitions are not exercised, or if they are systematically suppressed, they become atrophied, but it is doubtful whether they are ever actually lost.

THE PERIOD OF FORMAL OPERATIONS

After the age of 11–12, the child becomes capable of reasoning in a hypothetico-deductive manner in relation to *possibilities*, and not only realities. Such reasoning consists of operations of the second order, operations on operations, for which a propositional system is used.

The intuition of chance. According to Piaget and Inhelder, the adolescent groups the non-determined relations of random phenomena according to operational schemas. Once chance has been thus deal with by the use of operational schemas, it becomes *intelligible*, and the synthesis between the random and the operational leads the adolescent to the concept of probability.

As we have seen, however, things are more complicated than this. The synthesis between the random and the deducible is not realised spontaneously and completely at the level of formal operations. In experiments where the subject is required to recognise equal probabilities in different experimental conditions (an asymmetrical layout of forked channels) it is the adolescent who baulks at the unpredictable, and who looks for causal dependencies which would reduce uncertainty, even in situations where there can be no such dependencies.

The operational structure of formal thought alone cannot make chance intelligible, even though it can provide the schemas which are necessary for this, namely combinatory capacity, proportionality, and implication. The explanation which we have put forward for this deficiency is that the cultural and educational traditions of modern society orient thought toward deterministic, univocal explanations, according to which random events are beyond the bounds of the rational and scientific. The result is that the intuition of chance becomes irreconcileable with the structure of logical thought, and is relegated to an inferior status as an inadequate method of interpretation which does not meet scientific standards.

The logico-scientific thought of the adolescent is constructed in disregard of the intuition of chance, and therefore without the totality of formal structures which would be capable of translating the possible in terms of rational constructions.

The intuition of relative frequency. Research which has been carried out with different age levels has shown that probability matching becomes more rapid with age, and continues to improve even during adolescence, according to some authors. If only one response is reinforced, it is found that children at the level of concrete operations choose the reinforced response less often than pre-school children. But after the age of 11, the proportion of choices of the reinforced response is again higher (Weir, 1964). If the subject is punished for wrong predictions, the preference effect is intensified and becomes over-shooting (Gruen and Weir, 1964).

It can therefore be concluded that *the adolescent has made progress in comparison to previous age levels in so far as the intuition of relative frequency is concerned, particularly in cases where prediction has some practical outcome.* The maximisation strategy, when it is not the apparent result of a stereotypy, shows the favourable effect of the development of intelligence on prediction behaviour in certain experimental conditions.

Combinatorial procedures. Piaget and Inhelder claim that, during the formal operational level, the child becomes able to use systematic procedures in setting up inventories for all possible permutations, arrangements, and combinations of a given set of elements.

Our research has shown, however, that this is only a potentiality for the majority of subjects. In our view, it would be more accurate to say that these children are capable of assimilating combinatorial procedures with the help of instruction, and that this is also true for 10 year-old children. Although there are differences in performance between these two age levels, they are quite small.

The estimation of odds. The performance of adolescents in estimating odds is superior to that of younger children, except in the situation mentioned previously, where equal odds were determined by the geometrical lay-out of the experimental apparatus. When the experimental material consists of a jar of marbles, 12 year-old children give correct responses from the outset, even in cases where they have to compare ratios with unequal terms. Such a finding is predicted by Piaget's theory. What we have added to this is the fact that even 9–10 year-old children can respond correctly in such situations, if they have had appropriate instruction.

The effect of instruction. The experimental lessons which we have described mainly involved children aged 12–14. The lessons treated the following concepts and procedures: – event, sample space, elementary event and compound event, probability as a measure of chance, relative frequency, and combinatorial analysis.

These lessons revealed adolescents' great interest and receptivity as far as the ideas of probability and statistics are concerned. These subjects are able to understand and correctly apply the concepts taught, which must at the very least imply the beginning of a restructuring of the intuitive base. In our view, generative models (for example, tree diagrams, in the case of combinatorial operations) are the best teaching devices for the construction of secondary intuitions.

OPERATIONAL STRUCTURES AND THE PRIMARY INTUITIVE BASE

Our research with adolescents of 13, 15 and 17 has shown that if one attempts to go beyond situations in which the number of favourable and unfavourable outcomes can be directly enumerated, either false intuitions or simply an absence of intuitive resources are encountered. For example, subjects were asked the following question: "A warehouse contains 90% ripe apples, and 10% green apples. If three apples are taken at random, what is the probability that two of them will be ripe?" These subjects had all the knowledge required to solve this problem (including the knowledge of the addition and the multiplication laws of probabilities). However, their responses were generally of the form:

$$(\tfrac{9}{10})^2 \cdot \tfrac{1}{10} \text{ instead of: } 3 \cdot (\tfrac{9}{10})^2 \cdot \tfrac{1}{10}$$

Intuition is silent here, because what is required is not a primary intuition of odds, but an elaborated intuition, restructured by operational means. It should be stressed again that this is not a matter of lacking a method of calculation, but rather of the absence of an intuition (here the intuition of a compound event).

A different example is quoted by Weaver (1960, p. 95–98). There are two counters in a box. One counter (A) is red on both faces; the other counter (B) has one red, and one blue face. One counter is drawn at random and placed on the table. The visible face of the counter is red. What is the probability that its other face is also red? The natural reasoning here would be as follows: since there are two counters which could be drawn with equal probability, $P(A)=P(B)=0.5$. If the drawn counter is (A), then the other face will be red. If the drawn counter is (B), then the other face will be blue. Therefore the answer is: the probability of the other face being red is 0.5. The correct answer is, in fact, $\tfrac{2}{3}$!

The fact that the reasoning seems straightforward and obviously correct, while the answer which is in fact correct seems surprising, shows that we are not dealing here with a superficial, accidental error, but with a fundamental mechanism of thought. Intuition, in this case, has not developed in step with the operational schemas of thought.

The reasoning which is correct, but which seems bizarre, at least to anyone who is not familiar with this type of reasoning, is as follows. Call the two red faces of (A) r_1 and r_2; call the red face of (B) r_3, and the blue face of (B) a. If a counter is drawn at random, the following combinations of faces are possible:

$$r_1 \quad \text{and} \quad r_2$$
$$r_2 \quad \text{and} \quad r_1$$
$$r_3 \quad \text{and} \quad a$$
$$a \quad \text{and} \quad r_3.$$

The combination 'a and r_3' can be excluded from the list of possible combinations, because we already know that the visible face is red. We therefore have:

$$r_1 \quad \text{and} \quad r_2$$
$$r_2 \quad \text{and} \quad r_1$$
$$r_3 \quad \text{and} \quad a.$$

There are thus two chances out of three that the other face of the drawn counter will be red. The logical construction, once explained, seems perfectly clear. *Yet intuition does not accept it.* What is missing is the feeling of self-evidentness. Intuition remains distinct from the correct reasoning.

When naive subjects are asked to solve such a problem, they simply apply, inappropriately, logico-mathematical schemas and procedures which they have acquired either naturally, in the course of development during the stage of formal operations, or through instruction at school, as a superimposition on the primary intuitive base. The result is an incorrect solution which *apparently* satisfies both the demands of deductive reasoning and the bias of intuition.

Most of the paradoxes in probability can be explained in terms of the inappropriate application of operational schemas, because the intuitive base is not sufficiently elaborated.

The Chevalier de Méré knew that it was advantageous to bet on the occurrence of at least one 6 in four throws of a die. He then reasoned that in 24 throws, he would obtain at least one double six. His reasoning conformed to the 'rule of three' (according to Freudenthal, 1970, p. 152) and was part of the stock of logico-mathematical procedures available at the time. But it was inadequate in this case. The correct reasoning is quite different, although in fact it too uses the procedures of elementary logic.

Undeveloped probabilistic intuition is not able to follow the procedures of sophisticated reasoning, nor to guide the selection of such procedures, or evaluate the plausibility of the obtained result.

As we have indicated, our view is that this situation is explained by the quasi-systematic exclusion of statistical and probabilistic modes of thinking from education.

The general conclusion of our work, then, is this. In the contemporary world, scientific education cannot be profitably reduced to a univocal, deterministic interpretation of events. An efficient scientific culture calls for education in statistical and probabilistic thinking. Probabilistic intuitions do not develop spontaneously, except within very narrow limits. The understanding, interpretation, evaluation, and prediction of probabilistic phenomena cannot be entrusted to primary intuitions which have been neglected, forgotten, and abandoned in a rudimentary state of development under the pressure of operational schemas which cannot articulate with them.

But in order for this requirement of an efficient scientific culture to be met, it is necessary to train, from early childhood, the complex intuitive base relevant to probabilistic thinking; in this way a genuine and constructive balance between the possible and the determined can be achieved in the working of intelligence.

BIBLIOGRAPHY

Anderson, N. H.: 1960, 'Effect of a First Order Conditional Probability in a Two Choice Learning Situation', *Journal of Experimental Psychology* **59**, 73–93.

Atkinson, R. C., Sommer, G. R., and Sterman, M. B.: 1960, 'Decision Making by Children as a Function of Amount of Reinforcement', *Psychological Report* **6**, 299–306.

Atkinson, R. C., Bower, G. H., and Crothers, E. J.: 1967, *An Introduction to Mathematical Learning Theory*, J. Wiley, New York.

Bergson, H.: 1930, *L'évolution créatrice*, Alcan, Paris, pp. 191–192.

Berne, E.: 1944, 'The Nature of Intuition', *Psychiatric Quarterly* **23**, 223–226.

Bogartz, R.: 1966, 'Variables Influencing Alternation Prediction by Preschool Children: I. Previous Recurrent, Dependent and Repetitive Sequences', *Journal of Experimental Child Psychology* **3**, 40–56.

Brackbill, Y., Kappy, M., and Starr, R.: 1962, 'Magnitude of Reward and Probability Learning', *Journal of Experimental Psychology* **63**, 32–35.

Bruner, J. S., Olver, R. R., and Greenfield, P. M.: 1966, *Studies in Cognitive Growth*, J. Wiley, New York.

Brunswik, E.: 1939, 'Probability as a Determiner of Rat Behavior', *Journal of Experimental Psychology* **25**, 175–197.

Brunswik, E.: 1943, 'Organismic Achievement and Environmental Probability', *Psychological Review* **50**, 255–272.

Bunge, M.: 1962, *Intuition and Science*, Englewood Cliffs, N.Y., Prentice Hall.

Burke, C. J., Estes, W. K., and Hellyer, S.: 1954, 'Rate of Verbal Conditioning in Relation to Stimulus Variability', *Journal of Experimental Psychology* **48**, 153–161.

Bush, R. R. and Mosteller, F.: 1951, 'A Mathematical Model for Simple Learning', *Psychol. Review* **58**, 313–323.

Bush, R. R. and Mosteller, F.: 1955, *Stochastic Models for Learning*, J. Wiley.

Codirlă, R.: 1972a, 'Modelarea matematică a învăţării. Studiul influenţei recompensei asupra învăţării probabilităţii la copiii preşcolari cu ajutorul modelului liniar al învăţării', *Revista de Psihologie*, Nr. 1, 5–16.

Codirlă, A.: 1972b, 'Invăţarea probabilităţii la şcolarul mic şi modelarea matematică a învăţării', *Revista de Psihologie*, Nr. 3, 349–364.

Cohen, J., Dearncley, E. J., and Hansel, D. E.: 1957, 'Measures of Subjective Probability', *British Journal of Psychology* **48**, 271–275.

Cotton, J. W. and Rechtschaffen, A.: 1958, 'Replication report: Two and Three-Choice Verbal Conditioning Phenomena', *Journal of Experimental Psychology* **56**, 96.

Craig, G. L. and Myers, J. L.: 1963, 'A Developmental Study of Sequential Two Choice Decision Making', *Child Development* **34**, 483–493.

Crandall, V. J., Solomon, D., and Kellaway, R.: 1961, 'A Comparison of the Patterned and Nonpatterned Probability Learning of Adolescent and Early Grade School-Age Children', *The Journal of Genetic Psychology* **99**, 29–39.

Davies, C.: 1965, 'Development of the Probability Concept in Children', *Child Development* **36**, 779–788.

Davies, H.: 1970, 'The Role of Practical Experimentation in the Teaching of Probability and Statistics', in L. Råde (ed.), *The Teaching of Probability and Statistics*, Almqvist and Wiksell, Stockholm, pp. 69–86.

Detambel, M. H.: 1955, 'A Test for a Model for Multiple-Choice Behavior', *Journal of Experimental Psychology* 49, 97–105.

Dienes, Z. P.: 1963, *An Experimental Study of Mathematics Learning*, Hutchinson, London.

Dubosson, J.: 1957, *Le problème de l'orientation scolaire*, Delachaux et Niestlé, Neuchâtel, pp. 122–123.

Dumont, M.: 1968, 'Quelques jeux combinatoires', *Le courier de recherches pédagogiques* 33, 57–63.

Engel, A.: 1970, Teaching probability in intermediate grades in L. Råde (ed.), *The Teaching of Probability and Statistics*, Almqvist & Wiksell, Stockholm, pp. 87–150.

Estes, W. K.: 1950, 'Toward a Statistical Theory of Learning', *Psychological Review* 57.

Estes, W. K.: 1959a, in 'The Statistical Approach to Learning Theory', in S. Koch (ed.), *Psychology: A Study of a Science*, McGraw-Hill, New York, Vol. 2, 380–491.

Estes, W. K.: 1959b, 'Component and Pattern Model with Markovian Interpretation', in R. R. Bush and W. K. Estes (eds.), *Studies in Mathematical Learning Theory*, Stanford Univers. Press, Stanford, pp. 9–52.

Estes, W. K.: 1964, 'Probability Learning', in A. W. Melton (ed.), *Categories of Human Learning*, Academic Press, New York-London, pp. 89–128.

Estes, W. K. and Straughan, J. H.: 1954, 'Analysis of Verbal Conditioning Stimulus in Terms of Statistical Learning Theory', *Journal of Experimental Psychology* 47, 225–234.

Estes, W. K. and Suppes, P.: 1959, 'Foundations for Linear Models', in R. R. Bush and W. K. Estes (eds.), *Studies in Mathematical Learning Theory*, Stanford Univers. Press, Stanford, pp. 137–179.

Ewing, A.: 1941, 'Reason and Intuition', *Proceedings of the British Academy* XXVII, 67–107.

Feller, W.: 1968, *An Introduction to Probability Theory and Its Applications*, John Wiley, New York.

Fischbein, E., Pampu, I., and Mînzat, I.: 1967, 'L'intuition probabiliste chez l'enfant', *Enfance*, No. 2, 193–208.

Fischbein, E., Pampu, I., and Mînzat, I.: 1970a, 'Comparison of Ratios and the Chance Concept in Children', *Child Development* 41, 2, 377–389.

Fischbein, E., Pampu, I., and Mînzat, I.: 1970b, 'Effects of Age and Instruction on Combinatory Ability in Children', *The British Journal of Educational Psychology* 40, 261–270.

Fischbein, E., Bărbat, I., and Mînzat, I.: 1971, 'Intuitions primaires et intuitions secondaires dans l'initiation aux probabilités', *Educational Studies in Mathematics* 4, 264–280.

Fischbein, E., Mînzat, I., and Bărbat, I.: 1974, 'L'acquisition des stratégies expérimentales par les adolescents', *Revue Roumaine des Sciences Sociales, Série de Psychologie* 2, 131–148.

Flavell, J. H.: 1963, *The Developmental Psychology of Jean Piaget*, Van Nostrand, Princetown, N.Y.

Flood, M. M.: 1954, 'One Game Learning Theory and Some Decisionmaking Experiments', in R. M. Thrall, C. H. Coombs, and R. L. Davies (eds.), *Decision Processes*, J. Wiley.

Freudenthal, H.: 1970, 'The Aims of Teaching Probability', in L. Råde (ed.), *The Teaching of Probability and Statistics*, Almqvist and Wiksell, Stockholm, pp. 151–168.

Galperin, P. J.: 1963, 'Dezvoltarea cercetărilor asupra formării acţunilor intelectuale', în *Psihologia în U.R.S.S.*, Editura ştiinţifică, Bucureşti, pp. 278–311.

Gambino, B. and Myers, J. L.: 1966, 'Effect of Mean and Variability of Event Run Length on Two-Choice Learning', *Journal of Experimental Psychology* 72, 904–908.

Gani, J.: 1970, 'The Role of Mathematics in Conceptual Models', in L. Råde (ed.), *The Teaching of Probability and Statistics*, Almqvist & Wiksell, Stockholm, pp. 169–182.

Gardner, R. A.: 1957, 'Probability Learning with Two and Three Choices', *American Journal of Psychology* 70, 174–185.

Gardner, R. A.: 1958, 'Multiple-Choice Decision-Behavior', *American Journal of Psychology* 71, 710–717.

Gardner, R. A.: 1961, 'Multiple Choice Decision Behavior with Dummy Choices', *American Journal of Psychology* 74, 205–214.

Ginsburg, H. and Rapoport, A.: 1967, 'Children's Estimate of Proportions', *Child Development* 38, 205–212.

Goldberg, E.: 1966, 'Probability Judgment by Preschool Children; Task, Condition and Performance', *Child Development* 37, 157–167.

Goldman, D. E. and Denny, J.: 1963, 'The Ontogenesis of Choice Behavior in Probability and Sequential Programs', *The Journal of Genetic Psychology* 102, 5–18.

Gonseth, F.: 1936, *'Les mathématiques et la réalité. Essai sur la méthode axiomatique'*, Alcan, Paris.

Goodnow, J. J.: 1955, 'Determinants of Choice Distribution in Two-Choice Situations', *American Journal of Psychology* 68, 106–116.

Gratch, G.: 1959, 'The Development of the Expectation of the Non-Independence of Random Events in Children', *Child Development* 30, 217–227.

Gréco, P.: 1959, 'Induction, Déduction et Apprentissage', in *La logique des apprentissages (Etudes d'épistémologie génétique*, Vol. X), PUF, Paris.

Gruen, G. E. and Weir, M.: 1964, 'Effect of instruction, penalty and age on probability learning', *Child Development* 35, 265–273.

Hilgard, E. R. and Bower, G.: 1966, *Theories of Learning*, Ed. II, Appleton-Century-Crofts, New York.

Hoemann, H. W. and Ross, B.: 1972, 'Children's Understanding of Probability Concepts', *Child Development* 42, 221–236.

Hull, C. L., Hovland, C. I., Ross, R. T., Hall, M., Perkins, D. T., and Fitch, F. G.: 1940, *Mathematical Deductive Theory of Rote Learning*, New Haven, Yale Univ. Press.

Hull, C. L.: 1943, *Principles of Behavior*, Appleton-Century-Crofts, New York.

Humphreys, L. G.: 1939, 'Acquisition and Extinction of Verbal Expectations in a Situation Analogous to Conditioning', *Journal of Experimental Psychology* 25, 294–301.

Hyman, R. and Jenkins, N. W.: 1956, 'Involvement and Set as Determinants of Behavioral Stereotypy', *Psychological Report* 2, 131–146.

Inhelder, B. and Piaget, J.: 1955, *De la logique de l'enfant à la logique de l'adolescent*, PUF, Paris.

Iosifescu, M.: 1963, *Modele de învăţare cu mulţimi arbitrare de clase de răspunsuri şi de evenimente auxiliare*, I–II, Comunicările Acad. R.P.R., pp. 529–533.

Iosifescu, M. and Theodorescu, R.: 1965, 'On Bush-Mosteller Stochastic Models for Learning', *Journal of Mathematical Psychology* 2, 196–210.

Iosifescu, M. and Theodorescu, R.: 1969, *Random Processes and Learning*, Springer, Berlin.

Jarvik, M. E.: 1951, 'Probability Learning and a Negative Recency Effect in the Serial Anticipation of Alternative Symbols', *Journal of Experimental Psychology* **41**, 291–297.

Jones, M. H. and Liverant, S.: 1960, 'Effects of Age Differences on Choice Behavior', *Child Development* **31**, 673–680.

Jones, M. R. and Myers, J. L.: 1966, 'A Comparison of Two Methods of Event Randomization in Probability Learning', *Journal of Experimental Psychology*, 909–911.

Jung, C. G.: *L'homme à la découverte de son âme*, Payot, Paris, 1962.

Kahneman, D. and Tverski, A.: 1972, 'Subjective Probability: a Judgement of Representativeness, *Cognitive Psychology* **3**, No. 3, 430–454.

Kass, N.: 1964, 'Risk in Decision Making as a Function of Age, Sex and Probability Preference', *Child Development* **35**, 577–582.

Keller, H. R.: 1971, 'Children's Acquisition and Reversal Behavior in a Probability Learning Situation as a Function of Programed Instruction, Internal-External Control and Schedules of Reinforcement', *Journal of Experimental Child Psychology* **11**, 281–295.

Kessen, V. and Kessen, M. L.: 1961, 'Behavior of Young Children in a Two Choice-Guessing Problem', *Child Development* **32**, 779–788.

Kyburg, H. E. and Smokler, E. (eds.): *Studies in Subjective Probability*, J. Wiley, New York, 1964.

Klein, F.: 1898, *Conférences sur les mathématiques*, Conférence VI, A. Hermann, Librairie Scientifique, Paris.

Le Ny, J. F.: 1961, 'Généralisation et discrimination stochastique d'un stimulus verbal dans l'apprentissage stochastique chez des enfants', *L'Année Psychologique*, Nr. 1, 79–96.

Lewis, M.: 'Social Isolation: A Parametric Study of Its Effect on Social Reinforcement', *J. Exp. Child Psychol.* (1965), 2, 205–218.

Lindman, H. and Edwards, W.: 1961, 'Unlearning the Gambler's Fallacy', *Journal of Experimental Psychology* **62**, 630–631.

Longeot, F.: 1967, 'Aspects différentiels de la psychologie génétique, *BINOP*, 2-ème série, numéro spécial, 66–67.

Longeot, F.: 1968, 'La pédagogie des mathématiques et le développement des opérations formelles dans le second cycle de l'enseignement secondaire', *Enfance* **5**, 378–389.

Malpas, A. J.: 1972, *Experiments in Statistics*, Oliver and Boyd, Edinburgh.

Matalon, B.: 1959, 'Apprentissage en situations aléatoires et systématiques', in *La logique des apprentissages* (*Etudes d'épistémologie génétiques*, Vol. 10), Paris, PUF, pp. 61–80.

McCormack, P. D.: 1959, 'Spatial Generalization and Probability Learning in a Five Choice Situation', *American Journal of Psychology* **72**, 135–138.

McCullers, J. C. and Stevenson, H. W.: 1960, 'Effects of Verbal Reinforcement in a Probability Learning Situation', *Psychological Report* **7**, 439–445.

Messik, S. J. and Solley, Ch. M.: 1957, 'Probability Learning in Children: Some Exploratory Studies', *Journal of Genetic Psychology* **90**, 23–32.

Michaels, J. and Siegel, S.: 1960, 'Two-Choice Behavior in Children', paper presented at meeting of Psychonomic Society, Chicago.

Millward, R. B.: 1971, 'Theoretical and Experimental Approaches to Human Learning', in J. W. Kling and L. A. R. Riggs (eds.), *Woodworth and Schlossberg 'Experimental Psychology'*, Holt, Rinehart and Winston, pp. 905–1018.

Mînzat, I.: 1968, 'Unele aspecte ale învăţării probabiliste abordate în psihologia contemporană', *Revista de Psihologie*, Vol. 14, Nr. 2, 135–144.

Myers, J. L. and Fort, J. G.: 1961, 'A Sequential Analysis of Gambling Behavior', paper presented at meeting of Psychonomic Society, New York.

Neimark, E. D.: 1956, 'Effects of Type of Non-Reinforcement and Number of Available Responses in Two-Verbal Conditioning Situations', *Journal of Experimental Psychology* 52, 209–220.

Offenbach, S. J.: 1964, 'Studies of Children's Probability Learning Behavior. I: Effect of Reward and Punishment at Two Age Levels', *Child Development* 35, 709–715.

Offenbach, S. J.: 1965, 'Studies of Children's Probability Learning. II: Effect of Method and Event Frequency at Two Age Levels', *Child Development* 36, 952–961.

Ojemann, R. H., Maxey, E. J., and Snider, B. C.: 1965, 'Effects of Guided Learning Experiences in Developing Probability Concepts at the Fifth Grade Level', *Perceptual and Motor Skills* 21, 415–427.

Ojemann, R. H., Maxey, E. J., and Snider, B. C.: 'The Effect of a Program of Guided Learning Experiences in Developing Probability Concepts at the Third Grade Level', *Journal of Experimental Education* 33, 321–330.

Ojemann, R. H.: 1966, 'The Mental Health Effects of a Program for Teaching Elementary School Children the Elements of Probability Thinking', paper presented at Sixth International Congress of Child Psychiatry (cf. Harold Keller, *Journal of Experimental Child Psychology* 2, 1971).

Ojemann, R. H., Maxey, E. J., and Snider, B. C.: 1966, 'Further Study of Guided Learning Experience in Developing Probability Concepts in Grade Five,' *Perceptual and Motor Skills* 23, 97–98.

Piaget, J.: 1950, 'Une expérience sur la psychologie du hasard chez l'enfant', *Acta Psychologica* 7, 323–336.

Piaget, J. and Inhelder, B.: 1951, *La genèse de l'idée de hasard chez l'enfant*, PUF, Paris, p. 11.

Piaget, J.: 1956, 'Les stades du développement intellectuel de l'enfant et de l'adolescent', in P. Osterrieth (ed.), *Le problème des stades en psychologie de l'enfant*, PUF, Paris, pp. 32–41.

Piaget, J.: 1964, *La psychologie de l'intelligence*, Alcan, Paris.

Pire, G.: 1958, 'Notion du hasard et développement intellectuel', *Enfance*, Nr. 2, 131–143.

Poincaré, H.: 1906, *La science et l'hypothèse*, Flamarion, Paris.

Poincaré, H.: 1914, *Science et méthode*, Flamarion, Paris.

Pubols, B. H., Jr.: 1960, 'Incentive Magnitude Learning and Performance in Animals', *Psychol. Bull.* 57, 89–115.

Rosenblum, S.: 1956, 'The Effects of Differential Reinforcement and Motivation on Prediction Responses on Children', *Child Development* 27, 99–108.

Ross, B. M.: 1966, 'Probability Concepts in Deaf and Hearing Children', *Child Development* 37, 917–927.

Ross, B. M. and Levy, N.: 1959, 'Patterned Predictions of Chance Events by Children and Adults', *Psychological Report* 4, 87–124.

Rouanet, H.: 1967, *Les modèles stochastiques d'apprentissage*, Gauthier-Villars, Mouton, Paris.

Servais, W.: 1970, 'La dialectique de F. Gonseth et la pédagogie ouverte de la mathématique', dans *La Revue Internationale de Philosophie*, 24-e année, Nrs. 93–94, fasc. 3–4, p. 436.

Severi, F.: 1951, 'Intuizionismo e astratismo nella matematica contemporane', in

Atti del terzo Congresso dell'UMI, Ediz. Cremonese, Perella, Roma.

Siegel, S. and Goldstein, D. A.: 1959, 'Decision Making Behavior in a Two-Choice Uncertain Outcome Situation', *Journol of Experimental Psychology* 57, 37–42.

Siegel, S. and Andrews, J.: 1962, 'Magnitude of Reinforcement and Choice Behavior in Children', *Journal of Experimental Psychology* 63, 337–341.

Stevens, S. S. (ed.): 1951, *Handbook of Experimental Psychology*, J. Wiley, New York.

Stevenson, H. W. and Zigler, E. F.: 1958, 'Probability Learning in Children', *Journal of Experimental Psychology* 71, 473–490.

Stevenson, H. W. and Weir, M. W.: 1959, 'Variables Affecting Children's Performance in a Probability Learning Task', *Journal of Experimental Psychology* 57, 403–412.

Stevenson, H. W. and Hoving, K. L.: 1964, 'Probability Learning as a Function of Age and Incentive', *Journal of Experimental Child Psychology* 1, 64–70.

Suppes, P. and Ginsberg, R.: 1962, 'Application of a Stimulus Sampling Model to Children's Concept Formation of Binary Numbers with and without an Overt Correction Response', *Journal of Experimental Psychology* 63, 330–336.

Tolman, E. C. and Brunswik, E.: 1935, 'The Organism and the Causal Texture of the Environment', *Psychological Review* 42, 43–77.

Tverski, A. and Kahneman, D.: 1973, 'Availability: A Heuristic for Judging Frequency and Probability', *Cognitive Psychology*, No. 5, 207–232.

Varga, T.: 1970, 'Le langage des probabilités à l'école élémentaire', dans *Premier seminaire international, E. Galion – Le langage mathématique*, OCDL, Paris.

Vitz, P. C. and Hazan, D.: 1969, 'Memory During Probability Learning', *Journal of Experimental Psychology* 80, 1, 52–58.

Weaver, W.: 1969, *Doamna Sansa sau despre teoria probabilităţilor* (*Lady Luck: The Theory of Probability*), Editura ştiinţifică, Bucureşti.

Weir, M. W.: 1962, 'Effects of Age and Instruction on Children's Probability Learning', *Child Development* 33, 729–735.

Weir, M. W.: 1964, 'Developmental Changes in Problem Solving Strategies', *Psychological Review* 71, 473–490.

Weir, M. W.: 1964, 'Effect of Patterned Partial Reinforcement on Children's Performance in a Two-Choice Task', *Child Development* 35, 257–264.

Weir, M. W.: 1967, 'Age and Memory as Factors in Problem Solving', *Journal of Experimental Psychology* 73, 78–84.

Weir, M. W.: 1967, 'Children's Behavior in Probabilistic Tasks', in *The Young Child: Reviews of Research*, Published by the National Association for the Education of Young Children, Washington, pp. 136–154.

Weir, M. W.: 1972, 'Probability Performance: Reinforcement Procedure and Number of Alternatives', *American Journal of Psychology* 85, 2, 261–270.

Weir, M. W. and Gruen, G. E.: 1965, 'Role of Incentive Level, Number of Choices, and Type of Task in Children's Probability Learning', *Journal of Experimental Child Psychology* 2, 121–134.

Westcott, M. R.: 1968, *Toward a Contemporary Psychology of Intuition*, Holt, Rinehart and Winston, Inc. New York.

Wittig, M. A. and Weir, M. W.: 1971, 'The Role of Reinforcement Procedure in Children's Probability Learning as a Function of Age and Number of Response Alternatives', *Journal of Experimental Child Psychology* 12, 228–239.

Yost, P., Siegel, A. E., and Andrews, J. N.: 1962, 'Non Verbal Probability Judgement by Young Children', *Child Development* 33, 769–780.

E. FISCHBEIN, ILEANA BĂRBAT, AND I. MÎNZAT: PRIMARY AND SECONDARY INTUITIONS IN THE INTRODUCTION OF PROBABILITY*

In his writing on education, J. S. Bruner (1965) has emphasised the need to stimulate intuitive thinking in children, and to appeal to intuitive understanding (in association with analytical thought) in order to improve the assimilation of knowledge. This recommendation is not new. It has already been made by such great mathematicians as Felix Klein (1925, p. 127) and Henri Poincaré (1914, pp. 123–151) and it is being repeated today by specialists in mathematics teaching.

The different definitions of the term 'intuition' which have been put forward tend to reflect the point of view of the author concerning the nature of the phenomenon.

For Bergson, intuition is an extension of instinct, and consists of the ability to directly grasp the primary reality of life, of movement, and of pure duration (1930, pp. 191–201). This is a specialised philosophical sense which does not bear directly on the issues raised in this article.

For an author like Berne, who based his point of view on wide practical experience (in medicine), intuition is "knowledge based on experience and acquired through sensory contact with the subject without the 'intuiter' being able to formulate, to himself or others, how he came to his conclusions" (Berne, 1949, pp. 203–226).

For Westcott, and experimental psychologist, intuition is the phenomenon which occurs "when an individual reaches a conclusion on the basis of less explicit information than is ordinarily required to reach that conclusion" (Westcott, 1961, p. 100).

These few definitions will give an idea of the diversity of approaches. But if the differences between these authors, which derive from their individual points of view on the nature of intuition, are disregarded, there remains a common element in their definitions. The term *intuition*, in its most general accepted usage, denotes *immediate knowledge*, or, as Bruner says: "Intuition implies the act of grasping the meaning or significance of structure of a problem without explicit reliance on the analytical apparatus of one's craft" (Bruner, 1966, pp. 102–105).

Intuition is a very important factor to consider in the teaching process. The information and mental habits specific to a body of knowledge interact, at least in certain cases, with intuitive biases.

Compatibility between these intuitive biases and the logical structure of knowledge is an essential component of understanding, and a precondition of the independent and effective use of this knowledge in varying circumstances.

There are at least three situations which must be envisaged with regard to pre-existing intuitive biases:

(a) The information transmitted during the teaching process encounters a compatible intuitive bias, and this compatibility can be directly used in teaching (e.g. 'the shortest distance between two points is a straight line'). (b) Intuition is opposed; the relevant intuitive bias is not compatible, and there is a contradiction between the primary intuition and objective or demonstrable truth (e.g. 'the set of rational numbers is equipotent with the set of natural numbers'). (c) The absence of any prior intuitive bias relevant to the information taught (e.g. 'the medians of a triangle intersect at the same point').

The hypothesis could be put forward that, in order to be effective, the teaching of a subject should be preceded by a survey of the intuitive 'ground', just as the construction of a building is preceded by a survey of the nature and potential resistance of the ground on which it is proposed to build it.

The nature and, in particular, the origin of intuition is a great philosophical and psychological problem. We do not want to enter into the details here, but the problem is essentially this: is intuitive knowledge the expression of certain a priori mental structures (in the Kantian sense) or is it the result (as Berne's previously cited point of view would hold) of a series of individual experiences, condensed into mental habits? In what follows, we shall subscribe to the second view: intuition is founded on mental habits. It is possible that, in certain cases, hereditary structures are involved; however this would not preempt the need for adaptive, individual construction. If this is true, it implies that, in the teaching process, we are not obliged to accept as given and immutable the intuitive base on which we wish to construct a particular conceptual system. The process of teaching would, according to this hypothesis, by means of appropriate interventions during extended periods of intellectual development, correct or even construct cognitive attitudes having the same characteristics as intuitions. We will call *primary intuitions* those intuitions which exist before, and independently of, of any intentional systematic teaching (e.g. the intuition of the identity of the material object, despite its many different phenomenal appearances; elementary intuitions of space and time, etc). We will call *secondary intuitions* those which are systematically constructed during the teaching process (e.g. the idea that a body conserves its state of motion or rest until some external force intervenes).

A secondary intuition cannot be reduced simply to an accepted or automatised formula. What is most interesting about these acquisitions from the psychological point of view is that they are transformed into beliefs, convictions, even self-evident ideas.

It would be very difficult to draw a clear distinction between the two types of intuition.

The main objective of our research has been to study the intuitive biases corresponding to certain fundamental concepts and methods of the theory of probability. This is not simply a question of the general concepts of chance, or randomness, on which there are data already available. Research which has already been done by psychologists indicates the existence of a natural intuition of chance, or even of probability (cf. Fischbein *et al.*, 1967, 1970a, b). However, A. Engel, a mathematician, has written: "... we have a natural geometric intuition but no probabilistic intuition".

In order to elucidate this problem, we decided to go beyond the notion of chance, and try to follow the course of what, in fact, happens during the systematic teaching of certain concepts in the theory of probability.

We therefore decided to study the intuitive responses of subjects to certain concepts and calculational precedures which were introduced during some experimental lessons on probability, viz. chance, and probability as a metric of chance; the multiplication of probabilities in the case of an intersection of independent events, and the addition of probabilities in the case of mutually exclusive events.

In addition, the following variables were investigated:

– age (is there a spontaneous development of these intuitions which is determined by age?)

– prior ability in mathematics (are these intuitions superior in subjects who are gifted in mathematics?).

We were also interested in the question: if a favourable intuitive bias is found and rendered explicit (to the child) does this contribute to structural assimilation, which would be demonstrated by transfer?

METHOD

Subjects. The subjects were pupils at several secondary and grammar schools in Bucharest. We studied three age levels, corresponding to three general classes of secondary education; the 6th (subjects between 12:5 and 13:8 years); the 8th (subjects between 14:6 and 15:5); and the 10th (subjects between 16 and 16:9). Pupils from the 10th class were divided into two groups. One group was a representative sample of pupils from different types of schools and courses (classics, mathematics, general) and the other group was composed entirely of pupils from mathematical courses in grammar schools, who had received very good marks in mathematics. Each group was made up of 20 subjects, treated individually. The number of boys and girls in each group was equal.

None of the subjects had any prior knowledge of probability theory.

Procedure. We used a method of investigation which we have used in previous studies, and which we have called "instruction by programmed discovery" (Fischbein *et al.*, 1970a, b). The method combines certain features of programmed learning with the method of teaching through discovery. It consists of a sequence of standardised stages. Unlike programmed instruction, in which the stages in general begin by giving information, this method begins each stage with a question, which is formulated in such a way that the subject can give a meaningful answer, based either on intuition, or on transfer (from information or a procedure acquired previously). If the subject does not respond to the direct question, *auxiliary questions* are asked. Among these auxiliary questions, some appeal to more elementary intuitions which may, eventually, serve as the foundation of more specialised intuitions; others attempt to stimulate transfer from a previously learned solution.

The function of these auxiliary questions is not simply to keep the experiment going. They are designed to reveal the primary intuitive bias, which may not be able to respond to a too specialised question. Furthermore, it is important that information imparted or suggested by questions should not interfere with the intuitive bias, which we wish to observe in its 'pure state'.

This standardised sequence of questions, each kept to a minimum, has two useful features: (a) it permits the exact recording of the extent of spontaneous intuitive response in each subject in each stage; (b) it permits quantitative comparisons between different groups of subjects (in terms of each 'question-answer' step).

In order for the investigation to be effective, the sequence of questions must take the subjects as far as possible into a given domain in the shortest possible time, avoiding all side tracks.

The sequences of questions themselves are presented below, grouped according to the 4 main sections of the investigation. In certain cases, we have also shown the auxiliary questions, especially when they aim to uncover more elementary intuitions. A stands for auxiliary question, I for intuition, T for transfer, AI for auxiliary question aiming to stimulate transfer, and AIT for auxiliary question appealing simultaneously to intuition and to transfer.

I. PROBABILITY AS A METRIC OF CHANCE

The Concept of Chance

Introductory question: Do you know the word 'probable'? Give an example of the use of this word.*

(a) A white marble and a black marble are placed in a plastic box.

'If you take out a marble without looking, which one do you think it will be?'

Estimating Odds. (The same box)

(b) "Compare the chances of drawing the white marble with the chances of drawing the black marble. What are the chances?"

(c) Two plastic boxes. In the left box: one white and one black marble. In the right box: two white marbles and one black marble.

"Compare the chances of drawing a black marble from each box."

(d) Two black marbles are placed in one box.

"Is it possible to draw out a black marble?"

(e) "Is it possible to draw out a white marble?"

The experimenter concludes:

"The chances of a certain thing happening can be great or small. Sometimes the thing is certain, sometimes it is impossible. Since the chances can be so different, we might think of measuring them, or expressing them by means of different numbers."

(f) "What number would you use to express a certain outcome?"

Whatever the subject replies, the experimenter says that the most convenient number is 1.

(g) "What number would you use to express an impossible outcome?"

(h) "What number would you use to express the chances when there are only two possible outcomes?" (The chances of drawing a black marble from a box which contains one black and one white marble.)

If the subject does not give the correct response, resort is had to AI: "Let us show the chances on a scale. At one end we put 0, for an impossible outcome, and at the other end we put 1, for a certain outcome. Where now should we put the point to stand for equal chances?"

The Concept of Probability

The experimenter: "The number which measures the chance of an outcome, of an event, happening, is called the *probability* of this outcome or event, and we use the letter P to stand for 'probability'. Thus:

$P(\text{certain}) = 1,$

$P(\text{impossible}) = 0,$

$P(\text{equal chances}) = \frac{1}{2}.$

Let us now see how chances are measured in other situations.

"In a box there are two white marbles and a black marble. What is the probability of drawing:

(i) a white marble

(ii) a black marble."

AI: "When you worked out the probability of drawing a white marble (or a black marble) when there were two marbles in the box, you found $\frac{1}{2}$ (one white marble out of two possible marbles). Using the same reasoning now:

There are 3 white marbles and 2 black marbles in a box.

What is the probability of drawing

(*k*) a white marble?

(*l*) a black marble?

(*m*) How is the probability worked out? What calculation formula do we, in fact, use?"

II. THE MULTIPLICATION LAW OF PROBABILITIES

One white marble and one black marble are placed in a box.

(a) "If we make two draws, each time replacing the marble we have drawn in the box, what is the probability of drawing a black marble each time?"

If the correct answer is not given, the following auxiliary questions are put:

AI_1 (global comparison): "Which is easier, to draw a black marble in one draw, or to draw two black marbles in two successive draws?"

AI_2: "How much easier is it?"

A box with the same contents: one white and one black marble.

(b) "If we make *three* successive draws, replacing the marble after each draw, what is the probability of getting a black marble each time?"

AT – the calculation for $P(BB)$ is recapitulated.

III. THE DICE GAME (TRANSFER OF THE MULTIPICATION LAW. THE ADDITION OF PROBABILITIES)

Multiplication of probabilities. (Control of transfer)

(A die is shown.)

"If we throw the die, what is the probability of getting

(a) a 5

(b) a 6?"

AT: the rule for calculating probabilities.

(c) "We throw the die two times. What is the probability that we will get 5 the first time, and 6 the second time?"

AT: the multiplication law.

Addition of Probabilities

(*Two* dice are shown)

(d) "The two dice are thrown at the same time. What is the probability of getting the pair 5, 6?"

(It is essential for the subject to notice, in this case, that there are two possible ways in which this situation can occur, I: 5–6, II: 6–5, and that the probabilities of the two events must be added.)

AI_1: "Suppose that you have to choose between two games. Game X: you throw a die twice in succession. What is the probability of getting 5 on the first throw, and 6 on the second? Game Z: you throw two dice at the same time. What is the probability of getting the pair 5, 6? Are the chances of winning the same in both games?"

AT: After the two possibilities (5–6; 6–5) have been noted, the subject is asked to do the calculation.

(e) "Throw two dice at the same time. You will win if you get the pair 5,6. I win if I get a double, 5,5. Which of us has the greater chance of winning?"

AT: "Calculate the probabilities for 5–6 and 6–5; calculate the probability for 5–5."

IV. THE APPLES PROBLEM (TRANSFER OF THE MULTIPLICATION AND ADDITION OF PROBABILITIES)

A warehouse contains 90% ripe apples, and 10% green apples.

(a) "If we take 3 apples at random, what is the probability that they will all be ripe?"

(It is explained that taking out a few apples will not affect the initial probabilities, given the large number of apples in the warehouse.)
AT: (The multiplication law.)

(b) "What is the probability that there are just two ripe apples among the three we have taken out?" (From Knight, 1967, p. 98.)

AI: In cases where the response is: $\frac{9}{10} \cdot \frac{9}{10}$, the subject is reminded that the fact that the third apple is green has to be accounted for.

When a response has been obtained for a single possibility, $\frac{9}{10} \cdot \frac{9}{10} \cdot \frac{1}{10}$, the next question is:

AI_2: "Is that all there is to the calculation?" This question is essential in order to control for the intuition of several possibilities. If a satisfactory response is not obtained, the subject is asked:

AI_3T: "Is this the only order in which the apples can be taken out? What would we say if the order did not count?"

AI_4T: "Write down the three possibilities."

AT: "Do the final calculation."

V. RESULTS

The results are summarised in 4 tables representing the 4 sections of the experimental session.

The numbers indicate frequencies. Percentages would have unnecessarily complicated the tables, since the four experimental groups all contained the same number of subjects.

Errors are explicitly indicated (E) only when they are considered relevant to a systematic intuitive bias. If E (error) appears *after* AI or AT or AIT (auxiliary questions which are designed to assist the subject to correct a response) this indicates that the error or incomprehension persisted and that supplementary explanations were required.

The data indicate that:

1. *Probability as a Metric of Chance* (Table I)

(1) The concept of chance was used correctly from the beginning by all age groups. (As we have previously mentioned, data obtained by us and by other investigators have already shown that the idea of chance is understood even by pre-schoool children.)

(2) Although the use of the number 1 to quantify a certain event may be considered a convention, quite a large percentage of subjects (about 50%) spontaneously offered this device. Once 1 had been established as the number representing a certain event, almost all the subjects, in all age groups, intuitively assigned 0 to an impossible event.

(3) Equal chances in a situation with two alternatives were assigned the number 0.5 (in different numerical forms) by most subjects within each age group. The transition to other numbers quantifying the chances in a given situation was also made directly. We can therefore conlude that there is a favourable intuitive bias for: (a) the concept of chance, (b) the concept of a metric of chance, (c) the use of the values 1, 0, to denote certain and impossible events respectively, and (d) the quantification of chance as expressed by the relationship between the number of favourable events and the number of equally possible events. There is no systematic improvement in these intuitions which can be said to be due to age (over and above instruction).

2. *The Multiplication Law of Probabilities for Independent Events* (Table II)

(a) The operation of multiplying probabilities in the case of intersections of two independent events (successive draws of a black marble from a box containing a white marble and a black marble) did not appear spon-

TABLE I

Probability as a metric of chance

Question	Types of response	Class			
		6th	8th	10th	10th Mathematical
(a) prediction of draw for 1B:1W	RC: 'Impossible to say which' etc.	20	20	20	20
(b) comparison of chances 1B:1W	RC: 'chances equal'	20	20	20	20
(c) comparison of chances of drawing B 1B:1W 2B:1W	RC: $P(B/1B:1W) > P(B/1B:2W)$	20	20	20	20
(f) the number expressing a certain event	1	9	6	13	10
	10	3	3	1	–
	100%	7	7	4	6
	infinite	–	1	2	4
	other responses	1	3	–	–
(g) the number expressing an impossible event	0 (zero)	19	19	20	20
	other responses	1	1	–	–
(h) the number expressing equal chances	RC: 1/2	4	13	11	11
	RC: 0, 5	11	4	6	8
	RC: 50%	2	–	–	1
	other responses	3	3	3	–
(i) the probability of drawing B from 1B:2W	RC: 1/3	15	18	18	19
	AIT	2	1	2	1
	E	3	1	–	–
(j) the probability of drawing W from 1B:2W	RC: 2/3	17	16	17	19
	AIT	2	4	3	1
	E	1	–	–	–
(k) probability of drawing B from 2B:3W	RC: 2/5	18	16	20	20
	AT	–	4	–	–
	E	2	–	–	–
(l) probability of drawing W from 2B:3W	RC: 3/5	18	18	18	19
	AT	2	2	2	1
(m) calculation formula for probability	RC:	19	16	19	20
	A	1	4	1	–

$N = 20$. The numbers indicate frequencies. RC = responses correct. A = correct responses obtained with the help of auxiliary questions. E = errors. I = intuition. T = transfer. Results for questions (d) and (e) do not appear, since the correct responses were obvious.

TABLE II

The multiplication law of probabilities [a]

Question	Types of response	Class			
		6th	8th	10th	10th Mathematical
(a) the probability of consecutive BB draws from 1B:1W	RC: $1/2 \times 1/2 = 1/4$	–	2	2	8
	$1/2:1/2$ [b]	8	7	4	5
	E: $1/2 + 1/2$	–	–	3	2
	Other erroneous responses or S does not know	12	11	11	5
(a) AI$_1$: comparison of $P(N)$ $P(NN)$	RC: $P(N) > P(NN)$	18	14(+2)	12(+2)	12(+8)
	E: $P(NN) < P(N)$	–	3	–	–
	E: $P(NN) = P(N)$	1	1	2	–
	Other erroneous responses, or absence of response	1	–	4	–
(a) AI$_2$: How many times is $P(NN)$ smaller than $P(N)$?	RC: Twice	5	6(+2)	5(+2)	6(+8)
	E	15	12	13	6
(b) probability of drawing consecutively BBB from 1B:1W	RC: $\frac{1}{2} \cdot \frac{1}{2} \cdot \frac{1}{2} = \frac{1}{8}$	17	18	20	20
	E	3	2	–	–

[a] See legend, Table I.

[b] The subject (S) calculates the probability (P) of each draw separately, but does not carry out the multiplication.

The numbers in brackets indicate subjects who had done the correct calculation (question a) from the beginning, and who were therefore bound to make the comparison correctly.

taneously in any subject in the 6th class. It appeared only in 2 subjects in the 8th and 10th classes. But in the 10th mathematical group it appeared in 8 subjects (40%). In order to stimulate the intuitive substrate, appeal was made to a more elementary intuition: the global comparison between $P(B)$ and $P(BB)$. This time, most subjects responded correctly: $P(B) > > P(BB)$. Even so, the quantification of this comparison continued to present difficulties. It was only a relatively small number of subjects (about 25–30%) who were able to pass without assistance from this elementary global intuition $[P(B) > P(BB)]$ to the arithmetical operation $(\frac{1}{2} \cdot \frac{1}{2} = \frac{1}{4})$.

Age did not provide any detectable advantage in this case, either. Only the pupils of the mathematical group showed any advantage.

(b) Once the calculation rule for $P(BB)$ had been learned, the transfer was immediately made to $P(BBB)$. There was a slight age advantage (85% in 4th, 90% in the 6th, and 100% in the 10th classes made the transfer).

3. *The Dice Game (Transfer of Multiplication, Inventory of Elementary Events, the Addition Law of Probabilities)* (Table III)

(1) The multiplication law learned in the example with the marbles was spontaneously transferred by most subjects to the dice example.

(2) In contrast, in the case of two simultaneous throws of the dice, subjects failed to realise (with a few exceptions) that two distinct cases

TABLE III

The dice game (transfer of multiplication and addition of probabilities) [a]

Question	Types of response	Class			
		6th	8th	10th	10th Mathematical
(a, b) $P(5)$; $P(6)$	RC: $1/6$; $1/6$	13	18	15	18
	A	5	2	5	2
	E	2	–	–	–
(c) $P(5,6)$	RC: $1/6 \times 1/6 = 1/36$	19	14	18	20
	E: $1/6 + 1/6$	1	6	2	–
(d) $P(5,6; 6,5)$	RC: $2 \times 1/36 = 1/18$	1	2	4	3
	Other erroneous responses, or absence of response	19	18	16	17
(d) AI_1: comparison of $P_1(5,6)$ and $P_2(5,6; 6,5)$	RC: $P_2 > P_1$	7(+1)	4(+2)	4(+4)	4(+3)
	E: $P_1 < P_2$	7	4	3	2
	E: $P_1 = P_2$	4	6	6	7
	No choice	1	4	3	4
(d) AT: calculation after the two possible cases have been established $(5,6; 6,5)$	RC: $1/36 + 1/36 = 1/18$ or $2 \times 1/36$	18(+1)	17(+2)	16(+4)	17(+3)
	E	1	1	–	–
(e) comparison (game with two dice): $P_1(5,6; 6,5)$ $P_2(5,5)$	RC: $P_1 > P_2$	15	17	17	16
	AT (calculation)	5	3	3	4

[a] See legend, Table I.

were involved (5–6 and 6–5) of which the probabilities had to be added. There was only a slight age advantage (up to about 25% in the 10th class).

(3) The appeal to a more elementary intuition – the global comparison between $P_1(5,6)$ and $P_2(5,6) \cup (6,5)$ resulted in correct responses from a certain number of subjects (7 in the 6th, and 4 in the other classes). For a complete picture, those subjects should also be mentioned who immediately arrived at the numerical solution. But there were still 50% of subjects, in all age groups, who still did not grasp the difference between the two situations.

(4) Once the possibility of two favourable outcomes of the simultaneous throw of two dice had been understood, almost all subjects realised that the final calculation required was an addition (the addition of the probabilities of the simple events in order to calculate the probability of the compound event).

(5) The comparison between the probability of getting a 'double' (5,5) and the probability of getting two different numbers $(5,6) \cup (6,5)$ was correctly solved – through transfer – by 75–85% of subjects.

4. *The Apples Problem (Transfer of Multiplication, Transfer of the Operation of Enumerating Elementary Events, and Transfer of Addition)* (Table IV)

(1) Surprisingly, relatively few subjects spontaneously solved the problem of drawing 3 ripe apples, in the given conditions. Even among the mathematical group only 60% responded correctly.

Acquisition of the multiplication law was shown to be unstable. Transfer was difficult in the context of this problem.

(2) None of the subjects spontaneously saw the necessity of considering several possibilities, each of which contributed to an increase in the probability of the compound event.

The sequence of supplementary questions led only slowly to the complete response.

(3) After the three possibilities had been pointed out, almost all subjects saw, intuitively, that the final result was obtained by addition.

It is evident that the need to make an inventory of possibilities (at least in cases where there are no order restrictions) not only is not grasped spontaneously, but is counter-intuitive. The subject accepts this rule, but does not assent to it intuitively.

TABLE IV

The apples problem (transfer of multiplication and addition of probabilities)

Question	Types of response	Class			
		6th	8th	10th	10th Mathematical
(a) $P(R,R,R)$	RC: $9/10 \times 9/10 \times 9/10$	5	9	5	12
	AT	2	5	15	8
	E (or absence of response; supplementary suggestions made)	13	6	–	–
(b) $P(2R,1G)$	RC: $3 \times 9/10 \times 9/10 \times 1/10$	–	–	–	–
	RC: for a single possibility (R, R, G): $9/10 \times 9/10 \times 1/10$	12	13	17	18
	E: for a single possibility (or absence of response)	8	7	3	2
After subjects have established $9/10 \times 9/10 \times 1/10$ (b) AI_2: "Do you consider the calculation finished?"	RC: 'No'	2	2	–	1
	E: 'Yes' (or 'Don't know')	18	18	20	19
(b) AI_3T: "What would we say if order did not count?"	RC: There are three possibilities	1	–	3	7
	'Don't know'	19	20	17	13
(b) AI_4T: establishment of the three possibilities	RC: $1/10 \times 9/10 \times 9/10$ $9/10 \times 1/10 \times 9/10$ $9/10 \times 9/10 \times 1/10$	1	2	3	9
	E or 'Don't know'	19	18	17	11
AT: Show multiplication by three of $81/1000$	RC:	20	19	19	20
	'Don't know'	–	1	1	–

R = ripe apple.
G = green apple.

VI. DISCUSSION AND CONCLUSION

(1) The results of the investigation have shown that the introduction to probability theory may be based on compatible intuitive biases as far as the following concepts and procedures are concerned: the concept of

chance, and of the quantification of chance as the relationship between the number of favourable and of possible outcomes, with 1 as the representation of the probability of a certain event, and 0 as the representation of the probability of an impossible event. To this can be added the fact that subjects see intuitively that the operation by which the probability of the union of elementary events constitutes a compound event, is addition. The axioms of probability theory are:

$$(1)\ P(A) \geqslant 0; \quad (2)\ P(E) = 1;$$
$$(3)\ P(A \cup B) = P(A) + P(B)$$

for mutually exclusive events A and B. We can state, on the basis of our findings, that these axioms, and the classical definition of probability, derive from a primary intuitive source. With regard to the first axiom: no subject, in any circumstances, used a negative number to represent a probability. As far as the third axiom is concerned, we did not include the notion of 'mutually exclusive events' in the investigation, and so the extent to which intuition enters into the notion cannot be discussed here.

(2) In the case of the multiplication of probabilities, a distinction must be made between the primary, rudimentary intuition of the reduction of odds as a result of the multiplication of conditions (intersection of events) and the *calculation* relevant to this situation. The primary intuition of the reduction of odds is present, as we have seen, in the majority of subjects, but this does not guarantee an intuition of the appropriate calculation. Once the calculation has been learned, it transfers directly only to very closely related situations (proximal transfer): from two to three marbles; from marbles to dice. Transfer is severely restricted if the situations are remote in concrete modalities (the apples problem).

It might have been expected that, given the existence of an elementary intuitive bias, this bias would ensure direct transfer to more remote situations, after learning of the calculation rule. Since this, apparently, does not happen, it seems that articulation between the intuitive base and the logical structure of the operation is still weak in this case.

Different methods must therefore be sought for teaching the multiplication law of probability (and also preliminary exercises with a wide variety of concrete situations).

(3) In the case of the addition law, *there is an almost total lack of under-*

standing of the compound character of some events, and of the need to in-
ventory the different situations which can constitute the same event. In the
limited area of intuitive biases which we have studied, this represents the
most important intuitive lacuna observed. Very few subjects spontaneously saw the need to take into account different possible situations in the
extremely simple case of a dice game. Not a single subject saw this need
in respect of the (still simple) problem of the apples, even though it had
been preceded by the dice problem. *This is an instance, not simply of the*
absence of an intuition, but in fact of a contradicted intuition.

It therefore seems that a secondary intuition, destined to fill an intuitive
lacuna or to replace an inadequate primary intuition, cannot be constructed
as the result of a local explanation, however clear and convincing. Instead
is required prolonged exercise, which would interact, we believe, with the
broad stages of intellectual development (concrete and formal operations)
in such a way that the relevant construction would be organically incorpo-
rated within the mental structure as it develops. This is in line with the
hypothesis that a secondary intuition cannot be reduced to 'insight',
whether stimulated externally or not, but requires the construction of
mental habits over an extended period of time.

(4) It seems that there is no systematic and spontaneous improvement
in intuitive bias which is due to age, and this is important from the point
of view of the educational process. The bias exists, or it does not. There
was, however, a certain age advantage in the extent to which transfer was
possible, once a calculation rule had been learned for a given situation.

(5) We had supposed that, once an existing, correct, but rudimentary
intuition had been rendered explicit to the child, and associated with a
corresponding calculation technique, this would lead directly to the establishment of a viable intellectual structure, capable of transfer because
of the pre-existing intuitive bias which was now associated with the calculation technique. This was expected, for instance, in the case of the multiplication law of probabilities. But the data have proved this supposition
wrong. Prolonged exercise (in varied situations) is therefore necessary,
not only in order to construct an adequate intuitive base, i.e. a secondary
intuition, but also in order to ensure the articulation of a pre-existing
primary intuition with a corresponding calculation technique.

(6) The superiority of pupils from mathematical courses emerged particularly when they were induced to transfer a learned operation (e.g. the

application of the multiplication law to the cases of dice and apples, after it had been learned in relation to marbles).

The only other instance seems to be the following: the pupils from mathematical courses were outstandingly better (this was, in fact, the only instance in which they were outstandingly superior) than the other subjects when they were asked, for the first time, to determine the probability of drawing two black marbles in succession from a pair consisting of a black and a white marble. The results, in percentages, by class were: 0%, 10%, 10%, 40%.

This is no doubt an isolated finding, but we think it can give rise to the following hypothesis: *the aptitude for mathematics presupposes the ability to adapt a quantification procedure to pre-existing intuitions* (with the implication that it does not, or not necessarily, presuppose the existence of certain extra primary intuitions, or of a better capacity for generating such intuitions).

As far as the contradiction is concerned between the psychologists' finding of the spontaneous emergence of a probabilistic intuition, and Engel's observation that there is no such natural intuition, we would offer the following hypothesis: psychologists have mainly studied the concepts of chance and of the quantification of chance which have corresponding intuitive biases, while mathematicians deal either with more complex intuitive formations – which do not emerge spontaneously – or with the quantitative expression of certain existing intuitive formations, both of which call for extensive training. The practical truth is that the uneven and sometimes surprising intuitive 'ground' must be systematically prospected before the construction of a conceptual system is undertaken – particularly in the domain of probability.

NOTES

* Reprinted from *Educational Studies in Mathematics* **4** (1971), 264–280.
* The tables do not show data relevant to this question.

BIBLIOGRAPHY

Bergson, H.: 1930, *L'évolution créatrice*, Paris, Alcan, pp. 191–201.
Berne, E.: 1949, 'The Nature of Intuition', *Psychiatric Quarterly* **23**, 203–226.
Bruner, J. S.: 1965, *The Process of Education*, Harvard University Press, Cambridge, Massachusetts.

Bruner, J. S.: 1966, *On Knowing. Essays for the Left Hand*, Atheneum, New York.

Engel, A.: 1970, 'Teaching Probability in Intermediate Grades', in: L. Råde (ed.), *The Teaching of Probability and Statistics*, Almqvist, Wiksell, pp. 283–301.

Fischbein, E., Pampu, I., et Minzat, I.: 1967, 'L'Intuition probabiliste chez l'enfant', *Enfance*, No. 2, 193–208.

Fischbein, E., Pampu, I., and Minzat, I.: 1970a, 'Comparison of Ratios and the Chance Concept in Children', *Child Development* **41**, 2, 377–389.

Fischbein, E., Pampu, I., and Minzat, I.: 1970b, 'Effects of Age and Instruction on Combinatory Ability in Children', *The British Journal of Educational Psychology* **40**, 261–270.

Klein, F.: 1925, *Elementarmathematik vom höheren Standpunckte aus*, Ed. 2, vol. II, Berlin, Springer.

Knight, R. D.: 1967, *New Mathematics*, III, John Murray, London.

Poincaré, H.: 1914, *Science et méthode*, Paris, Flammarion.

Westcott, M.: 1961, *Psychology of Intuition*, Holt, Rinehart and Winston Inc., New York.

E. FISCHBEIN, ILEANA PAMPU, AND I. MÎNZAT:
THE CHILD'S INTUITION OF PROBABILITY*

INTRODUCTION

Over the past few years, there have been a number of studies on the development of the concept of probability in the child. This interest was initially stimulated by the growing concern in psychology – particularly after 1950 – with stochastic models of learning and perception, matching behaviour, and decision and choice behaviour. The relevance of probability calculation to secondary education has also led to a demand for psychological and educational research in this field. Both of these motivations clearly stem from the increasing importance of probability and statistics in contemporary scientific thought. Using specially adapted techniques of modern mathematics, the analysis of stochastic processes in physics, biology, sociology, psychology, and so on, makes possible deeper and more heuristic interpretations of phenomena, and ultimately a closer grasp of the dynamic dialectical features of objective reality.

Piaget in 1950, and Inhelder and Piaget in 1951, carried out a series of detailed studies. Their conclusion was that the child has no understanding of probability before the age of seven: the pre-school child does not distinguish between the possible and the necessary. This conclusion is reiterated in an important later work (1955, pp. 286–287). In general, according to Piaget and Inhelder, understanding of probabilistic situations occurs only at the level of concrete operations. Cohen, Dearncley and Hansel (1957 – in N. Kass, 1964, pp. 577–582) raise the age of acquisition of the concept still higher; in their estimation, the child has no concept of probability before the age of sixteen. They believe that the decisions of younger children are based on variable subjective preferences such as superstition, etc.

There is a large body of data to support a contrary point of view (Messick and Solley, 1957; Stevenson and Weir, 1959; Braine, 1962 – in S. Goldberg, 1966; Siegel and Andrews, 1962; Brackbill *et al.*, 1962, etc.). The crucial finding on which these authors base their point of view is that children even younger than seven adapt their responses in accordance with the objective frequencies of certain events (called 'matching behaviour' by Edwards, 1954 – in S. L. Offenbach, 1965, p. 952). This is analogous to the behaviour of adults in probability learning tasks, in which the frequency of the prediction of an event approaches the objective frequency of the event.

Offenbach considers that the argument based on this similarity of behaviour is not valid. He asserts that the ability of the child to discriminate frequencies of events is not the same as probabilistic behaviour, and therefore does not indicate possession of the concept of probability. In other words, Piaget's view of the child's concept of probability is not invalidated by the fact that the child possesses this discriminative capacity (Offenbach, 1965). Offenbach's argument raises a very interesting problem, which we shall discuss later.

Yost *et al.* (1962, p. 769), and later Goldberg (1963) attempted to directly verify Piaget and Inhelder's account by comparing the results from two different types of experiment. In what these authors call Piagetian experiments, children are asked to determine which of two colours has the greatest chance of being selected in a random selection from a group of counters in the two colours, unequally represented. In 'decision making' experiments, the other type, the child compares two groups of counters in which a particular colour is unevenly represented. The child has to judge which group is most likely to yield a counter of the desired colour. Yost *et al.* added material reinforcement (toys, sweets) for correct choice to this type of experiment. The conclusion is that, in Piagetian experiments, the behaviour of the children confirms Piaget's view; but in the decision making type of experiment, children of the same age demonstrate probabilistic behaviour.

The development of comprehension of probabilistic relations as a function of age has been relatively little studied, and what data have been obtained are generally inconsistent. According to Piaget and Inhelder, it is only after seven years of age that the child becomes capable of understanding the distinction between the determined and the undetermined at the level of concrete operations – a distinction which permits discrimination between the possible, the actual, and the necessary to begin. This in turn makes possible an elementary understanding of the idea of probability, in the context of situations directly accessible to the child. At the level of formal operations – i.e. after eleven to twelve years of age– understanding of the concept of probability is widened to include all possible combinations of considered elements, and the child arrives at an integrated concept of chance and predictability (1951, pp. 226–229; 1955, pp. 286–287).

The main aim of our research has been to contribute to an elucidation of the following problem: from what age, and in what sense, is it possible to speak of an intuition of chance and probability in the child? Taking Piaget's view as our starting-point, we have assumed that the central feature is that of the relationship between the possible and the necessary. At the same time, we have looked at other aspects which seemed likely to throw light on the problem as a whole:

(a) Probability can be expressed either as a prediction of a single isolated event (without specifying the hypothetical multiplicity of its origin), or as a prediction of several events – which may be repetitions of a single event, or a succession of different events. We therefore need to know to what extent children of different ages understand the concept of relative frequency, and the extent to which this enters into their understanding of probabilistic situations.

(b) How far is the child able to abstract a common probabilistic structure from different specific contexts and situations? It seemed important to us to include series of events described by equal probabilities, as well as events described by unequal probabilities.

METHOD

Subjects were children aged from 6 to 14 years, divided into 5 age groups: (5 years: 10 months – 7 years: 6 months), (7:0–8:3), (9:2–10:5), (11:3–12:10), and (13:5–14:5). We used 50 subjects from each age group for the first tests. Since it was not possible to use all these subjects for the final test, the actual numbers of subjects used in this test were: $N1 = 50$, $N2 = 18$, $N3 = 35$, $N4 = 43$, $N5 = 42$ (youngest to oldest).

Materials

A set of experimental materials was specially constructed. These consisted of a set of boards (22×30 cm) on which systems of channels had been constructed with thin strips of wood. The channels were progressively

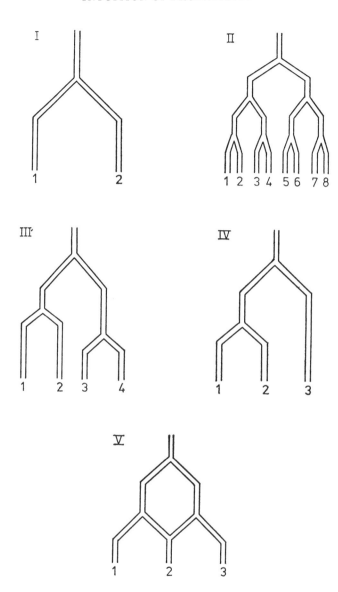

Fig. 1.

bifurcated and branched toward the base of the board, which was held inclined vertically so that a marble released at the top of the main channel could follow any one of a number of paths down through the system. Five different boards were used (Figure 1).

On board I (Figure 1, I) the marble necessarily arrives at a point of uncertainty. The probability of entering either channel is $\frac{1}{2}$. If the child has the idea of uncertainty as the opposite of certainty, this must become apparent in this elementary situation. If the idea can be given a probabilistic form, it must be expressed, not simply by a response such as "I don't know where the marble will go", but by the response "The marble can go *either* into one channel, or the other."

Board II is merely a more complex version of the first test (Figure 1, II). In this case, we were interested to see whether the reasoning appropriate to the first case would resist the distracting complication of an added number of articulations. The channels in this case are arranged in such a way that the probability of the marble exiting at any one of the exits is $\frac{1}{8}$.

Board III (Figure 1, III) also represents a situation where the marble is equally likely to drop through any one of the exits. But here the child must be able to distinguish between the probabilistic situation and the changed spatial situation (lengthened right channel). To what extent can the probabilistic structure be detached from differing perceptual contexts?

Board IV (Figure 1, IV) goes a step beyond simple equiprobability. Channels 1, 2, and 3 represent the probabilities $\frac{1}{4}$, $\frac{1}{4}$, and $\frac{1}{2}$. Here, concretised, is the multiplication of probabilities. (Multiplicative probabilities occur also in tests II and III, but are masked by the symmetry of channel branching and the final equivalence of outcomes.) In the case of two independent events A_1 and A_2, $P(A_1 \cap A_2) = P(A_1) P(A_2)$. The paths leading to exits 1 and 2 are the outcomes of just such a multiplication of probabilities: $P = \frac{1}{2} \times \frac{1}{2} = \frac{1}{4}$. The experimental model provides the conditions for direct intuition, without recourse to actual mathematical calculation.

Board V (Figure 1, V) is a concrete model of the addition of probabilities, according to the theorem: $P(A_1 \cup A_2) = P(A_1) + P(A_2)$, A_1 and A_2 being mutually exclusive events. Exit of the marble at 2 is the outcome of this set of probabilities: $P(E_2) = \frac{1}{4} + \frac{1}{4} = \frac{1}{2}$. Tests IV and V therefore allow the possibility of determining whether the child has an elementary intuition of these two fundamental rules of probability calculation.

The final model used (Figure 2) permits the generalisation of the idea of unequal probabilities beyond situations where there are only binary branches or junctions (as in the inclined planes of the other experimental conditions). This generalisation is made possible by distributing channels in space, as Figure 2 indicates schematically.

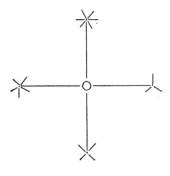

Fig. 2.

A marble is dropped through a funnel onto a small metal sphere. From this sphere radiate 4 downward-sloping channels, each of which terminates above another funnel, through which the marble falls onto another metal sphere. From each of these 4 spheres at the second level radiate another set of channels, arranged as follows: from sphere 1 they radiate in 3 directions, from sphere 2 in 4 directions, from sphere 3 in 5 directions and from sphere 4 in 6 directions. Thus, overall, the marble enters one of the four initial channels with a probability of $\frac{1}{4}$, and entry into one of the second-level channels is subject to the following probabilities: $\frac{1}{12}$, $\frac{1}{16}$, $\frac{1}{20}$, and $\frac{1}{24}$. We have called this apparatus *the pagoda* because this is the image that its form suggests.

As will be understood from the description of this apparatus, the paths taken by the marble result from the alternation of strictly determined sequences of movements and nodes of uncertainty (branchings and junctions of channels). The experimental materials also had to satisfy other requirements: the conditions of the various problems were fully and continuously accessible to the subjects' perception. The children's responses could be simply a gesture or an elementary verbal response; this ruled out the potentially complicating effects of language difficulties. Despite the alternation of deterministic and probabilistic aspects, we were dealing here with essentially elementary phenomena.

Procedure

The sessions were begun with explanations of a general nature. ("This is a sort of guessing game. Do you see these channels here? I am going to put in a marble at the top, and I want you to guess where it will come out.") The main questions put to the subjects were formulated as follows: (A) "I am going to drop a marble in here (pointing to the top of the main channel) – where will it come out at the bottom?" After the subject's first response, the question was then asked: "Will it always come out there, or can it come out in other places?"; (B) "If I drop the marble a lot of times, one after the other, will it come out at each place the same number of times, or will it come out of some places more often than others?" After each response to this question, the child was asked for a justification: "What makes you think that?" or "What did you think of, that made you say that?" Each subject was seen individually, and the session lasted between 30 and 40 minutes. The subject went through each trial in succession. When responses were wrong, some supplementary questions were used ("How many places are there where the marble can come out?"; "Follow where the marble can go with your finger") so that the continuation of the experiment was not meaningless. On tests IV, V, and VI, which dealt with unequal probabilities, the subject was also asked to say which of the exits the marble would come out at most often.

RESULTS

The quantitative results are shown in Tables I–VI; each table corresponds to one test. The numbers indicate correct responses as percentages. Only initial responses were counted, not those obtained after supplementary questions. Since there were two questions (A, concerning a single drop of the marble; B, concerning several successive drops, and therefore involving the concept of frequency), we have used a double notation in the discussion. For example, the notation III B refers to test III, question B.

As can be seen from Table I, question I A caused no difficulty, even for pre-school children. In this situation, the element of uncertainty is clear-cut and easily separable from the other aspect of the situation, the strictly

TABLE I

Percentage of correct responses

	Pre-school (%)	7:0–8:3 (%)	9:2–10:5 (%)	11:3–12:10 (%)	13:5–14:5 (%)
Single drop (A)	100	88	98	98	98
Successive drops (B)	80	82	84	98	98

determined movement *per se* of the marble. At all levels, almost all children gave responses of the form: "The marble can come out either one way or the other." On question I B, there were fewer correct responses by the youngest children, but this was probably due to the novelty of the question, since they did not perform worse on this question in the other tests. There was a significant difference overall on test I in favour of the older children (comparing ages 13:5–14:5 with the pre-school children, $t = 3$, $p < 0.01$). The important point arising from this elementary test is that almost all the children, including those of pre-school age, *demonstrated that they could distinguish clearly between certainty and uncertainty.* Slight differences in the form of response as between older and younger children, while not affecting the meaning of the solution, nevertheless provide some insight into their mental attitude. Thus we find that *older children hesitate very often*, even though they finally arrive at the conclusion that the chances are equal.

Here is an example of a response from a pre-school child: C. F. (6:9): "I think it will be the same, because the paths are the same. They both turn a corner, and then go straight."

As examples of responses from older children: F. G. (13:9): "The marble will come out one side more often than the other…no, I just guessed. The point is in the middle, so it will be equal for both coming out". N.I. (13:6): "About the same, because the two ways have the same slant." A.D. (13:6): "Equal, because the marble can fall anywhere… about equal." The idea of approximation is very common in the older children, and, to a certain extent, compensates for the lack of assurance they seem to feel.

Test II: As was foreseen, because of the greater complexity of this test, the number of correct responses is less for all age groups on this test as compared to the first (see Table II).

For many of the children, the complexity of the situation meant that the idea of equiprobability, which could be directly appealed to in the first test, could no longer be held to in the context of so many other dis-

TABLE II

Percentage of correct responses

	Pre-school (%)	7:0–8:3 (%)	9:2–10:5 (%)	11:3–12:10 (%)	13:5–14:5 (%)
Single drop (A)	76	66	61	56	58
Successive drops (B)	90	88	82	94	88

tracting features. In giving erroneous responses, subjects said that the paths were determined. It should be noticed that there was nothing in the lay-out to justify such a choice. The channels were perfectly symmetrical within the limits of unaided perception. The best proof of this was that the preferred path was not the same for all subjects: some chose a path which was at the extreme left or right, while others chose a more central path. Apart from this general depression of performance, the data obtained point to a surprising fact: *the number of correct responses decreases systematically from the younger to the older children* (with the small exception of the last age-group). The difference between the youngest and oldest groups is significant ($t = 2$, $p < 0.05$). Question B restored somewhat the age balance, correct responses clustering around 90%. It was the older children who made most correct responses on B (successive drops of the marble). The responses of the older children continued to be hesitant.

These are examples of hesitant responses: N.N. (14:0): "It won't be the same everywhere, but I don't know where it will be more or less." G.G. (13:8): "It is more likely to come out here (7). – Why? – The marble can go anywhere…If I let the marble drop a lot of times, one after the other, where do you think it will come out? – Perhaps it will come out through all of them the same…or through some more often. – When would the marble be likely to come out of all the exits the same number of times? – "Perhaps if you did it a lot of times it would be the same number ... or nearly".

Test III: It will be recalled that, on this test, the chances were equal in regard to the final exits, but, instead of having symmetrical channels, an asymmetry had been created in this case by lengthening one of the channels. This test seemed essential, in order to determine the subject's ability to separate the probabilistic component (equiprobability) of the situation from its objective structure.

TABLE III

Percentage of correct responses

	Pre-school (%)	7:0–8:3 (%)	9:2–10:5 (%)	11:3–12:10 (%)	13:5–14:5 (%)
Single drop (A)	62	54	36	43	40
Successive drops (B)	78	63	72	80	64

This time, there was a reduction in the frequency of correct responses at all ages, the percentage for each group approximating 50% (see Table III). It is clear, then, that the intuition of equiprobability, which manifests itself so rapidly in a simple situation, is not sufficiently integrated into the system of logical operations to be able to resist a complication of the situation. But what is more surprising is the fact that it is not the younger children who are most sensitive to complications of the situation, but the older ones. *The percentage of correct responses decreases with age.* The difference between the oldest and youngest groups is significant ($t = 2.1$, $p < 0.05$). As in the earlier tests, the older children did better on question B (successive drops of the marble). But, in spite of this advantage, the overall percentage of correct responses is higher for the pre-school children than for the oldest age-group (although the difference is not significant, $t = 1.5$).

In general, the younger children continue to respond immediately and without hesitation, but with justifications which indicate a certain failure to distinguish between objective conditions and subjective choice.

L.D. (6:3): "I think it will come out here (4) because it's easier ... they are all easy. – Why did you choose this one? – They're all easy, I just guessed...I think it will come out of all of them the same, because they are all easy...The marble goes where it wants, not where I want. We can't know where it will go".

The older children show the same uncertainty as on the previous tests, clearly because an unequivocal choice was demanded whereas in reality the conditions of the problem do not permit of such a choice. The child offers all kinds of explanations, suggested by the mechanical-geometric aspects of the channels, in order to justify a choice. This is a typical example of this type of reasoning from an older child: P.M. (13:6): "It will go along the far right channel, this one (4) because it is more to the side, because objects try to get out of a closed space." He was asked for further explanation; "There will be more in the far right channels, some in this one and some in that one (3 and 4). In these there will always be less (1 and 2)." The experimenter insisted again on a clearer explanation; "The marble will come more often down the channel with a longer bend." The experimenter pointed out that the number of bends and branches was equal, and that it was only the length which differed. "It will come more often down (3 and 4) because it has a longer and narrower trajectory."

Test IV: With tests IV, V, VI we pass on to cases of unequal probabilities. The results change radically, correct responses in general increasing with age.

The situation is less clear-cut in the case of question IV A (see Table IV). The percentage of correct responses is higher for the oldest age-group than for the youngest, but this difference is not significant. On question IV B, however, the superiority of the older children is clear. There is an increment of correct responses from each age-group to the next higher, and the difference between the oldest and youngest groups is highly signi-

TABLE IV

Percentage of correct responses

	Pre-school (%)	7:0–8:3 (%)	9:2–10:5 (%)	11:3–12:10 (%)	13:5–14:5 (%)
Single drop (A)	76	84	78	84	82
Successive drops (B)	54	64	66	88	92

ficant ($t = 6.33$, $p < 0.001$). This indicates, firstly, that, as in the previous tests, making the frequency aspect explicit benefits the older children (but increases the difficulty of the problem for the younger children). Secondly, the shape of the curve for question B indicates two complementary tendencies; the improvement on question A for the older children, which at first appeared equivocal, can be accepted as real.

Test V: In this case, the problem was to notice that the probability of exit at (2) was double that at (1) and (3); ($\frac{1}{4} + \frac{1}{4} = \frac{1}{2}$).

TABLE V

Percentage of correct responses

	Pre-school (%)	7:0–8:3 (%)	9:2–10:5 (%)	11:3–12:10 (%)	13:5–14:5 (%)
Single drop (A)	40	40	40	53	62
Successive drops (B)	54	58	62	68	82

The results (see Table V) are in general poorer than those obtained in test IV. Here also, the percentage of correct responses increases with age, but more markedly than in the previous test, even on question A (the difference between the oldest age-group and the pre-school group is significant: $t = 2.44$, $p < 0.05$). Making frequency explicit (question B) benefited all subjects, but particularly the older ones, so that the difference between the two extreme age-groups is greater ($t = 3.11$, $p < 0.002$).

Test VI (the pagoda): On this last test, subjects were asked only question B. Essentially, they were to indicate where the marble would exit most frequently. It will be recalled that, after the first branching in four directions (each channel therefore having a probability of $\frac{1}{4}$ of receiving the marble) there was a second branching from each of the four initial channels. The four resulting sub-systems of channels were called 'little pagodas'. It is clear that the 3 channels radiating from sphere 1 (or 'little pagoda 1') have the highest probability of receiving the marble ($\frac{1}{4} \times \frac{1}{3} = \frac{1}{12}$), and that the 6 channels radiating from sphere 4 ('little pagoda 4') have the smallest probability ($\frac{1}{4} \times \frac{1}{6} = \frac{1}{24}$).

The correct response would therefore indicate little pagoda 1. But there were also responses which specified a particular channel in this sub-system. Such a response was considered partially correct. Even though the sub-system was correctly chosen, choice of a particular channel showed that only a single path had been taken into consideration. The results are shown in Table VI.

TABLE VI

	Overall total	Little pagoda				Single channel			
		Correct (a)		Incorrect (b)		Partially correct (c)		Incorrect (d)	
		Total	(%)	Total	(%)	Total	%	Total	(%)
Pre-school	50	0	0	3	6	4	8	43	86
7:0–8:3	18	2	11	4	22	2	11	10	56
9:2–10:5	35	9	25	2	6	7	20	17	49
11:3–12:10	43	25	58	10	25	3	7	5	12
13:5–14:5	42	29	69	9	21	0	0	4	10

Responses were divided into the following categories: (a) correct response (correct indication of a little pagoda, without specifying a particular channel); (b) errors consisting of a wrong choice of little pagoda; (c) partially correct responses (choice of a particular channel in the correct sub-system); (d) errors consisting of the choice of a particular channel in the wrong sub-system.

The increase with age of correct responses (a) is spectacular. It is very highly significant. The distribution of partially correct responses (c) takes the form of a concave curve with the maximum at the third age-group (9:2–10:5). The increment in fully correct responses from one age-group to the next is much more significant in this test than in the previous tests.

INTERPRETATION OF RESULTS

1. The pre-school children achieved a high level of correct responses in the tests with equal probabilities; how can this be explained? In our opinion, there are two factors responsible for this. Firstly, there is syncretism characteristic of this age-group. The intuition of equiprobability, which was sufficient in the case concerned, is in fact supported by

a reduced capacity for analysis and a relative indifference to detail. "It can come out anywhere" responds the child, without bothering to scrutinise the situation more closely. The second factor is the relative lack of discrimination in pre-school children between equiprobability as objectively conditioned fact and as subjective whim. Explanations such as the following are very frequent: "That's how the marble wants to go, it goes where it wants". This lack of discrimination leads to a certain indifference as to what other possible determining elements there may be. This is a phenomenon which we have called 'mental symbiosis': a correct, objectively sufficient solution is in fact supported by a motivation properly belonging to a previous stage of development.

2. But what is the explanation of the surprisingly poorer responses among the older children? We believe that the explanation is as follows. The teaching process – particularly as it is determined by schools – orients the child toward a deterministic interpretation of phenomena, in the sense of looking for and explaining in terms of clear-cut, certain, and univocal relations. The child is taught to seek the causes of phenomena in the form of univocally operating factors. Theoretically, the concepts of chance and necessity, certainty and uncertainty are mutually defined and balanced in the course of mental activity. But, in fact, during the intellectual development of the child, this mutual definition and balance are disturbed by the fact that school instruction systematically cultivates only one of these terms. As we have shown, older children often appeal to mechanical-geometric principles, mistakenly of course, to justify their choice of certain paths. The most telling of such responses were in the third test, where a spatial modification to the lay-out which had practically no effect on the probabilities of the situation misled particularly the older children.

The difficulties which Piaget found in children younger than 11–12 in reconciling the stochastic and the determined can be explained, not only with reference to the corresponding stage of intellectual development (that of concrete operations) but mainly, in our view, by the existence of a disequilibrium. The hesitant, oscillating responses of these children – *a type of response which increases with age* – strongly argue in favour of this explanation.

3. We have seen that in the case of problems concerning unequal proba-

bilities, in which the addition and multiplication of probabilities are involved, the frequency of correct responses increases with age. At least
two factors seem to be relevant here. Firstly, in these situations, the child
is not confronted with what would be totally repugnant, namely a complete lack of certainty. The uncertainty which is present in these situations
is compensated for, to a certain extent, by the presence of an option which
is objectively justified: the marble will exit more frequently at one loca-
tion than at another. Thus the child's 'scientific scruples', which are in the
process of being developed, are satisfied. This means something which to
us seems to be of fundamental importance for the whole problem – that
discussion cannot be reduced to a question of *what intellectual resources
are available to the child.* What we are really and specifically concerned
with here is the *orientation of knowledge,* a factor of cognitive 'set', or a
kind of 'mentality' on the intellectual level (which Lévy-Bruhl confounded
with the level of logical operations).

On the other hand, we should also consider, in the situations involving
unequal probabilities, the general level of development of the logical
operations themselves. Correct solutions here imply certain logical constructions which are only gradually elaborated. The path of a marble
exiting at (2) on board V concretises reciprocal exclusion, and the progressive bifurcations concretise logical conjunctions (the event depends on
the realisation of several conditions).

These elements could explain the improvement of performance with
age observed in the tests with unequal probabilities. This improvement
is rather slow, not reaching its peak until the age of 13–14. The explanation of this slowness may be found in the restraining effect of a negative
attitude towards uncertainty. In the case of unequal probabilities, the
random element is part of a larger scheme which has a more salient
quantitative aspect, but it is not totally submerged.

The final consideration which we must take into account emerges from
the data obtained from test VI, the 'pagoda'. Firstly, the sheer complexity
of the problem here, including that of the conformation of the apparatus,
excluded the younger children from the race, and explains, to a certain
extent, the systematic improvement in responses from one age level to the
next. The biggest jump was to the 11:3–12:10 age group, which partly
confirms the conclusions and recommendations of Piaget. But what seems
particularly striking is the following. In choosing one little pagoda out of

four, the child must understand the fact that each of its channels may receive the marble more frequently (or more rarely) than the others. The problem therefore combines two aspects: the option of a unique solution and the admission of equiprobability. The number of subjects responding adequately to both aspects was not greater than chance, except for the two oldest age groups. And this is a result of the fact that, up to the age of 10, the number of children choosing correctly the 'little pagoda' *but specifying a particular channel, is increasing.* All these results seem to confirm the view expressed above. The drop in the number of correct responses in situations involving equiprobability is due to 'cognitive set', and not to a lack of intellectual capacity. If the child's 'scientific scruples' are satisfied (by choosing a *single* group of channels) equiprobability is admitted within the framework of this unique solution. Naturally, this is a situation of conflict, which means that the frequency of correct responses is lower than for the other problems.

The discussion may be summarised thus: the synthesis of the stochastic and the determined, which the concept of probability theoretically presupposes, is to a certain extent prevented by the fact that schools, and the whole intellectual environment of the child, conspire to favour only one of these terms – that of explanation by strict necessity – and create a 'cognitive set' in this direction. The child is gradually and fundamentally convinced that to fully know and understand a phenomenon means referring it to a unique causal relationship. This is a belief which has, in fact, dominated modern scientific thought for centuries, and which is still cultivated in schools. If this explanation is correct, it poses an important educational problem: is it useful for schools to go on cultivating this orientation exclusively, or would it be better to prepare the child early for the synthesis of the possible and the determined by providing familiarisation with stochastic phenomena and the possibilities of 'rationalising' them? We are not only referring here to the introduction of probability calculation to older children – this question has been in principle resolved – but also to the introduction of certain practical and theoretical problems of this type even to very young children.

4. The thesis we have put forward enables us to explain a series of apparently disparate results obtained by other investigators.

(a) Stevenson and Weir (1959, p. 404) found that, where the subject can make one of three possible responses (pressing one of three response buttons) of which one is confirmed with a certain frequency, it is the older children who experiment with non-rewarded buttons, which depresses their performance. This phenomenon, which seems curious, can be explained if it is accepted that the older children are less able to accept randomness (the apparent absence of any determining factors) and, looking for *a rule*, address themselves to the other possibilities with the hope of finding one in relation to them. Since this is not a matter of random responding, but an effect of rationality, of intention, it follows that if a sufficient reward is introduced into the situation the numbers of responses on the rewarded button will decrease, not increase.

(b) Results obtained by Matalon (1959, pp. 61–80) who looked at the behaviour of 5–9 year-old children in stochastic and determined situations, lead to the same conclusion. In a situation with two possible responses and a frequency of confirmation of A is 70% and B is 30% respectively, the youngest children predicted the event in 80% of instances, and the older children in 65%. Of course the strategy which maximises gain is the pure strategy (100% prediction of the most frequently rewarded response). But the pure strategy, although the most useful, implies unconditional surrender to the random.

As in the experiments of Stevenson and Weir, it was predominantly the older children who refused this solution. Among the 23 5 year-old children in this experiment, 5 adopted the pure strategy, while only one among the 17 children aged 8 did so (1959, p. 74). In conjunction with the data of Stevenson and Weir, these data of Matalon's show that older subjects attain a better performance than would be indicated by an attempt at mathematical calculation of expectations, since even in the case of random alternations they succeeded in finding certain useful dependencies in avoiding long series of A or B.

(c) It could be supposed, in accordance with our thesis, that in general, the negative recency effect is an expression of the tendency of the subject to rationalise chance. This effect is very strong in these age groups – particularly at 7 years – (Gratch; Kessen and Kessen; Stevenson and Weir; Gruen and Weir; c.f. Gruen and Weir, 1964, pp. 271–72). *In trying to 'mimic' chance, the subject is really trying to 'rationalise' it.*

(d) It has been found that subjects between 5 and 9 years, and in particular 7 year-olds, show an increasing tendency to stereotyped responses of the form left-centre-right, or vice versa (in reference to the positions of three buttons) (Stevenson and Weir – 1959, pp. 405–406; Gruen and Weir – 1964, p. 270). The percentage of these stereotyped responses decreases with age as the tendency to seek more complex sequences becomes more apparent (Gruen and Weir, 1964, p. 272).

This phenomenon can also be explained as stemming from the inability to accept randomness, and the attempt to find *some* kind of regularity (in fact, really to *impose* a regularity, since the search is not, of course, successful).

(e) Offenbach, who has also investigated matching behaviour, found that older children (9 year-olds) took more account than younger children (5 year-olds) of the confirmation or disconfirmation of the preceding response (1965, p. 957). Brackbill *et al.* (1962, pp. 34–35) found a similar dependency in 8 year-old children. Offenbach (1965, p. 957) was interested to see whether and to what extent children in an experimental situation where event E_2 (25% frequency) was always followed by event E_1 (75% frequency) could learn to predict the order of events (i.e. discover the sequencing rule); succesful prediction would consist of responding A_1 after E_2. The analysis showed that the older children were more receptive to such rules. According to Offenbach, the concept of probability is evidenced precisely in adapting predictions to such sequencing rules, and not in the discrimination of frequencies (c.f. Piaget, 1965, pp. 960–961). Our opinion is that, in such cases, the behaviour of the child does not involve the concept of probability as such, but merely demonstrates the dominant orientation toward univocal relations.*

In conclusion, not only our own results, but also those of several other authors are explained by the thesis which we have outlined here.

The synthesis of the possible and the necessary, of the indeterminate and the determined, which is presupposed by the understanding of probabilistic phenomena, is in reality handicapped by a structural disequilibrium in the mental development of these two components. Under the influence of the teaching process, chance events are rejected as being inexplicable and beyond human control, while univocally determined relations are accepted, sought, even imposed in the form of different attempts to 'rationalise' phenomena.

NOTES

* Reprinted from *Enfance* 2 (1967), 193–206.
* Schiopu (1966) discusses thinking strategies in prediction contexts.

BIBLIOGRAPHY

Brackbill, I., Kappy, M. S., and Starr, R. H.: 1962, 'Magnitude of Reward and Probability Learning', *J. of Exp. Psychol.* **63**, No 1, 32–35.

Goldberg, S.: 1966, 'Probability Judgements by Preschool Children: Task Conditions and Performance', *Child Developm.* **37**, No. 1.

Gruen, G. E. and Weir, M.: 1964, 'Effect of Instructions Penalty and Age on Probability Learning', *Child Developm.* **35**, No. 1, 265–273.

Inhelder, B. and Piaget, J.: 1955, *De la logique de l'enfant à la logique de l'adolescent*, Paris, PUF.

Kass, N.: 1964, 'Risk in Decision Making is a Function of Age, Sex and Probability Preference', *Child Developm.* **35**, No. 2.

Matalon, B.: 1959, 'Apprentissage en situations aléatoires et systématiques', dans *La logique des apprentissages* (*Etudes d'Epistémologie génétique*, Vol. 10), Paris, PUF, 1959, pp. 61–80.

Messik, S. J. and Solley, C. M.: 1957, 'Probability Learning in Children: Some Exploratory Studies', *J. Genet. Psychol.* **90**, 23–32.

Offenbach, S. I.: 1964, 'Studies of Children's Probability Learning Behavior: I. Effect of Reward and Punishment at Two Age Levels', *Child Developm.* **35**, No. 3, 715.

Offenbach, S. I.: 1965, 'Children's Probability Learning Behavior: II. Effect of Method and Event Frequency at Two Age Levels', *Child Developm.* **36**, No. 4, 952–961.

Piaget, J.: 1950, 'Une expérience sur la psychologie du hasard chez l'enfant, le tirage au sort des couples', *Acta psychologica* **7**, 325–336.

Piaget, J. and Inhelder, B.: 1951, *La génèse de l'idée de hasard chez l'enfant*, Paris, PUF.

Schiopu, U.: 1966, 'Operativitatea si strategia gîndirii in situatii de predictie', *Revista de psihologie* **12**, No. 1, 47–59.

Siegel, S. and Andrews, J. M.: 1962, 'Magnitude of Reinforcement and Choice Behavior in Children', *J. of Exp. Psychol.* **63**, No. 4, 337–341.

Stevenson, H. W. and Weir, M. W.: 1962, 'Variables Affecting Children's Performance in a Probability Learning Task', *J. of Exp. Psychol.* **57**, 403–412.

Yost, P., Siegel, A. E., and Andrews, J. M.: 1962, 'Nonverbal Probability Judgements by Young Children', *Child Developm.* **33**, No. 4.

E. FISCHBEIN, ILEANA PAMPU, AND I. MÎNZAT:
COMPARISON OF RATIOS AND THE CHANCE
CONCEPT IN CHILDREN*

ABSTRACT. Children (preschoolers and third-, and sixth-grade pupils) were asked to choose out of 2 sets of marbles of 2 colors the set which they believed offered more chances of drawing a marble of a given color. It was found that a short instruction enabled the third-grade Ss to make their correct decisions, as did the sixth-graders, through a comparison of quantitative ratios.

Yost *et al.* (1962) and Goldberg (1966), following some investigations of Piaget (1950) and Piaget and Inhelder (1951), concluded that preschool children in decision-making situations are able to make appropriate probabilistic judgments. Davies (1965) studied practically the same problem in 3- to 9-year-olds. Using a somewhat different technique, he found that the grasp of the probability concept is a progressive process and that non-verbal probabilistic behaviours precede verbal ones.

In the experiment we devised, a decision-making technique was used in order to study a variety of variables.

(1) In contrast with the aims of Yost *et al.* (1962) and Goldberg (1966), our goal was a systematic exploration of the evolution with age of the three major stages: (*a*) the preoperational (*b*), the concrete operational, and (*c*) the formal operational.

(2) In the technique of Yost *et al.* and of Goldberg, the Ss had to choose between two sets with the same number of chips for one of the two colors (e.g., four blue, one white; four blue, 16 white). We used, as will be seen, three categories of trials in order to extend the scope of our investigation.

(3) Since all the above-mentioned experiments were limited to the investigation of spontaneous behavior, we thought it of interest to study the effects of *prior systematic instruction.*

(4) We also intended to examine differences between sexes in performance, as this is still a controversial point (Davies, 1965; Pire, 1958).

(5) Finally, our aim was to study the influence of the total number of marbles, in either set, on the correctness of the response.

In preliminary experiments we noticed that Ss tended to estimate chance by using ratios of the form W_1/B_1 and W_2/B_2, rather than $W_1/(W_1+B_1)$

and $W_2/(W_2 + B_2)$ (W_1 and B_1, W_2 and B_2 stand for the number of white and black marbles in the first and second boxes, respectively). The mathematical concept of probability takes the form $W/(W + B)$ (the number of expected cases/the total number of equally possible cases). Since the response is the same (in the kind of trials we have used), it was acceptable that the children continue to use the same procedure. Therefore, we shall henceforth refer to *chance* and not to the probability concept.

METHOD

The Ss were at three age levels: preschool children (from 5–0 to 6–4), third-graders (from 9–0 to 10–0) and sixth-graders (from 12–4 to 13–7); they were selected from among pupils of various Bucharest kindergartens and schools.

The three groups consisted of 60 Ss each, divided into three subgroups of 20, corresponding to the three experimental conditions I_1, I_2, I_3 (see Procedure). Each subgroup comprised an equal number of boys and girls.

The experimental groups were equivalent with respect to school achievement as measured by school marks. Only Ss with marks ranging from 6 to 10 were selected, thus excluding those who failed in their school tasks.

The Trials

The Ss, seen individually, were presented with 18 problems, structured as shown in Table I. Each figure represents the number of marbles of one color in either box.

The problems were devised according to the following criteria: Nine were basic trials (the small sets, left column), and nine (the large sets, right column) were obtained by multiplying by two each element of the first nine.

The 18 trials also fell into three categories with the following structure: In C_1 the choice was facilitated by the structure of the ratios to be compared. Thus in trials 1, 2, 3, and 4 there was an equal number of marbles of the same color in the two boxes (e.g., one white with two black and five white with two black). In trials 5 and 6, one of the boxes contained the same number of white and black marbles (i.e., two white two black marbles and four white four black). In the C_2 category of trials no restriction was imposed. In C_3 trials the ratios to be compared were equal; thus

TABLE I

Description of trials

		Small sets		Large sets
C_1	(1)	1/2:5/2	(2)	2/4:10/4
	(3)	3/1:3/2	(4)	6/2:6/4
	(5)	2/2:6/3	(6)	4/4:12/6
C_2	(7)	6/2:10/5	(8)	12/4:20/10
	(9)	2/1:5/2	(10)	4/2:10/4
	(11)	4/2:5/3	(12)	8/4:10/6
C_3	(13)	2/4:1/2	(14)	4/8:2/4
	(15)	3/1:6/2	(16)	6/2:12/4
	(17)	4/2:2/1	(18)	8/4:4/2

the correct decision was: "We have the same chance of drawing a marble of a given color from either box."

The trials were balanced to prevent any possible artifact.

Out of the 18 trials, in six the correct response consisted in pointing to the box on the right side; in six, in pointing to the left box; and in the last six, in stating the equivalence. In the first 12 trials the number of marbles of a given color in one of the boxes, out of which the expected marble had to be randomly drawn, was smaller, equal to, or larger than that of the marbles of different color in the same box or the number of marbles of the same color in the other box. In this way it was impossible for the S to give correct responses relying on a criterion other than the proportion estimate.

We utilized black and white marbles placed in plastic boxes (8 cm in diameter). In each of the experimental groups half of the 20 Ss were to draw a white marble and the other half a black one, the problem remaining practically the same (for instance, if to draw a white marble the trial was 2 W/2 B:6 W/3 B, to draw a black marble it became 2 B/2 W:6 B/3 W). On the other hand, within each subgroup of 10 Ss the position of the favorable box was changed; thus 2 W/2 B on the left and 6 W/3 B on the right for five Ss was changed to 6 W/3 B on the left and 2 W/2 B on the right for the other five. The purpose was always the same, namely, to remove any possible artifact. *The problems were presented in random order.*

Procedure

At each of the three age levels, three instructional conditions were used. Under each condition a different group of 20 Ss was investigated. All three instructional variants began in the same manner: "Here is a nice little guessing game with black and white marbles (the child counts the marbles). Now, you see these two boxes; take a good look at them, for I'll cover them and then you'll have to draw a marble from one. You are expected to draw a white marble (or black, according to the model used). But before the boxes are covered you have to decide from which box, the left or the right one, you feel you are more likely to get the white marble without looking. Or, maybe, you feel equally sure; I mean, you feel that the chance for you to get a white marble is the same with either box."

Further instructions specific to each of the three variants were given thereafter.

Under the I_1 condition we merely illustrated the three possible reponses. The problems used for this purpose were other than the 18 mentioned above. The situation in which the left-hand box had to be chosen was illustrated by the 10 B/2 W and 3 B/8 W pair of ratios (if a black marble was expected). If the right-hand box had to be chosen, the 5 B/4 W and 4 B/1 W pair was presented. For equal ratios the 2 B/2 W and 1 B/1 W pair was shown. The S was first required to choose the box himself. If his answer was correct, it was verbally reinforced. If the response was wrong, the E indicated the correct one. Finally, the three possible responses were summed up: (a) the right, (b) the left, and (c) same chance with either box.

Under the I_2 and I_3 conditions our aim was to instruct the Ss systematically on a solving procedure. The instruction was devised in such a way that it did not involve the arithmetic concept of ordinary fractions, unknown to preschool Ss and insufficiently known to third-graders. The main point we intended to make clear to the S was that chance could not be estimated by relying only on the number of favorable cases. The whole content of the box had to be considered. During the instruction we followed the manner in which the children were spontaneously coping with the task, that is, comparing the favorable cases with the unfavorable ones.

Let us remember that for any of the three (I_1, I_2, I_3) conditions the experiment was carried out on different groups of Ss.

Under the I_2 condition the instruction was given in two stages: (a)

Boxes were presented containing 4 B/1 W and 8 B/2 W marbles. The S drew 20 times from each box. It was noted that black marbles were drawn from either box four times as frequently as white ones. (We always managed to have the trial develop in this way in order to avoid complicated explanations. Yet we stated: "It doesn't always turn out so exactly.") The conclusion, therefore, was that the chance to draw a black marble was the same with either box. (b) Next, the S was instructed how to use a grouping technique to answer questions. Thus, assuming that we had 4 B/1 W and 8 B/2 W, the right-box marbles could be grouped as follows: 4 B/1 W + 4 B/1 W; so the S was just as likely to draw a black marble from the right as from the left box. Assuming we had 4 B/1 W and 9 B/2 W, by grouping it was possible to bring out the surplus of black marbles in the right box.

Under the I_3 condition, the instruction technique consisted only in illustrating the grouping procedures leading to the solution. For any of the three alternatives, examples and cues to the solution were given: (a) 2 B/1 W and 4 B/2 W, equal chances; (b) 2 B/1 W and 5 B/2 W, more chances on the right side; (c) 4 B/1 W and 6 B/2 W, more chances on the left side (i.e., left box: four black marbles to one white; right box: three black to one white).

Under any of the three conditions – I_1, I_2, I_3 – the winning color during the instruction was the same as that to be used throughout the 18 trials.

A full description of the instruction technique would take too much space; so we have confined ourselves to describing the essential aspects. Actually, a complete standardization was not possible in view not only of the ages but also of the individual characteristics of the children. Each S was seen individually over a session lasting from 30 to 60 minutes (according to the S's age). With younger children we had one or two breaks during the experiment.

Under the three experimental conditions – I_1, I_2, I_3 – the Ss were informed at first that if they scored a sufficient number of correct responses, they would be rewarded (toys, pencils, india rubbers, etc.). This minimum number of correct responses certainly varied with age: 12 for preschool children, 16 for third-graders, and 18 for sixth-graders. Throughout the experiment the prizes were set on the table before the S, who at the end, was allowed to choose what he liked best. After each of the 18 trials the response was confirmed (or not) by the E.

Experimental Design

The research was devised as a $3 \times 3 \times 3$ factorial design – three age levels, three instructional conditions, and three categories of trials with repeated measures of the last factor (the same Ss). In all, there were 180 Ss. As the number of boys and girls was the same in any of the nine groups, we could perform a preliminary analysis with 10 Ss in a group taking into account the factors of sex (two), age (three) and instruction (three) and disregarding the type of trial.

RESULTS

Means of correct responses according to age, sex, and instructional conditions are shown in table 2. A global, preliminary analysis of variance taking into consideration the three factors 2 (sex) $\times$ 3 (age) $\times$ 3 (instructional conditions) (see Table II) revealed only two main significant effects: age, for which $F(2.162) = 203.18$, $p < 0.001$; and instructional conditions, for which $F(2.162) = 16.13$, $p < 0.001$ (further reference will be made to

TABLE II

Means of correct responses according to age, sex, and instructional conditions

Age level	I_1			I_2			I_3		
	Boys	Girls	Both	Boys	Girls	Both	Boys	Girls	Both
Preschool	8.00	7.90	7.95	9.00	9.30	9.15	8.30	8.60	8.45
Third grade	10.7	10.6	10.65	14.8	12.9	13.85	14.6	12.0	13.30
Sixth grade	14.90	15.30	15.10	17.20	16.50	16.85	17.60	16.90	17.25

these data). The factor of sex was found to be nonsignificant $(F[1.162] = 3.15)$, and so were all the interactions.

In a further analysis the factor of sex was disregarded. The data have been reorganized according to the following factors: age, instructional conditions, and categories of trials $(3 \times 3 \times 3)$. Table III shows the means of correct responses.

An analysis of variance of the above data with repeated measures on the last factor (trial category) was performed. The summary of this analysis is given in table 4.

As regards the factors of age and instructional conditions the data differ slightly from those found in the previous analysis. This small difference is due to the fact that the error was computed on the basis of a different arrangement of scores.

The factor *age* is highly significant, and inspection of Tables I and II reveals an increasing number of correct responses from younger to older children. The factor *instruction* also is highly significant. Altogether, under the I_2 and I_3 conditions the results were better than those obtained under the I_1 condition. The third factor (category of trial) is also highly significant. The data in Table II show important differences in the results obtained for each category of trial, especially in preschool children and thirdgraders

TABLE III

Means of correct responses according to instructional conditions, age, and trial category

Age level	Instructional condition and category of trial								
	I_1			I_2			I_3		
	C_1	C_2	C_3	C_1	C_2	C_3	C_1	C_2	C_3
Preschool	4.25	2.70	1.00	4.35	2.70	2.10	3.90	2.80	1.75
Third grade	5.05	2.65	2.95	5.35	4.00	4.50	5.45	3.50	4.35
Sixth grade	5.65	4.55	4.90	5.85	5.35	5.65	5.70	5.65	5.90

TABLE IV

Analysis of variance for scores tabulated per category of trials

Source	Sum of squares	df	Variance estimate	F
Between subjects	950.33	179	–	–
Age	621.74	2	310.87	199.27 [b]
Instruction	49.36	2	24.68	15.82 [b]
Age × instruction	11.95	4	2.98	1.91 (N.S.)
Subjects within groups	267.28	171	1.56	–
Within subjects	718.34	360	–	–
Categories of trials	215.83	2	107.91	99.92 [b]
Age × categories of trials	104.05	4	26.01	24.08 [b]
Instruction × categories of trials	19.53	4	4.88	4.52 [a]
Age × instruction × trials	7.96	8	0.99	< 1
Category of trials × subjects within groups	370.97	342	1.08	–

[a] $p < 0.01$.
[b] $p < 0.001$.

The age × trial interaction is highly significant. Indeed, progress from one age to another is not parallel with respect to the three categories of trial. The most important changes produced by age are revealed by C_3 trials (equal ratios), whereas the changes observed on C_1 trials are the slightest. Therefore, C_3 trials may be considered as indicators of the level of intellectual development.

The instruction × trial interaction is also significant. Instruction, usually, is not of equal advantage to Ss in the three types of trials. An increase in the number of correct responses was noted especially with C_2 and C_3 trials. In C_1 trials the instruction, as was to be expected, did not produce important changes. The number of correct responses on C_1 trials was, even without instruction, much above the chance level $(=2)$ for any of the three age levels because of the simplicity of the problem.

The age × instruction interaction was not significant; yet it approached the significance level 0.05. Apparently, Ss at any of the three age levels drew approximately the same advantage from instruction. The apparently similar profiles are, in fact, only masking structural differences.

Preschool children gave, under the I_1 condition, a number of correct responses on C_3 trials which was definitely inferior to the chance level ($\bar{M} = 1$). This may be accounted for by the fact that, even with equal ratios, preschool children systematically estimate the chances to be unequal because of the global, perceptual difference between the number of marbles in the two boxes.

Following instruction (under I_2 and I_3) the mean number of correct responses increased. Actually, by this increase preschool children only reached the chance level. So, from *systematic errors they shifted to randomly correct or wrong responses*. On C_2 trials the instruction did not improve the responses in preschool children.

Twelve-year-old Ss significantly improved their responses following instruction. Thus C_2 $(I_1 : I_2)$, $t = 2.22$, $p < 0.05$; C_2 $(I_1 : I_3)$, $t = 3.14$, $p < 0.01$; C_3 $(I_1 : I_2)$, $t = 2.20$, $p < 0.05$; and C_3 $(I_1 : I_3)$, $t = 3.22$, $p < 0.01$. But this was only a quantitative and not an essential improvement, as the Ss in question, regardless of the type of trial, also gave spontaneously (I_1) a mean number of correct responses which placed them above the chance level.

The most important change brought about by instruction was noted in 9- to 10-year-old Ss. With C_2 and C_3 trials (where the correct comparisons required the explicit estimation of two ratios and therefore the concept of proportionality) these Ss shifted from almost blind to systematically correct responses. Thus for C_2 $((I_1:I_2)$, $t=3.21$, $p<0.01$; C_2 $(I_1:I_3)$, $t=2.43$, $p<0.02$; C_3 $(I_1:I_2)$, $t=3.16$, $p<0.01$; and C_3 $(I_1:I_3)$, $t=3.11$, $p<0.01$.

A comparison of the effects produced by I_2 and I_3 conditions did not reveal any significant difference at any of the three age levels.

Small Sets and Large Sets

Table V shows the mean number of correct responses separately for large and small sets and as a function of age.

As may be seen from Table V, the differences between small and large sets are rather slight. By applying Wilcoxon's test for correlated samples, we found that only two out of the nine pairs exhibited significant differences: preschool children, I_3 condition $(N'=N-13=17$; $T=21$, $p<0.01)$; and third-grade Ss under the same I_3 condition $(N'=N-7=13$; $T=16$, $p<0.05)$.

Learning during the Experiment

The experimental design enabled us to test the extent to which the Ss were improving their responses by training over the 18 trials. The data discussed above have referred to reactions grouped per category of trial, irrespective of the actual, random succession in time in which the trials were given to the Ss. The initial values for each experimental group (defined by age and instructional condition) were again taken and added in

TABLE V

The means of correct responses for small and large sets

Age level	I_1		I_2		I_3	
	Small sets	Large sets	Small sets	Large sets	Small sets	Large sets
Preschool	8.77	8.88	10.55	9.77	10.77	8.00
					$p<0.01$	
Third grade	11.66	12.00	15.22	15.55	14.11	15.44
					$p<0.05$	
Sixth grade	16.42	17.22	18.77	18.66	19.22	19.11

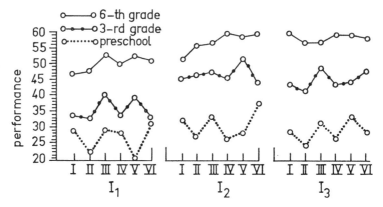

Fig. 1.   Graphs representing the number of correct responses successively obtained
(each value represents a block of three trials).

the random order of presentation, irrespective of the category of trial.

We then grouped the values obtained into six blocks of three trials each. The curves in figure 1 illustrate the chronological order of the performances for each of the nine experimental groups.

A slight increase may be noted in a few cases only. In order to estimate the extent to which this trend was significant, we utilized Page's (1963) test, which, however, required elimination of the blocks 3 and 4 (so each of the remaining four columns corresponded to four possible values: 0, 1, 2, and 3, namely, the possible number of correct responses in one block). The critical value for four treatments and 20 Ss is 522 – as indicated in Page's tables; it was never reached, however, which means that in no group was it possible to demonstrate any significant improvement from trial to trial during the experimental session.

Verbal Reports on Solving Procedures

After each trial the Ss were asked to account for their responses. A preliminary examination suggested the following types of solution procedures used by the Ss: (a) Choice was based on a simple binary comparison (for instance, "I chose this box because there are more black marbles here than in the other box"). (b) The reasoning took into account all four terms, but the numerical ratios were not indicated (for instance, "Here it is easier to pick a white marble for there are more white than black marbles as compared with the other box"). (c) Both ratios are considered, and their numerical relations are set forth explicitly for instance. "In this box there are three times and in the other two times more black than white marbles").

In order to establish for each S the category into which he was falling, we used the following criterion: if S indicated at least 12 (out of the 18 possible) procedures of a category, he was placed in that category. If he failed to attain this criterion, he was placed in the 'transition' category.

The statements of type (b) were very infrequent and never reached the criterion established. Consequently, only the following categories were left: (1) comparison reduced to one ratio, (2) transitional stage, and (3) correct comparison of the numerical ratios. The data in Table VI show the number of Ss per type of procedure, grouped according to age and instructional conditions.

In preschool children the first type of solution procedure was evidently predominant. Under the I_2 and I_3 conditions some changes did occur; yet the first type was still prevalent. Here, as was to be expected, the third type never appeared. A χ^2 test did not reveal any significant differences between either I_1 and I_2 or I_1 and I_3 conditions.

In third-graders and under the I_1 condition the first type of procedure

TABLE VI

Number of subjects classified according to solving procedures

Type of solution procedure	Instructional conditions		
	I_1	I_2	J_3
Preschool:			
I	19	14	15
II	1	6	5
III	0	0	0
Third grade:			
I	15	1	0
II	5	2	8
III	0	17	12
Sixth grade:			
I	2	0	0
II	5	0	0
III	13	20	20

was still predominant, but under the I_2 and I_3 instructional conditions a shift toward the third type occurred. We utilized the Kolomogorov-Smirnov test to evaluate the change that the instructional conditions brought about in the distribution of the procedure types. For $I_1:I_2$, N being equal to 20, $K_D = 17$, $p < 0.01$. For $I_1:I_3$, $N = 20$, $K_D = 15$, $p < 0.01$. *So, in third-graders a short systematic instruction induced significant shifts of procedure toward the superior type* (explicit statement of numerical relationships).

In sixth-graders the third type was predominant from the outset; yet the I_2 and I_3 instructional conditions caused all the Ss to turn to this type of procedure. However, the Kolomogorov-Smirnov test did not reveal any significant differences.

Comparisons were also made between different age levels under the same instructional condition.

Under the I_1 condition, the difference between preschool children and third-graders was not significant, whereas that between third- and sixth-graders was $(N = 20, K_D = 13, p < 0.01)$. Under the I_2 and I_3 conditions the difference between preschool children and third-graders become significant. Under I_2 (preschool:third grade), $N = 20$, $K_D = 17$, $p < 0.01$. On the other hand under both I_2 and I_3 the difference between third- and sixth-graders was not significant.

Thus, in preschool children, judgments based on simple binary relations were prevalent, while most of the sixth-grade children based their decisions on explicit correct estimations (relations between ratios). Instruction did not produce essential changes at these levels. *In third-grade pupils the spontaneous type of solution procedure was of much the same kind as that expressed by preschool children; instruction, however, produced a shift toward the the sixth-grade pupils' solution procedure.*

DISCUSSION

(1) Our data confirm the finding that preschool children can correctly understand and cope with situations involving chance, and that this is a progressive phenomenon. What may account for the preschool Ss' ability to give correct responses, certainly under the simpler conditions of C_1 trials, when, generally, they cannot do elementary calculations? It is possible to assume that their responses are based on spontaneous perceptual sampling. This assumption is supported by our finding that the responses

do not differ significantly in the case of large (requiring harder calculations) and small marble sets. This hypothesis is also in agreement with the results obtained by Ginsburg and Rapoport (1967) showing that 6- to 11-year-olds' estimates of proportions are correct.

(2) Our data show that 9- to 10-year-old Ss' spontaneous responses scarcely differed from those of preschool children; however, following a brief systematic instruction, their responses became comparable with those of 12- to 13-year-old Ss. They became able to estimate chances by comparing the ratios correctly.

Piaget and Inhelder (1951) concluded that such a twofold comparison – including the proportionality concept – is accessible only at the formal operational stage. The conclusions of these authors, however, were based only on spontaneous responses. What might account, however, for the spectacular effect which was produced by instruction and which seems to contradict the law of stages?

A first hypothesis is that 9- to 10-year-olds' responses on C_2 and C_3 trials were wrong only because they had not been trained before. Indeed, if a mental structure existed, it would have to manifest itself either spontaneously or following an inductive process (admitting, like Piaget and Gréco [see Gréco, 1959], that "induction is the application of deduction to experience"). Preparative instruction under I_2 and I_3 conditions might have played the part of eliciting the mental mechanisms in question.

This hypothesis is, however, contradicted by our finding that although the Ss received feedback concerning the correctness of each of their responses they did not exhibit any progress over the 18 trials.

A second hypothesis is that the data now available in genetic psychology with regard to the difficulty of accelerating the transition to a higher developmental stage refer mostly to the transition from the intuitive to the concrete operational stage. Would it not be reasonable to assume that during the process of mental development the differences between the successive stages are gradually reduced? If so, instruction might be able to set up structures corresponding to formal operations already at the concrete operational stage with much greater ease and more stability than would be the case for the transition from the preoperational to the operational stage.

In any case, the finding that 9- to 10-year-old Ss, after a brief instruction, become able to perform chance estimates by comparing numerical ratios and to understand the concept of proportionality might be an argument for starting to teach probabilities while children are still in primary school.

NOTE

* Reprinted from *Child Development* **41** (1970), 377–389.

BIBLIOGRAPHY

Davies, Carolyn M.: 1965, 'Development of the Probability Concept in Children', *Child Development* **36**, 779–788.

Ginsburg, H. and Rapoport, A.: 1967, 'Children's Estimate of Proportions', *Child Development* **38**, 205–212.

Goldberg, S.: 1966, 'Probability Judgments by Preschool Children: Task Conditions and Performance', *Child Development* **37**, 157–167.

Gréco, P.: 1959, 'Induction, déduction et apprentissage', in *La logique des apprentissages* (*Etudes d'épistemologie génétique*, Vol. 10), Presses Universitaires de France, Paris, p. 6.

Page, E. B.: 1963, 'Ordered Hypotheses for Multiple Treatments: A Significance Test for Linear Ranks', *Journal of the American Statistical Association* **58**, 216–230.

Piaget, J.: 1950, 'Une expérience sur la psychologie du hasard chez l'enfant – le tirage au sort des couples', *Acta Psychologica* **7**, 323–336.

Piaget, J., Inhelder, Bärbel: 1951, *La genèse de l'idée de hasard chez l'enfant*, Presses Universitaires de France, Paris.

Pire, G.: 1958, 'Notion du hasard et développement intellectuel', *Enfance* **2**, 131–143.

Yost, Patricia, Siegel, Alberta, and Andrews, Julia: 1962, 'Nonverbal Probability Judgments by Young Children', *Child Development* **33**, 769–780.

E. FISCHBEIN, ILEANA PAMPU, AND I. MÎNZAT:
EFFECTS OF AGE AND INSTRUCTION
ON COMBINATORY ABILITY IN CHILDREN*

ABSTRACT. The aim of the study was to investigate the effect of direct instruction on the ability to handle permutations and arrangements, as an example of a problem at the level of formal operations. 60 Bucharest school children, 20 aged 10 years, 20 aged 12 and 20 aged 14, tested individually, were first asked to estimate the number of possible permutations with 3, 4 and 5 objects. Results showed that these subjective estimates improved with age, with a threshold (or marked improvement) at age 12, though there was serious underestimating at all ages. A step-by-step teaching strategy using generative 'tree diagrams' was then used. Even the 10-year-olds learned the use of the tree diagrams and the appropriate procedures for permutations and arrangements.

I. INTRODUCTION

Previous studies have demonstrated that children at different age levels can adequately use the concept of probability. According to some authors (Yost *et al.*, 1962; Siegel and McAndrews, 1962; Goldman and Denny, 1963; Davies, 1965; Fischbein *et al.*, 1967, 1969) judgments even in pre-school children may involve the idea of probability (or, at least, of chance). According to other authors (Piaget and Inhelder, 1951; Offenbach, 1964, 1965) the concept of probability can be used only after the age of 7 years; between 7 and 12 years of age it can be used only in concrete situations; later, at the formal-operational stage, it becomes an abstract general strategy (i.e., the capacity to consider all the alternatives conceivable in a given situation). However, in previous papers we reported that the process may be greatly accelerated by systematic instruction (Fischbein *et al.*, 1969, 1970).

We realised, however, that we had to consider also the possibility of developing by instruction the combinatory ability at the formal-operational stage. Piaget and Inhelder's data demonstrate, in fact, only combinatory potentialities in adolescents; the question that concerned us was to find out whether such potentialities could be actualized by specific instruction.

According to Piaget and Inhelder (1951, 1955) the development of combinatory ability can be related to the well-known stages described by their theory: at the pre-operational level, the absence of any systematic strategy which would permit an exhaustive inventory of possibilities; at the concrete-operational level, the search for a system and the acquisition by the child of partial results; and, finally, at the formal-operational level, i.e., after 12 to 13 years of age, the progressive discovery of a strategy.

This conclusion does not exactly fit the facts. Firstly, according to the authors quoted, only some subjects discover at this age the procedure of combinatory construction (1951, p. 183). We do not know what proportion do so, nor what happens with the others. Tasks involving arrangements are not mastered before the age of 13. In the case of permutation, though it seems to be a simpler operation, Piaget and Inhelder (1951, p. 189) showed that subjects did not discover a procedure before the age of 14 or 15. Secondly, the responses obtained by these authors cannot be considered spontaneous (or resulting from the general experience of the child), because their investigatory technique included a certain amount of implicit instruction. (For instance, the subject is successively questioned about the number of permutations obtainable with two, three and four different objects. This gradual amplification is itself instructive). Such analysis suggests two hypotheses: (a) at the formal operational stage combinatory ability is still developing, even though, theoretically, formal operations should be regarded as acquired; (b) this process is likely to be accelerated by systematic instruction.

The close connection between combinatory ability and some characteristics of logical thinking – i.e., reversibility, composition, ability to inventory the possibilities in a given situation – has suggested to some authors the use of combinatory activities for testing the intelligence level (Claparède, in Dubosson, 1957; Longeot, 1967). The use of combinatory tests at different age levels (Dubosson with ages 5 to 9 and Longeot with 9 to 16-year-olds) showed a tendency for the responses to improve with age. Longeot studied, in addition, the effect of a mathematically mediated instruction, i.e., the effect of learning the cartesian product on solving permutation tests.

The present study was designed mainly to investigate systematically *the effect of direct instruction* upon combinatorial ability (arrangements and permutations) in children and adolescents.* Within this context we thought it of interest to examine also the opposite aspect of the phenomenon, i.e., the *spontaneous subjective estimation* of the number of permutations possible with three, four and five objects. Naturally, within each experimental session the subjective estimation was tested first, passing on afterwards to the requirement of a systematic inventory based on an explicit strategy.

II. METHODS AND RESULTS

Subjects were pupils in the fourth grade (ages 10:3 to 11:5) sixth grade (ages 12:2 to 13:4) and eighth grade (ages 14:0 to 15:2), enrolled in public schools of Bucharest, 20 subjects for each of the three age levels.

The materials consisted of letters and numbers printed on small cards, coloured geometric figures cut out in cardboard (squares, triangles, ellipses).

Within the same experimental session we investigated: (a) the subjective estimation of the number of permutations; (b) the acquisition of a systematic strategy in reckoning the number of outcomes (arrangements and permutations). The details of procedure and the results concerning the two aspects investigated will be presented separately. The subjects were tested individually.

(a) *Subjective Estimation*

Procedure. The letters A, B, C were set on the table. By way of example, the child was shown that, by altering the position of the letters, he could obtain various groups (permutations) and he was asked to estimate how many permutations were possible with the three letters, then with the three numbers and three figures. The procedure with four and then with five letters, numbers and figures was the same.

Results. The mean values and the standard deviation of the subjects'

TABLE I

Means and standard deviations of subjective estimations of number of permutations possible with 3, 4 and 5 objects

Grade	Three letters		Four letters		Five letters	
	M	sd	M	sd	M	sd
IV	4.30	1.95	6.70	3.74	9.10	6.32
VI	5.50	2.09	9.85	4.03	14.65	7.23
VII	5.30	1.68	9.60	4.36	16.05	8.02

responses for letters, numbers and geometrical figures were almost identical. Therefore, Table I shows the results with letters only.

As these responses are to be judged against the correct values obtained by calculations, we present in Table II the relative values obtained by dividing the mean values of Table I by 6 for P_3, 24 for P_4 and 120 for P_5.

TABLE II

Means and standard deviations of subjective estimations relative values, of number of permutations possible with 3, 4 and 5 objects

Grade	Three letters		Four letters		Five letters	
	M	sd	M	sd	M	sd
IV	0.71	0.32	0.28	0.16	0.07	0.05
VI	0.91	0.35	0.41	0.17	0.12	0.06
VIฦ	0.87	0.28	0.40	0.18	0.13	0.06

An analysis of variance was performed with two factors, i.e., age and number of objects (3×3), on the data summarised in Table II (with repeated measures on the factor *number of objects*). The category of elements (letters, numbers, figures) was no longer considered in view of the very close values. The result of this analysis shows that the *age* factor is significant $(F = 3.89, df = 2/57, P < 0.05)$ and that the number-of-elements factor is highly significant $(F = 268.80, df = 2/114, P < 0.001)$. The interaction is not significant.

Inspection of the data led us to the following findings: there is a general tendency towards *under-rating the number of possible permutations. The underrating is more significant the larger the number of objects considered.* While for P_3 the values indicated by subjects are as high as 80–90% of the correct number, for P_5 the under-rating is striking. While there is improvement with age, in fact only the age of 12 years (6th grade) represents an evident threshold. Thus, on testing the significance of the discrepancy in mean values obtained in fourth- and sixth-graders (data in Table I) we obtain: for P_3, $t = 1.93$, $P \simeq 0.05$; for P_4, $t = 2.76$, $P < 0.01$; for P_5, $t = 4.86$, $P < 0.001$. On comparing the sixth- with the eighth-graders we did not note any significant difference for P_3 and P_4. For P_5 $t = 1.86$, P just short of

0.05. For P_5 there was an improvement even from age 12 to age 14, which was not the case with either P_3 or P_4. It is thus reasonable to assume that age differences become wider as the number of objects considered increases.

(b) *The Effects of Instruction*

Two guiding principles were followed in the design of this stage of the experiment session:

(a) We felt that some techniques of programmed instruction might be combined with some of learning by discovery; we thus devised a procedure which we termed *instruction by programmed discovery*. The whole process of instruction was divided into sequences according to the following criteria: (i) each sequence started with a question which it was possible for the subject to answer by himself, and this enabled him to solve by himself all the subsequent elements of the sequence; (ii) after solving a sequence, the subject became able to solve the next one by transfer and generalisation.

(b) In a previous paper we formulated the following hypothesis: by learning a concept the pupil builds a variety of diagrammatic models which are implicit, in that they escape conscious check-up by the conceptual network. Such implicit figural patterns may become a source of errors. It is desirable, therefore, that the process should be systematically guided by the teacher so that the pattern established should be correct and should lend itself to conscious control and handling. In fact, such a model may be considered a generative one, in view of its self-proliferating property. The figural pattern used in this experiment was that of tree diagrams currently used in probability reasoning.

Procedure. Arrangements of two different objects in groups of three. The letters A and B were introduced into a small opaque bag. S was asked to draw from it three times, *replacing each time the previously drawn letter*, and to write down the group obtained. E: 'How many such groups, different from one another, may be obtained?" After S had answered he was asked to write down the groups he expected to draw from the bag. E: "Couldn't we find out all the possible groups more easily, I mean by a method? Go ahead, try!" E: "Which is the letter that you expect to draw first?" If S fails to answer, E indicates the response: "Either A or B." Next, we proceeded in the same way with the second draw, obtaining in this way two-letter groups that S had to read. E: "Let's think further; let's draw the third time."

We thus obtained the sequences shown in Figure 1.

The dotted circles are what might be called the *nodal moments* of the process. These nodal moments actually mark the steps of understanding.

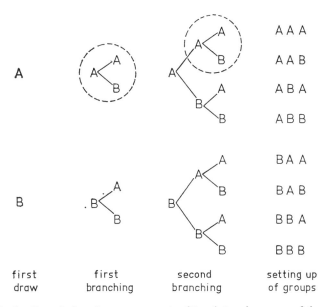

| | first draw | first branching | second branching | setting up of groups |

Fig. 1. Steps in learning arrangements of two letters in groups of three.

Each moment is indicated by a question designed to arouse, by a limited generalisation, the leap toward the succeeding step in the process of constructive thinking. After building the diagram S has to interpret it, writing down the groups obtained. The last questions are designed to guide S to the computing formula. E: "Couldn't we get this result by a simple computation? Let's examine the diagram." When S fails to pass directly from the diagram to computation, he is reminded of the principle of construction: "We had two alternatives at first. Either was followed by two more and so forth..."

Arrangements of two different objects in groups of four. The subject was asked *to compute* the number of possibilities in arranging two objects in

groups of four *without turning to the diagram*. If he failed, he was asked
to build first the diagram from which he was then to infer the solution.

Permutations. The letters, A, B, C were put in the bag and mixed and
the subject was asked to draw one letter at a time *without putting back the
preceding one*. The subject, who already knew the term *permutation* from
the beginning of the session (subjective estimations), wrote down the
groups thus formed. He was asked to write also the groups he expected
to draw. Next, he was asked to use, as in the previous task, a method. In
principle, the instructional technique used by the experimenter was the
same as that previously used with arrangements. The diagram-construc-
tion steps are shown in Figure 2.

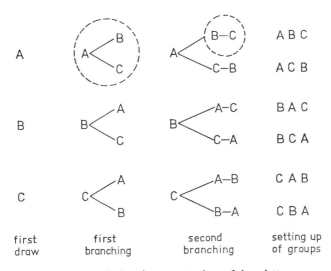

| first draw | first branching | second branching | setting up of groups |

Fig. 2.   Steps in learning permutations of three letters.

After the diagram was built, the subject was asked to determine the
value of P_3 by computation. Subsequently he had to compute the P_4. If
he failed he was asked to build the diagram first, computing afterwards.
The final question required computation of P_5. The basic idea of the instructional procedure is that a proper alternation between diagrammatic
intuitive techniques and abstract synthesizing concepts stimulates the
pupil's mental activities and thereby leads to structural acquisitions.

TABLE III

Successes in arrangements of two letters in groups of three
S: number of subjects solving unassisted
S + E: number of subjects solving with minimum hints from experimenter.
E: solution indicated by experimenter.
*: hints necessary only for diagram construction.
**: hints necessary only for computation.

Grade	Arrangements of two letters in groups of three								
	Diagram Construction						Computation		
	First branching		Second branching		Setting up of groups		Solution by computation		
	S	E	S	E	S	S+E	S	S+E	E
IV	$2_{(10)}$	$18_{(90)}$	$7_{(35)}$	$13_{(65)}$	$13_{(65)}$	$7_{(35)}$	$9_{(45)}$	$10_{(50)}$	$1_{(5)}$
VI	$0_{(0)}$	$20_{(100)}$	$13_{(65)}$	$7_{(35)}$	$18_{(90)}$	$2_{(10)}$	$8_{(40)}$	$8_{(40)}$	$4_{(20)}$
VIII	$7_{(35)}$	$13_{(65)}$	$14_{(70)}$	$6_{(30)}$	$16_{(80)}$	$4_{(20)}$	$12_{(60)}$	$7_{(35)}$	$1_{(5)}$

Grade	Arrangements of two letters in groups of four					
	I Computation / II Diagram		I Diagram / II Computation		Failure	
	S	S+E*	S	S+E**	Computation	Diagram
IV	$15_{(75)}$	$2_{(10)}$	$1_{(5)}$	$1_{(5)}$	$1_{(5)}$	–
VI	$17_{(85)}$	–	$1_{(5)}$	$1_{(5)}$	–	$1_{(5)}$
VIII	$19_{(95)}$	–	–	$1_{(5)}$	–	–

Results. The results are summarised in Tables III (arrangements) and IV (permutations).

On the basis of the data set out in Tables III and IV the following can be stated:

(a) Pupils assimilate the model of the tree diagram during the first phase of the experimental session (arrangement of two different letters in groups of three). An improvement is to be noted, from sequence to sequence, for each of the three age levels, which confirms the principal effect pursued by the learning-by-discovery method, i.e., *the ability to transfer by generalisation the previously acquired skills.*

(b) The solving by computation ($2 \times 2 \times 2$), however, appears spontaneously only in few subjects after the first diagram has been drawn. Even

TABLE IV

Successes in permutations of three, four and five letters after learning of arrangements

Grade	Permutations of three letters							
	First branching		Second branching		Setting up of groups	Solving by computation		
	S	S+E	S	S+E	S	S	S+E	E
IV	$17_{(85)}$	$3_{(15)}$	$16_{(80)}$	$4_{(20)}$	$20_{(100)}$	$14_{(70)}$	$1_{(5)}$	$5_{(25)}$
VI	$15_{(75)}$	$5_{(25)}$	$15_{(75)}$	$5_{(25)}$	$20_{(100)}$	$17_{(85)}$	$2_{(10)}$	$1_{(5)}$
VIII	$18_{(90)}$	$2_{(10)}$	$15_{(75)}$	$5_{(25)}$	$20_{(100)}$	$19_{(95)}$	–	$1_{(5)}$

Grade	Permutations of four letters						Knows only		Knows nothing
	I Computation II Diagram			I Diagram II Computation			Computation	Diagram	
	S	S+E*	S+E**	S	S+E*	S+E**			
IV	$12_{(60)}$	$1_{(5)}$	–	$2_{(10)}$	–	$1_{(5)}$	$2_{(10)}$	–	$2_{(10)}$
VI	$12_{(60)}$	–	$1_{(5)}$	$2_{(10)}$	–	$2_{(10)}$	$1_{(5)}$	–	$2_{(10)}$
VIII	$12_{(60)}$	$1_{(5)}$	–	$4_{(20)}$	$1_{(5)}$	–	–	$1_{(5)}$	$1_{(5)}$

Grade	Permutations of five letters Computation	
	Correct	Wrong
IV	$16_{(85)}$	$4_{(20)}$
VI	$17_{(80)}$	$3_{(15)}$
VIJI	$18_{(90)}$	$2_{(10)}$

* (Same legend as in Table III: percentages in brackets).

among eighth-graders, those spontaneously transposing the diagram into a numerical operation numbered 12 out of 20 (60%).

(c) The progress achieved during the first phase of the session proves to be a structural one, as in passing from groups of three to groups of four letters the majority of the subjects succeed in performing the computation and building the diagram unassisted.

(d) Passing on to permutations of three letters (Table IV) we find, this time, that around 80 per cent of the subjects can build the diagram unassisted, which may denote the effect of a remote transfer.

(e) As may be seen from Table IV, it is only among fourth-graders that those who discover the computational solution ($P_3 = 1 \times 2 \times 3$) are fewer than those who build the diagram (70% against 85%). Among sixth- and eighth-graders, the number of those who discover the computational way of solving without any assistance exceeds the rest (amounting to 95% in eighth-graders).

(f) Permutations with four letters: at this phase of the session, from the outset we asked the subjects to solve the task by extension of the previously used computational procedure (passing from $1 . 2 . 3$ to $1 . 2 . 3 . 4$) and to build the diagram by themselves. Subjects who failed to do the computation were asked to build the diagram first. In order to find out the number of subjects who had succeeded in building the diagram by themselves, we added up the two columns of correct answers for P_4 (Table IV) (I computation, II diagram; I diagram, II computation). We thus obtained 70%, 70% and 80% for the three age levels considered, of which 60% only, at each age level, performed the computation unassisted from the outset. But going also through this phase of the session greatly consolidates the understanding of the computational formula ($n!$) as is shown by the P_5 column of correct unassisted answers, i.e., 80%, 85% and 90% for the three age levels, respectively.

We point out the fact that in practice it proved a much easier task for the subjects to pass to the computational formula $n (n-1) (n-2) ... -$ in fact the one we used with them – than to $1.2.3...n$.

(g) The vertical comparisons among the three age levels indicate generally a progressive improvement of responses with age. Such improvement, however, is far from being as spectacular as it should have been according to the Piaget-Inhelder concept of intellectual development by stages. *It was only in the first phase of the session that the discrepancies were striking.* The differences diminished during the instructional session.

III. DISCUSSION

1. As shown by the data on subjective estimation of the permutations, included in Table 1, the mean values for the estimations (and, as a matter of fact, the standard deviations, too) made by the 12- to 15-year-old subjects are surprisingly close. In so far as these estimations are not, at least apparently, based on any exhaustive inventorying strategy and do not

rely on any direct preceding experience, the responses may be assumed to be 'blind,' that is, given absolutely casually and thus unable to express anything significant. The fact that for tasks using three and four elements the mean values obtained for subjects at different age levels were almost equivalent and that for tasks using five elements the mean values were so close, points, we believe, to the existence of a covert mechanism of estimation of the permutations which determines a statistically stable resultant beyond the aleatory influences and, within certain limits, even beyond the age factor.

What this mechanism consists of and how it operates we do not know, but it must be assumed to be intimately interlocked with the dynamics of plausible reasoning, in fact with the dynamics of productive thinking. Marcel Dumont said, in this connection: "The fact must be recognized that if a fair proportion of people can write and if they know, more or less, the four elementary operations with the natural integers, the majority are absolutely perplexed before a plain combinatorial problem, confused by a kind of computation that they have not been trained for. And as this is precisely the sort of problem which comes up whenever we are to consider one eventuality among others, in other words, at every moment of life as a matter of fact, the majority turn to 'chance', a more or less metaphor-laden chance."

What our findings show, in addition, is the fact that actually the relative chance is to a certain extent controlled by a mechanism of evaluation which, however, leads to a striking *under-rating of the number of possibilities*, an underrating that is the more striking the larger the number of alternatives. It may be inferred from this that our judgments involving estimations of possible combinations (and this is, as Dumont states, always the case) will be biased by a strong tendency to under-rate the gamut of alternatives involved.

2. The differences due to age are evident with subjective estimations and at the first stage of the instruction. In this situation it is possible to speak of thresholds, of *leaps* that spectacularly fit the stages indicated by Piaget. *Instruction, however, reduces these differences.* Even though not inducing a complete levelling, instruction diminishes the differences in such a degree that all that remains is but a slightly upward curve. Hence, a first inference that seems to be basic to the whole problem of intellectual development:

the effect of stage differences is partly counterbalanced by the higher receptivity of younger subjects, at least for some patterns of activity.

As far as combinatory ability is concerned, a well-conducted instruction may determine structural acquisitions, the efficiency of which is demonstrable by the remote transfer effects we have ourselves ascertained.

In the previously quoted paper Dumont made also the following remark: "Until we get more evidence on the way intelligence is operating,
imagination may be considered as an unconscious mechanism of combination ('une combinatoire'), on the level of recollection, viz., recollections
of activities, or more or less elaborate concepts. Imagination presupposes
a great mobility and a considerable flexibility in exploring the field of
memory" (Dumont, p. 57). According to Dumont, the inclusion in school
instruction of educational games stimulating combinatory activities may
contribute to developing the imagination (and thus the intelligence too),
a point too frequently overlooked by scientific education nowadays.

Our findings suggest, we hope, something more: the possibility for the
child to attain *systematically, yet at the concrete operational stage, a body
of knowledge and mental skills and intuitions concerning combinatory analysis.*

Associated with concepts of statistics and probability these might contribute substantially to the development of the pupil's scientific thinking
and imagination.

NOTES

* Reprinted from *The British Journal of Educational Psychology* **40** (1970), Part 3.
* Our paper is in fact dealing with arrangements with replacement, the formula for
which is n^p.

BIBLIOGRAPHY

Davies, C.: 1965, 'Development of the Probability Concept in Children', *Child Dev.*
  36, 779–788.
Dumont, M.: 1968, 'Quelques jeux combinatoires', *Le courrier de recherche pédagogique*
  33, 57–63.
Dubosson, Z.: 1957, *Le problème de l'orientation scolaire*, Delachaux et Niestle,
  Neuchâtel, pp. 122–133.
Fischbein, E., Pampu, I., and Minzat, I.: 1967, 'L'intuition probabiliste chez l'enfant',
  Enfance **2**, 193–208.
Fischbein, E., Pampu, I., and Minzat, I.: 1969, 'Initiation aux probabilités à l'école
  élémentaire', *Educ. Studies in Mathematics* **2**, 16–31.

Fischbein, E., Pampu, I., and Minzat, I.: 1970, 'Comparison of Ratios and the Chance Concept in Children', *Child Dev.* **41**, 377–389.

Fischbein, E.: 1969, 'Modèles figuraux implicites et apprentissage conceptuel', paper presented at the XIXth International Congress of Psychology, London.

Goldman, D. E. and Denny, J.: 1963, 'The Ontogenesis of Choice Behavior in Probability and Sequential Programs', *J. of Genet. Psychol.* **102**, 5–18.

Inhelder, B. and Piaget, J.: 1955, *De la logique de l'enfant à la logique de l'adolescent*, PUF, Paris.

Longeot, F.: 1967, 'Aspects différentiels de la psychologie génétique', *Binop*, 2ème série, numéro spécial, 66–67.

Longeot, F.: 1968, 'La pédagogie des mathématiques et le développement des opérations formelles dans le second cycle de l'enseignement secondaire', *Enfance* **5**, 378–389.

Offenbach, S. I.: 1964, 'Studies of Children's Probability Learning Behavior: Effect of Reward and Punishment at Two Age Levels', *Child Dev.* **35**, 715.

Offenbach, S. I.: 1965, 'Studies of Children's Probability Behavior: Effect of Method of Event Frequency at Two Age Levels', *Child Dev.* **36**, 952–961.

Piaget, J. and Inhelder, B.: 1951, *La genèse de l'idée de hasard chez l'enfant*, PUF, Paris.

Siegel, S. and McAndrews, J.: 1962, 'Magnitude of Reinforcement and Choice Behavior in Children', *J. Exp. Psychol.* **63**, 337–341.

Yost, P., Siegel, A. E., and Andrews, J. N.: 1962, 'Non-Verbal Probability Judgment by Young Children', *Child Dev.* **33**, 769–780.

INDEX OF NAMES

SYNTHESE LIBRARY

Monographs on Epistemology, Logic, Methodology,
Philosophy of Science, Sociology of Science and of Knowledge, and on the
Mathematical Methods of Social and Behavioral Sciences

Managing Editor:

JAAKKO HINTIKKA (Academy of Finland and Stanford University)

Editors:

ROBERT S. COHEN (Boston University)
DONALD DAVIDSON (The Rockefeller University and Princeton University)
GABRIËL NUCHELMANS (University of Leyden)
WESLEY C. SALMON (University of Arizona)

1. J. M. BOCHEŃSKI, *A Precis of Mathematical Logic.* 1959, X + 100 pp.
2. P. L. GUIRAUD, *Problèmes et méthodes de la statistique linguistique.* 1960, VI + 146 pp.
3. HANS FREUDENTHAL (ed.), *The Concept and the Role of the Model in Mathematics and Natural and Social Sciences, Proceedings of a Colloquium held at Utrecht, The Netherlands, January 1960.* 1961, VI + 194 pp.
4. EVERT W. BETH, *Formal Methods. An Introduction to Symbolic Logic and the Study of Effective Operations in Arithmetic and Logic.* 1962, XIV + 170 pp.
5. B. H. KAZEMIER and D. VUYSJE (eds.), *Logic and Language. Studies dedicated to Professor Rudolf Carnap on the Occasion of his Seventieth Birthday.* 1962, VI + 256 pp.
6. MARX W. WARTOFSKY (ed.), *Proceedings of the Boston Colloquium for the Philosophy of Science, 1961–1962,* Boston Studies in the Philosophy of Science (ed. by Robert S. Cohen and Marx W. Wartofsky), Volume I. 1973, VIII + 212 pp.
7. A. A. ZINOV'EV, *Philosophical Problems of Many-Valued Logic.* 1963, XIV + 155 pp.
8. GEORGES GURVITCH, *The Spectrum of Social Time.* 1964, XXVI + 152 pp.
9. PAUL LORENZEN, *Formal Logic.* 1965, VIII + 123 pp.
10. ROBERT S. COHEN and MARX W. WARTOFSKY (eds.), *In Honor of Philipp Frank,* Boston Studies in the Philosophy of Science (ed. by Robert S. Cohen and Marx W. Wartofsky), Volume II. 1965, XXXIV + 475 pp.
11. EVERT W. BETH, *Mathematical Thought. An Introduction to the Philosophy of Mathematics.* 1965, XII + 208 pp.
12. EVERT W. BETH and JEAN PIAGET, *Mathematical Epistemology and Psychology.* 1966, XII + 326 pp.
13. GUIDO KÜNG, *Ontology and the Logistic Analysis of Language. An Enquiry into the Contemporary Views on Universals.* 1967, XI + 210 pp.

14. ROBERT S. COHEN and MARX W. WARTOFSKY (eds.), *Proceedings of the Boston Colloquium for the Philosophy of Science 1964–1966, in Memory of Norwood Russell Hanson*, Boston Studies in the Philosophy of Science (ed. by Robert S. Cohen and Marx W. Wartofsky), Volume III. 1967, XLIX + 489 pp.
15. C. D. BROAD, *Induction, Probability, and Causation. Selected Papers*. 1968, XI + 296 pp.
16. GÜNTHER PATZIG, *Aristotle's Theory of the Syllogism. A Logical-Philosophical Study of Book A of the Prior Analytics*. 1968, XVII + 215 pp.
17. NICHOLAS RESCHER, *Topics in Philosophical Logic*. 1968, XIV + 347 pp.
18. ROBERT S. COHEN and MARX W. WARTOFSKY (eds.), *Proceedings of the Boston Colloquium for the Philosophy of Science 1966–1968*, Boston Studies in the Philosophy of Science (ed. by Robert S. Cohen and Marx W. Wartofsky), Volume IV. 1969, VIII + 537 pp.
19. ROBERT S. COHEN and MARX W. WARTOFSKY (eds.), *Proceedings of the Boston Colloquium for the Philosophy of Science 1966–1968*, Boston Studies in the Philosophy of Science (ed. by Robert S. Cohen and Marx W. Wartofsky), Volume V. 1969, VIII + 482 pp.
20. J. W. DAVIS, D. J. HOCKNEY, and W. K. WILSON (eds.), *Philosophical Logic*. 1969, VIII + 277 pp.
21. D. DAVIDSON and J. HINTIKKA (eds.), *Words and Objections: Essays on the Work of W. V. Quine*. 1969, VIII + 366 pp.
22. PATRICK SUPPES, *Studies in the Methodology and Foundations of Science. Selected Papers from 1911 to 1969*. 1969, XII + 473 pp.
23. JAAKKO HINTIKKA, *Models for Modalities. Selected Essays*. 1969, IX + 220 pp.
24. NICHOLAS RESCHER *et al.* (eds.), *Essays in Honor of Carl G. Hempel. A Tribute on the Occasion of his Sixty-Fifth Birthday*. 1969, VII + 272 pp.
25. P. V. TAVANEC (ed.), *Problems of the Logic of Scientific Knowledge*. 1969, XII + 429 pp.
26. MARSHALL SWAIN (ed.), *Induction, Acceptance, and Rational Belief*. 1970, VII + 232 pp.
27. ROBERT S. COHEN and RAYMOND J. SEEGER (eds.), *Ernst Mach; Physicist and Philosopher*, Boston Studies in the Philosophy of Science (ed. by Robert S. Cohen and Marx W. Wartofsky), Volume VI. 1970, VIII + 295 pp.
28. JAAKKO HINTIKKA and PATRICK SUPPES, *Information and Inference*. 1970, X + 336 pp.
29. KAREL LAMBERT, *Philosophical Problems in Logic. Some Recent Developments*. 1970, VII + 176 pp.
30. ROLF A. EBERLE, *Nominalistic Systems*. 1970, IX + 217 pp.
31. PAUL WEINGARTNER and GERHARD ZECHA (eds.), *Induction, Physics, and Ethics, Proceedings and Discussions of the 1968 Salzburg Colloquium in the Philosophy of Science*. 1970, X + 382 pp.
32. EVERT W. BETH, *Aspects of Modern Logic*. 1970, XI + 176 pp.
33. RISTO HILPINEN (ed.), *Deontic Logic: Introductory and Systematic Readings*. 1971, VII + 182 pp.
34. JEAN-LOUIS KRIVINE, *Introduction to Axiomatic Set Theory*. 1971, VII + 98 pp.
35. JOSEPH D. SNEED, *The Logical Structure of Mathematical Physics*. 1971, XV + 311 pp.
36. CARL R. KORDIG, *The Justification of Scientific Change*. 1971, XIV + 119 pp.

37. MILIČ ČAPEK, *Bergson and Modern Physics*, Boston Studies in the Philosophy of Science (ed. by Robert S. Cohen and Marx W. Wartofsky), Volume VII, 1971, XV + 414 pp.
38. NORWOOD RUSSELL HANSON, *What I do not Believe, and other Essays* (ed. by Stephen Toulmin and Harry Woolf), 1971, XII + 390 pp.
39. ROGER C. BUCK and ROBERT S. COHEN (eds.), *PSA 1970. In Memory of Rudolf Carnap*, Boston Studies in the Philosophy of Science (ed. by Robert S. Cohen and Marx W. Wartofsky, Volume VIII. 1971, LXVI + 615 pp. Also available as a paperback.
40. DONALD DAVIDSON and GILBERT HARMAN (eds.), *Semantics of Natural Language*. 1972, X + 769 pp. Also available as a paperback.
41. YEHOSHUA BAR-HILLEL (ed)., *Pragmatics of Natural Languages*. 1971, VII + 231 pp.
42. SÖREN STENLUND, *Combinators, λ-Terms and Proof Theory*. 1972, 184 pp.
43. MARTIN STRAUSS, *Modern Physics and Its Philosophy. Selected Papers in the Logic, History, and Philosophy of Science*. 1972, X + 297 pp.
44. MARIO BUNGE, *Method, Model and Matter*. 1973, VII + 196 pp.
45. MARIO BUNGE, *Philosophy of Physics*. 1973, IX + 248 pp.
46. A. A. ZINOV'EV, *Foundations of the Logical Theory of Scientific Knowledge (Complex Logic)*, Boston Studies in the Philosophy of Science (ed. by Robert S. Cohen and Marx W. Wartofsky), Volume IX. Revised and enlarged English edition with an appendix, by G. A. Smirnov, E. A. Sidorenka, A. M. Fedina, and L. A. Bobrova. 1973, XXII + 301 pp. Also available as a paperback.
47. LADISLAV TONDL, *Scientific Procedures*, Boston Studies in the Philosophy of Science (ed. by Robert S. Cohen and Marx W. Wartofsky), Volume X. 1973, XII + 268 pp. Also available as a paperback.
48. NORWOOD RUSSELL HANSON, *Constellations and Conjectures* (ed. by Willard C. Humphreys, Jr.), 1973, X + 282 pp.
49. K. J. J. HINTIKKA, J. M. E. MORAVCSIK, and P. SUPPES (eds.), *Approaches to Natural Language. Proceedings of the 1970 Stanford Workshop on Grammar and Semantics*. 1973, VIII + 526 pp. Also available as a paperback.
50. MARIO BUNGE (ed.), *Exact Philosophy – Problems, Tools, and Goals*. 1973, X + 214 pp.
51. RADU J. BOGDAN and ILKKA NIINILUOTO (eds.), *Logic, Language, and Probability*. A selection of papers contributed to Sections IV, VI, and XI of the Fourth International Congress for Logic, Methodology, and Philosophy of Science, Bucharest, September 1971. 1973, X + 323 pp.
52. GLENN PEARCE and PATRICK MAYNARD (eds.), *Conceptual Chance*. 1973, XII + 282 pp.
53. ILKKA NIINILUOTO and RAIMO TUOMELA, *Theoretical Concepts and Hypothetico-Inductive Inference*. 1973, VII + 264 pp.
54. ROLAND FRAÏSSÉ, *Course of Mathematical Logic* – Volume I: *Relation and Logical Formula*. 1973, XVI + 186 pp. Also available as a paperback.
55. ADOLF GRÜNBAUM, *Philosophical Problems of Space and Time*. Second, enlarged edition, Boston Studies in the Philosophy of Science (ed. by Robert S. Cohen and Marx W. Wartofsky), Volume XII. 1973, XXIII + 884 pp. Also available as a paperback.
56. PATRICK SUPPES (ed.), *Space, Time, and Geometry*. 1973, XI + 424 pp.
57. HANS KELSEN, *Essays in Legal and Moral Philosophy*, selected and introduced by Ota Weinberger. 1973, XXVIII + 300 pp.

58. R. J. Seeger and Robert S. Cohen (eds.), *Philosophical Foundations of Science. Proceedings of an AAAS Program, 1969.* Boston Studies in the Philosophy of Science (ed. by Robert S. Cohen and Marx W. Wartofsky), Volume XI. 1974, X + 545 pp. Also available as a paperback.

59. Robert S. Cohen and Marx W. Wartofsky (eds.), *Logical and Epistemological Studies in Contemporary Physics,* Boston Studies in the Philosophy of Science (ed. by Robert S. Cohen and Marx W. Wartofsky), Volume XIII. 1973, VIII + 462 pp. Also available as a paperback.

60. Robert S. Cohen and Marx W. Wartofsky (eds.), *Methodological and Historical Essays in the Natural and Social Sciences. Proceedings of the Boston Colloquium for the Philosophy of Science, 1969–1972,* Boston Studies in the Philosophy of Science (ed. by Robert S. Cohen and Marx W. Wartofsky), Volume XIV. 1974, VIII + 405 pp. Also available as paperback.

61. Robert S. Cohen, J. J. Stachel, and Marx W. Wartofsky (eds.), *For Dirk Struik. Scientific, Historical and Political Essays in Honor of Dirk J. Struik,* Boston Studies in the Philosophy of Science (ed. by Robert S. Cohen and Marx W. Wartofsky), Volume XV. 1974, XXVII + 652 pp. Also available as paperback.

62. Kazimierz Ajdukiewicz, *Pragmatic Logic,* transl. from the Polish by Olgierd Wojtasiewicz. 1974, XV + 460 pp.

63. Sören Stenlund (ed.), *Logical Theory and Semantic Analysis. Essays Dedicated to Stig Kanger on His Fiftieth Birthday.* 1974, V + 217 pp.

64. Kenneth F. Schaffner and Robert S. Cohen (eds.), *Proceedings of the 1972 Biennial Meeting, Philosophy of Science Association,* Boston Studies in the Philosophy of Science (ed. by Robert S. Cohen and Marx W. Wartofsky), Volume XX. 1974, IX + 444 pp. Also available as paperback.

65. Henry E. Kyburg, Jr., *The Logical Foundations of Statistical Inference.* 1974, IX + 421 pp.

66. Marjorie Grene, *The Understanding of Nature: Essays in the Philosophy of Biology,* Boston Studies in the Philosophy of Science (ed. by Robert S. Cohen and Marx W. Wartofsky), Volume XXIII. 1974, XII + 360 pp. Also available as paperback.

67. Jan M. Broekman, *Structuralism: Moscow, Prague, Paris.* 1974, IX + 117 pp.

68. Norman Geschwind, *Selected Papers on Language and the Brain,* Boston Studies in the Philosophy of Science (ed. by Robert S. Cohen and Marx W. Wartofsky), Volume XVI. 1974, XII + 549 pp. Also available as paperback.

69. Roland Fraïssé, *Course of Mathematical Logic – Volume II: Model Theory.* 1974, XIX + 192 pp.

70. Andrzej Grzegorczyk, *An Outline of Mathematical Logic. Fundamental Results and Notions Explained with all Details.* 1974, X + 596 pp.

71. Franz von Kutschera, *Philosophy of Language.* 1975, VII+305 pp.

72. Juha Manninen and Raimo Tuomela, *Essays on Explanation and Understanding.* 1975, approx. 450 pp.

75. Jaakko Hintikka and Unto Remes, *The Method of Analysis. Its Geometrical Origin and Its General Significance.* Boston Studies in the Philosophy of Science (ed. by Robert S. Cohen and Marx W. Wartofsky), Volume XXV. 1974, XVIII+ 144 pp. Also available as paperback.

76. John Emery Murdoch and Edith Dudley Sylla, *The Cultural Context of Medieval Learning. Proceedings of the First International Colloquium on Philosophy, Science, and Theology in the Middle Ages – September 1973.* Boston Studies in the

Philosophy of Science (ed. by Robert S. Cohen and Marx. W. Wartofsky), Volume XXVI. 1975, X+566 pp. Also available as paperback.

77. STEFAN AMSTERDAMSKI, *Between Experience and Metaphysics. Philosophical Problems of the Evolution of Science.* Boston Studies in the Philosophy of Science (ed. by Robert S. Cohen and Marx W. Wartofsky), Volume XXXV. 1975, XVIII+193 pp. Also available as paperback.

80. JOSEPH AGASSI, *Science in Flux.* Boston Studies in the Philosophy of Science (ed. by Robert S. Cohen and Marx W. Wartofsky), Volume XXVIII. 1975, XXVI+ 553 pp. Also available as paperback.

SYNTHESE HISTORICAL LIBRARY

Texts and Studies
in the History of Logic and Philosophy

Editors:

N. KRETZMANN (Cornell University)
G. NUCHELMANS (University of Leyden)
L. M. DE RIJK (University of Leyden)